ASKING QUESTIONS

Asking Questions

Using Meaningful Structures to Imply Ignorance

ROBERT FIENGO

OXFORD

UNIVERSITY PRESS

OXFORD

UNIVERSITY PRESS

Great Clarendon Street, Oxford OX2 6DP

Oxford University Press is a department of the University of Oxford.
It furthers the University's objective of excellence in research, scholarship,
and education by publishing worldwide in

Oxford New York

Auckland Cape Town Dar es Salaam Hong Kong Karachi
Kuala Lumpur Madrid Melbourne Mexico City Nairobi
New Delhi Shanghai Taipei Toronto

With offices in

Argentina Austria Brazil Chile Czech Republic France Greece
Guatemala Hungary Italy Japan Poland Portugal Singapore
South Korea Switzerland Thailand Turkey Ukraine Vietnam

Oxford is a registered trade mark of Oxford University Press
in the UK and in certain other countries

Published in the United States
by Oxford University Press Inc., New York

© Robert Fiengo 2007

The moral rights of the authors have been asserted
Database right Oxford University Press (maker)

First published 2007

British Library Cataloguing in Publication Data

Data available

Library of Congress Cataloging in Publication Data

Fiengo, Robert, 1949-
Asking questions : using meaningful structures to imply ignorance /
Robert Fiengo.
p. cm.
Includes bibliographical references and index.
ISBN 978-0-19-920841-8 (alk. paper)
1. Ignorance (Theory of knowledge) 2. Knowledge, Theory of—
Methodology. 3. Questioning. 4. Rhetoric. I. Title.
BD221.F54 2007
401'.4—dc22
2007007678

Typeset by Laserwords Private Limited, Chennai, India
Printed in Great Britain
on acid-free paper by
Biddles Ltd, King's Lynn, Norfolk

ISBN 978–0–19–920841–8

1 3 5 7 9 10 8 6 4 2

Preface

The present book derives from my belief that linguistic theory, as currently practiced, suffers from not doing justice to the fact that people talk, and my belief that pragmatics, as currently practiced, suffers from underestimating the importance of sentence-structure. Somehow, it has seemed to me, the proper balance between these two pursuits has gone wrong. Mostly, I have mulled this sad fact over by myself, but there have been some steady influences. First I would mention the almost constant irritant of reading and listening to pragmatics being syntacticized. This practice never yields good pragmatics or good syntax, and should create revulsion in anyone who values either one of them in its pure form. Nevertheless, it was a stimulant; absent this, I would not have been impelled to write this book. Another influence, more positive, has been Austin's writings, in particular his essays. There are echoes of some particular views of his here, but there is a more general debt: in his talk of use and meaning, he seems to me to get the balance right. More episodically, I have, on a few occasions, presented some of my views concerning questions in courses at the Graduate Center of CUNY. Those in attendance have often been helpful, and always polite. In addition, I would like to express my gratitude to two anonymous readers for their perceptive and constructive criticism. Finally, most important to the formulation of the ideas this book contains, I wish to cite my discussions with Barbara Bevington. There are few sentences in this book that have not benefited from her advice. On countless occasions, both on matters of fact and matters of analysis, she has shown me the shortest and clearest path to the truth.

RF

Contents—Summary

Contents

Note on Punctuation

The reader should be alerted to certain conventions of punctuation that I will be following. Italicized sentences may be representations of utterances or sentence-types; context will decide. Italics are also used for emphasis. Single quotes are used when citing particular words; these are also occasionally used as shudder quotes, and as corner quotes when displaying schemata. My use of the question mark deserves special mention. I use it to indicate that the sentence it appears after is being used to ask a question. *Bernini designed that?* is not, in virtue of the question mark, indicated to have rising intonation. Insofar as punctuation is concerned, it might have rising intonation, or it might not.

1

Introduction: Ignorance and Incompleteness

If you do not keep the multiplicity of language-games in view, you will
perhaps be inclined to ask questions like: 'What is a question?'

Wittgenstein (*Philosophical Investigations* §24)

1.1 Ignorance of items and ignorance of predicates

Ignorance is a lack, and one can address it by asking questions. When we
ask questions, we utter sentences that are noticeably incomplete in one respect
or another. Those incompletenesses correspond to our lacks. The activities we
engage in when we utter them display the lacks that we wish to relieve ourselves
of. If those incompletenesses are filled in, our lacks are relieved, and the questions
we ask are answered.

There are two major sorts of ignorance that we display. On the one hand, we
may wish to indicate that we lack either a thing-in-the-world or a bit of language.
To indicate that we have either of these lacks, we use sentence-types that are
incomplete in specific ways. On the other hand, we may wish to indicate that we
lack certain beliefs, or that we lack the ability to complete certain utterances. To
indicate that we have either of these lacks, we reveal our lacks through our using
of a sentence.

The former domain of ignorance is more commented on. In this domain, there
is no limit to those things that we are ignorant of, and no way to gauge the extent
of them. We do not know what we do not know. The domain across which that
ignorance spreads cannot be charted; nevertheless, we can isolate areas within it
concerning which we can reasonably ask in what ways we might be ignorant in
them. Suppose, for example, we consider just those ignorances we might have
concerning carpenters' tools. Given one of those tools, we might wonder what
it is called. Our ignorance in this case can be characterized by saying that what
we lack is a name, a word the tool is called by. So in one type of ignorance,
the type of ignorance illustrated here, an item is given, a carpenters' tool, and
we seek its name. Once the name is produced, our ignorance is addressed; if
the right name is produced, we know what we wanted to know. Of course the
list of names is long, and we are perhaps never so desperate that any name

will do. Our normal needs are more specific, and language allows us to be more specific.

Another kind of ignorance in this domain complements the first. We might wonder which of the carpenters' tools measure angles, which are called rabbet planes, which are light enough to carry, or which were made by Stanley. In this kind of case, we have predicates, but are ignorant as to what item or items fall under them. Once the tool or tools are produced, our ignorance is addressed, and if the right tool or tools are produced, we know what we wanted to know. There are many items, of course, and we are seldom so desperate that any item will do. But again, language allows us to be more specific.

So, within the domain of ignorance concerning carpenters' tools, there are two kinds of ignorance that may be distinguished. Given a tool, we may be ignorant as to which name or predicate it falls under, or, given a name or predicate, we may be ignorant as to which tool falls under it. How far beyond the domain of carpenters' tools do these complementary kinds of ignorance spread? That is a hard question. It is fair to say that that wider domain is coincident with the domain in which one may be ignorant as to whether a name or predicate applies to an item. How wide is that domain? Note that, with very few exceptions, in assertions, items and predicates are joined.[1] If we consider that that joining is in question, we are ignorant as to whether it obtains. So this kind of ignorance would appear to extend to that domain concerning which assertions may be made, a very wide domain. Of course, the domain of ignorance might be exhausted in many ways. But there will be few kinds of ignorance that are potentially more widespread.

Language allows us to make plain, when we ask questions, what it is we wish to know, what ignorance we want relief from. In particular, we can make it clear which of the two kinds of ignorance just distinguished we want relief from. Sometimes, when we are ignorant in both ways, we succeed in relieving our ignorance step by step. Suppose I want to know who stole the tarts. I can move things along by saying *Who stole the tarts?* And you, if you know the answer, and you wish to answer me, may do so by pointing at a person, the person that you think stole the tarts. So now you have told me, or at least shown me, who stole the tarts: that person did. So now I have the item I sought. But still I may be ignorant concerning the identity of the person. I can move things along on that front by asking *Who is that?* And you, if you know and you wish to answer me, might say *That is the Jack of Hearts.* In answering the first question, you provided me with a thing-in-the-world, an 'item' as I will often say; in answering the second question, you provided me with a bit of language, that item's title. In other circumstances, in this second case, you might have provided me with the item's name, or with a description that that item falls under. But pointing at the item again would not be helpful; I have the item already; what I seek is a bit of language, and by pointing at the Jack of Hearts you cannot demonstrate a bit of language.

---

[1] As potential exceptions, I have in mind 'subjectless' sentences such as *It's raining.*

These are examples of the first kind of ignorance that I referred to. This kind of ignorance is addressed by asking what I call an open question. The other kind of ignorance is addressed by asking a confirmation question, to be discussed below. But so far, I have distinguished two kinds of ignorance of the former kind, and observed that we can direct our use of language in such a way as to ask questions which, if answered, will relieve each of them. As will be seen, there are in fact many kinds of question that can be asked, and many kinds of circumstance to consider, when trying to determine how a speaker decides which sentence-type to use when asking them. That is the focus of this book. In this chapter, I will survey only the most prominent features of the terrain.

1.1.1 On the tendency to syntacticize distinctions of use

In common talk, there is the noun 'question' and the verb 'question'. We label some of our sentences 'questions', and we call the activity we engage in when we use such sentences 'questioning'. In common talk, we use questions to question. English is notorious for such noun–verb pairs for a tool and its use: we use a mop to mop, we use a hammer to hammer. In the case of questions, this behavior of English may tend to cause confusion between the tool itself—the sentence-type being used—and the activity of questioning.

One might, for example, hold that there are three basic speech-acts, three overridingly important things that one can do with language: to assert, to question, and to command. This view might derive from: (i) the fact that sentences used to ask questions or give commands are, in the world's languages, quite often grammatically distinguished from sentences used to make assertions, and (ii) from a failure to distinguish sentences from the acts they are used to perform. Austin (1962) did a great deal to counter some of this, in part by pointing to the thousands of speech-acts other than the three mentioned, and in part by insisting on a distinction between sentences and the acts they may be used to perform. But still, it has been suggested that just three classes of sentence—declaratives, questions, and imperatives—are syntactically distinguished, a common move being to *add* syntactic structure to sentences used to ask questions and issue commands.

Katz and Postal (1964) proposed that question and imperative sentence-types be syntactically distinguished from declarative sentence-types by placing 'Q' and 'I' morphemes in their syntactic representations. The morphemes served two purposes: to trigger the application of the question and imperative transformations as then conceived, and to express the meanings characteristic of questions and commands.[2] In the case of 'Q', they suggested that this morpheme

---

[2] The term 'meaning' raises a flag. Is the claim that all sentence-types used to ask questions share some aspect of meaning? Does the account claim that one can tell, by inspecting the meaning of a sentence-type, what it is (must be?) used to do?

is paraphrasable as 'I request that you answer . . .', a proposal that anticipated the sentential performative analysis of Ross (1970), which has it that an often tacit full clause of the form 'I Verb you that . . .' is prefixed to every sentence, including declarative sentences, the verb being taken from a very long list of performative verbs.

Now one should not infer from Katz and Postal's proposal that there are only three basic speech-acts: asserting, questioning, and ordering. Their proposal touches syntax and semantics, not speech-act theory. They distinguish question and imperative sentence-types from declarative sentence-types, but presumably do not countenance a 'B' morpheme for sentences used to perform bettings, owing to the lack of syntactic evidence. Ross (1970), in contrast, allows all of the performative verbs to appear in his higher performative sentences, including such verbs as 'bet', allowing the speech-act to drive the syntax. But the two accounts agree that sentences used to ask questions contain a bit of structure whose meaning is the meaning that all questions share. That, I think, is a mistake. I do not oppose the spirit of Katz and Postal's syntactic arguments in support of 'Q'; there is nothing in principle wrong with syntactic arguments in support of unheard structure. Given the assumptions they were working with, they needed such a device. Given the syntactic assumptions that will be presented in Chapter 5, and my views concerning the semantics of questions developed in Chapter 3, I do not. My complaint, rather, is against syntacticizing distinctions of use. There can be no syntactic evidence for syntacticizing distinctions of use.

First, let's get the facts straight. What is it about questions that the 'Q' morpheme analysis seeks to capture? I agree that syntactic evidence is criterial to the postulation of syntactic structure; suppose it be granted that that structure, whether it be a 'Q' morpheme or a full performative clause, triggers the application of syntactic rules such as inversion (as in *Is it raining?*) and *wh*-movement (as in *Who did you see?*). What is gained? It can be said neither that the 'Q' morpheme occurs in all sentence-types used to ask questions nor that a performative clause does. One can perfectly well ask a question using a sentence-type in which neither inversion nor *wh*-movement applies. *Some* of the sentence-types used to ask questions show their application, but others do not (as in *It's raining?*). So to say that there is structure meaning 'I ask you . . .' which triggers inversion or *wh*-movement and appears in all sentence-types used to ask questions would be false to the facts. But the point does not end there. As it happens, there is a speech-act distinction between asking *Is it raining?* and *It's raining?*, which I will discuss in detail in Chapter 3. There, I distinguish open questions from confirmation questions, arguing that if one wants to ask the former, one should use a sentence-type in which either inversion or *wh*-movement has applied, and that if one wants to ask the latter, one should use a sentence-type in which they have not. Against the point just made, the syntacticizer could respond by stipulating that only an 'open Q' morpheme triggers inversion, and that a 'confirmation Q' morpheme, if it were held to exist, does not. But, now that the facts are at least partially straightened out, the issue is joined. Why syntacticize distinctions of use at all?

The tools that we use must be distinguished from the uses to which they are put. Sentences are tools we use for various purposes. Those sentences have the structures that they do, but it in no way follows from the fact that a sentence is used to ask a question that it contains added structure in its syntactic representation. There are many formal ways to distinguish one kind of sentence from another that do not involve adding anything. If sentences used to ask questions (or issue commands) are generally syntactically distinguished in the world's languages, that could just as well be because they *lack* structure that other sentences have. Or it might be because the same elements that other sentences contain are, in these sentences, arranged in a different way. Furthermore, if there is some formal characteristic of certain sentences that makes them particularly suitable for the asking of questions, we may of course observe that this is so, and seek to explain why that structural characteristic would make them suitable tools for the asking of questions. I will be arguing that incompleteness is in fact one such characteristic. But we should not conclude that only sentences with that characteristic can be used to ask questions, nor should we conclude that it is only asking questions that those sentences may be used for. If we distinguish tools from the uses to which they are put, we must acknowledge that generally a tool may be used for different tasks, and that generally a task may be performed using structurally different tools. 'Q'-type proposals seem to ignore these simple points. Generally, we do not say that the use of a tool is *part of* the structure of that tool. Rather we say that, because a tool has a particular structure, it can be used for a certain purpose, or that because a certain purpose imposes certain requirements, a certain tool might be used to accomplish it, and another tool might not be. This is the right way to talk about both sentences used to ask questions and questioning and also the right way to talk about hammers and hammering.

If sentence-types are distinguished from their uses (as one would distinguish any tool from its uses), an interesting topic can be discerned. How do speakers decide which sentence-type to utter a token of? If a speaker intends to do something with language, how does the speaker find a tool which, when brought forward, will pull it off? Clearly, if we are to take on such topics, we must do justice to our actual behavior. One complicating factor is that there are many kinds of questioning speech-acts, and many different sentence-types that may be used to ask any one of them. Contrariwise, there are sentence-types that may be used to ask certain kinds of question that may also be used to do other things, such as to express hopes or to venture guesses. But, as in the case of tools generally, there are limits in both directions. Generally, sentence-types are such that they may be readily used for some purposes and not for others. And generally speech-acts are such that they may be readily performed by using some sentence-types and not others. This isolates the respect in which syntax, and grammar more generally, plays a role in the study of questioning. We want to be able to ask why tools with certain structures may readily be used for certain purposes and not for others, and we cannot even state that question without assuming that the syntactic structures of sentence-types play a role.

1.1.2 The incompleteness of sentence-types used to ask *wh*-questions, and the incompleteness of sentence-types used to ask *yes-no* questions

The tendency to syntacticize distinctions of use results in the mistaken belief that a class of questions can be isolated and defined syntactically. But the mistake does not end there. English contains two kinds of sentence-types, which are commonly called, on this view, the *yes-no* questions and the *wh*-questions. That distinction, once acknowledged, can lead to the view that, within the *use* of language, the primary distinction among the questioning speech-acts is between asking a *yes-no* question and asking a *wh*-question. Thus can a mistake in one direction feed another mistake in the opposite direction, once use and form are confounded.

Ignorance, I repeat, is a lack. So it should not be surprising that people, in asking questions, reveal what they lack, what ignorance they want relief from. Sentence-types that suit this purpose are those that are themselves incomplete in one way or another, thus revealing the speaker's lacks. So, as I have already suggested, it is not that there is something that sentence-types used to ask questions have that other sentence-types do not have; rather, many of the sentence-types used to ask questions do not have something that other sentence-types do have. The kinds of incompleteness are telling, and, in what follows, the speciation of the questioning speech-acts will in part reflect the various incompletenesses in the tools used to perform them.

Incompleteness is obvious in the case of *wh*-questions. A speaker uttering *Who is John talking to?* offers an incomplete sentence-type, a sentence-type that is traditionally awarded the logical form '[who x [John is talking to x]] ', the final 'x' position being a variable bound by 'who x'. The sentence, as well as its logical form, is noticeably incomplete in that there is no referring expression following the preposition 'to'.[3] That noticeable incompleteness corresponds to an incompleteness in what is expressed: it is not expressed what person John is talking to. I will argue that it is a convention of use that the reason for using an incomplete sentence-type is so as to have the addressee provide the completion. In the case at hand, that item should be a person John is talking to, produced either by name, by description, or by demonstration. The initial *wh*-expression

---

[3] That is to say, no expression that has a reference. It has been common in the syntactic literature to include both variables and names under the term 'r-expression', a technical term whose only flaw is that the 'r' suggests 'reference'. Variables do not refer, a point Geach (1962) noted.

in sentence-types used to ask (simple) *wh*-questions serves to provide conditions on the identity of that which the speaker lacks. There are options: by using *who, what, where,* or *when,* the speaker may require of her addressee that a person, a thing, a place, or a time be produced. In *wh*-questions, the site of the incompleteness is occupied by a variable; by producing an item or a predicate, the speaker's lack is addressed.

With respect to sentence-types used to ask questions, and the questioning speech-acts, the standard of completeness is the declarative sentence and assertion, a point that I will clarify and expand upon in Section 5.7. But while it may seem obvious that the sentence-types used to ask *wh*-questions are incomplete in the way I have mentioned, it may not seem obvious that the sentence-types used to ask *yes-no* questions are incomplete. *Is Jack fat?* does, after all, appear to contain the same parts as *Jack is fat,* and surely that sentence-type is complete. But enumerating words does not guarantee completeness: there is much in the structure of a sentence that is unheard. Frege (1882, 1891), for example, proposed that saturation joins an argument to a function. Saturating a function with an argument allows the determination of a truth-value for a sentence containing expressions referring to that function saturated by that argument. But he did not hold that there was a word in the sentence that referred to the process of saturation; saturation was the completion of incomplete things (functions) by complete things (objects). Similarly, in an account in which truth is cashed in in terms of set-membership, there need not be a word that refers to set-membership. So, in many accounts, there is more in what a sentence speaks to than meets the ear; that thing might even make it possible for a sentence to have a truth-value. For convenience, I will use the term 'the glue' in a functional way, meaning by it whatever it is in a theory that joins subject and predicate, thus giving rise to the possibility of a truth-value being determined. My claim is that, in *yes-no* questions, the glue is missing. The sentence-type *Is Jack fat?* is incomplete in that it lacks the glue between the subject and the predicate, the question being directed toward whether it should be supplied. By answering *Yes,* or by asserting *Jack is fat,* the respondent indicates that the subject and predicate should be glued together, yielding a sentence, which, if asserted, would say that the predicate 'fat' does apply to Jack. But no word refers to the glue.[4]

It should be said that Frege's view concerning *yes-no* questions is in direct contradiction to what I have just suggested. A short history. In Frege 1892, unembedded sentences express thoughts and refer to truth-values. When embedded, sentences refer to the thoughts that they express when unembedded: at least in an interesting range of cases this is so. Some embedded sentences are indirect

---

[4] I am ignoring various differences in doctrine and terminology. Does the glue relate bits of language or an object to a bit of language? Should the distinction be given as function–argument or predicate–subject? By 'subject' does one mean a bit of language or a thing-in-the-world? I only am interested here in naming the relation, however it is given.

questions; these, he argues, have indirect reference, referring not to truth-values but to requests. Requests, like commands, "are indeed not thoughts, yet they stand on the same level as thoughts" (Frege 1892: 68). So indirect questions refer to things that are not thoughts, but are senses of some sort. It is not clear that Frege meant to include *whether*-questions, the embedded analog of *yes-no* questions, under this early account, since he only lists 'who', 'what', 'where', 'when', 'how', and 'by what means'. However, in 'Negation', he does focus strictly on *yes-no* questions, which he calls 'propositional questions', whose senses, he assumes, are complete thoughts. Further:

The very nature of a [propositional] question demands a separation between the act of grasping a sense and of judging. And since the sense of an interrogative sentence is always also inherent in the assertoric sentence that gives the answer to the question, this separation must be carried out for assertoric sentences too. (Frege 1918*a*: 119)

Here Frege is in the midst of arguing that since the senses of assertions and *yes-no* questions are the same, sense and judging must be distinguished, and that therefore the being of a thought does not consist in its being true.[5] We can therefore surmise that had Frege included indirect *whether*-questions in the earlier paper, he would have said that unlike *who*-questions and the rest, *whether*-questions refer to complete thoughts, not merely something like them on the same level. In any event, he assumes in the later paper that *Is the Sun bigger than the Moon?* and *The Sun is bigger than the moon* contain the same thought, but that, in the terminology of Frege 1879, only the second contains the 'judgment stroke'. In 'Thought', much of the same ground is covered, but he adds the remark that, "In a word-question [*wh*-question] we utter an incomplete sentence, which is meant to be given a true sense just by means of the completion for which we are asking" (Frege 1918*b*: 329).

This last is an insight that I try to develop here, but I diverge from Frege in other respects. I do not hold that an assertoric sentence contains both a thought and assertion, that a *yes-no* question contains a thought and a request, or that a *yes-no* question expresses a complete thought. Having no pragmatics in which to place distinctions of illocutionary force, Frege indicated force and thought together. We are not now limited in that way. Against Frege 1879, in which the distinction between asserted thoughts and supposed thoughts is represented as the difference between the presence and the absence of the judgment stroke, I would distinguish asserting a sentence expressing a thought from supposing a sentence expressing that thought, these being different speech-acts that a speaker may perform using the same sentence-type. The use to which a sentence is put is not contained in, or represented within, the structure of the sentence.

---

[5] He is arguing to the *conclusion* that the being of a thought does not consist in its being true. I am arguing that, since the assumption that the senses of assertions and propositional questions are the same is false, his argument does not go through. I think his conclusion is better supported in Frege 1892.

I also cannot agree, as Frege suggests in 'Thought', that "in saying 'yes' the speaker presents as true the thought that was already completely contained in the interrogative sentence" (Frege 1918*b*: 329). He does not argue his claim about the use of 'yes', and it can be quickly seen that the use of 'yes' actually contradicts what Frege claims. One can say *Yes* after an assertion (*It's a fine day. Yes*), after a question (as Frege notes), but also after a command (*Go to bed! Yes, mommy*). This last fact is important, since Frege is clear in 'Thought' that the sense of a command is not a complete thought, that the sense of a command is "not such that the question of truth could arise for it" (Frege 1918*b*: 329). Here, then, we have 'yes' in response to a sentence which, by Frege's own lights, expresses an incomplete thought. So the fact that *Yes* can be used to respond to a question in no way argues that the question expresses a complete thought. Furthermore, certainly the easiest way to say that a thought is true, which is what Frege is saying *Yes* is doing, is to say *True* after the thought is expressed, which, in fact, does happen after assertion. One person says *It's a fine day* and the other says *True*. But we don't see this response after open *yes-no* questions. *True* would be an impossible answer to *Is it a fine day?*[6] So the use of 'yes' provides no evidence that the sense of a *yes-no* question is a complete thought, and the impossibility of using 'true' as an answer to a *yes-no* question leads to the suspicion that, by saying 'yes' in such a case, the speaker is not in the business of presenting a previously expressed complete thought as true.

Frege is right, however, to say in 'Thought' that many sentence-types used to issue commands are incomplete. But what is the site of that incompleteness? In *Take your shoes off!*, there is no overt subject, but the addressee is understood, so this is not the site of incompleteness.[7] Rather, the incompleteness characteristic of commands is the incompleteness that distinguishes the imperative mood from the indicative, a distinction that involves matters of temporal reference. Characterizing that difference is no simple matter, but it may be said that while the indicative mood is used to place an event at a time, the imperative mood is used to enjoin an addressee to make an event come about. Assertoric indicatives place facts in time, whether present, past, or future, while imperatives urge their coming. The imperative is incomplete in that it does not place an event in time, but the predicate is saturated.[8] By using an unplaced sentence-type

---

[6] Although we *can* respond *True* (or *Right*) after the confirmation question *It's a fine day?*, since in confirmation questions a complete thought *is* expressed, the incompleteness in this case often reflecting a lack of confidence, as will be argued.

[7] Of course, one can overtly refer to the addressee by saying *You take your shoes off!* It makes a difference whether the 'you' is overt or not. Imagine the drill sergeant saying, instead of *Present arms!*, *You present arms!* Or imagine saying to the waiter *You bring me the check!* As with the questioning speech-acts, there is a lot a sorting out to do among the ordering speech-acts.

[8] Here also there is much work to be done, much of it involving grammatical tense. One task is to explain the curious use of the present tense in *I (hereby) promise to leave*. Perhaps only in performative occurrences may the present tense on an active (non-stative) verb actually denote simple present time. The present tense in *Max promises to leave* is different; there is a generic use,

expressing the doing of an action by the addressee, the speaker can perform a variety of speech-acts, including not only ordering the addressee to perform that action, but also suggesting, cajoling, or entreating him to do so. Since sentence-types in the imperative mood are saturated, they cannot be confused with *yes-no* questions. Since they lack *wh*-expressions, they cannot be confused with sentence-types used to ask *wh*-questions. Sentence-types normally used to ask questions and issue commands are both incomplete, but they differ in the site of the incompleteness. On the speech-act side, there is a similarity between questioning and ordering. Commands are like requests to perform activities and questions are like requests for information. Neither commands nor questions should be generally identified with requests, but there are similarities. Many sentences used to issue commands and many sentences used to ask questions are incomplete; the site of incompleteness generally differs. But complete sentence-types may be used to issue commands; *You will take your shoes off* may be used to predict a future event or to urge the addressee to bring it about.

So, putting aside commands and returning to the topic of asking questions, I will be adopting an analysis for *yes-no* questions that I believe Frege could have adopted but did not. In his terms, I will be claiming that inverted sentence-types such as *Is it raining?* express incomplete thoughts, the incompleteness consisting in an absence of saturation. But there is a distinction of form and a distinction of use that applies more broadly, and cuts more deeply, than the classical distinction between *yes-no* questions and *wh*-questions. Beyond these there is another kind of question, and this kind of question embodies another kind of incompleteness.

1.2 Open questions, confirmation questions, and the standard of completeness

The fundamental distinction among the questioning speech-acts is between open questions and confirmation questions. It cross-cuts the sentence-type differences between *yes-no* questions and *wh*-questions. This has not, however, been generally recognized, since open questions have received virtually all of the attention. This bias is not inexplicable, since many of the things that researchers have found interesting about questions are characteristic of open questions. The questions posed by science, for example, are open questions. But the resulting tendency has been to equate all questions with open questions. Furthermore, since open questions and confirmation questions stand in direct contrast with each other, both have been misunderstood. The distinction between these two speech-acts involves the sort of ignorance a speaker presents himself as having.

---

and an historical present use. Austin (1962) held that this use of tense perhaps came closest to a grammatical criterion for performative sentences. Another task is to understand the uses of the grammatical tenses in the non-indicative moods.

Sentences must be distinguished from the uses to which they are put. In asking a question, there are two possible sites of incompleteness. The incompleteness might reside in the structure of the sentence used, or the incompleteness might reside in the using of the sentence. Sentences used to ask open questions are incomplete in structure. Sentences used to ask confirmation questions may well be complete in structure, but there is an incompleteness in the using of them.

In asking an open *wh*-question, the speaker presents himself as not knowing what item, or what predicate, rightly fills the incompleteness in the sentence-type he has uttered a token of. In asking an open *yes-no* question, the speaker presents himself as not knowing whether a predicate ought rightly to be glued to some item. In Chapter 3, we will encounter some deviations from this, but these are the central cases. In general, by using a sentence-type that is incomplete in a particular way, the speaker presents himself as being unable to complete that sentence-type in that way. The question asked is open in that respect. And, if he does use an incomplete sentence-type, he generally intends to be taken to be asking the hearer to complete it for him.

In contrast, consider the question *You are talking to who?* That might be said in many different circumstances; one such circumstance must suffice here. Suppose, seeing you talking on the telephone, I ask you who you are talking to and you reply that you are talking to the Queen of England. Hearing you perfectly well, and believing what you have said, I might nevertheless respond: *You are talking to who?* In that case, I do not consider the question open, I consider it quite closed in fact, but I may achieve the effect of surprise by presenting myself as needing you to confirm what you have said. Take now a *yes-no* case. If you walk in soaking wet, and I say to you *It's raining?* I present myself as wanting you to confirm my belief, based on your appearance, that it is raining. In contrast with earlier open-question examples, in which the speaker considered the range of possible answers open, in these confirmation-question examples, he does not. But the distinction between the two kinds of question cuts even deeper. In the Queen of England example, I make as if I cannot complete what I set out to say; in the raining example, I make as if I do not quite have enough confidence to assert that it is raining. These are incompletenesses not in the structures of the sentences used but in the using of them.

Austin (1962) saw large parts of this, distinguishing among various infelicities that an utterance may suffer from. Among the infelicities are hitches—cases in which a speech-act is incompletely performed, and abuses—cases in which the performer of a speech-act lacks the thoughts, feelings, or intentions that one should have if one is to perform that act. These two kinds of infelicity correspond, in an interesting way, to the two kinds of confirmation question I have just exemplified. I do not mean to say that confirmation questions are infelicitous; they are not. Rather, the speaker of a confirmation question presents himself as lacking what he would have to have to perform the corresponding assertion felicitously. Since the speaker of a confirmation question does not present himself as making an assertion, the incompletenesses that would give rise to (assertive) infelicities have no teeth. The incompletenesses are intentionally and openly displayed, thereby furthering the goal of asking a question.

When I say that a speaker, when asking a question, 'presents himself' as having a particular lack, I mean that in a quite literal way. The presentation is performed either through the choice of a noticeably incomplete sentence or through the noticeably incomplete using of a sentence. The nature of the incompleteness reveals the nature of the lack. The lack is the ignorance the speaker wants relief from.

But what is the standard of completeness? It is tempting simply to suggest that the declarative sentences and the assertive use of them provide the standards of completeness: that, on the side of open questions, declarative sentences are structurally complete in a way that sentences used to ask questions are not and that, on the side of confirmation questions, asserting is complete in a way that asking a confirmation question is not. But this will not quite do. The problem is that, among assertions, it is arguable that there are degrees of completeness. If we contrast *Jack ate* with *Jack ate the fish*, it would seem that the second is more complete than the first, since it specifies what Jack ate while the first does not. But then the question comes, is not *Jack ate* incomplete in the same way that *What did Jack eat?* is? Are they not both incomplete in that they do not specify what Jack ate?

If assertions as a class do not provide a standard of completeness for questions as a class, we are left with the natural alternative of defining completeness on a case-by-case basis. The idea would be that, corresponding to each question, there are assertions that are complete in a way that the question is not. On the open question side, corresponding to the sentence *What did Jack eat?* there is a structurally related set of sentences containing *Jack ate the fish*, but not *Jack ate*, since *Jack ate*, though an assertion, is not complete with respect to the question, since it, like the question, fails to specify what Jack ate. On the other hand, the question *What did Jack do?* will find *Jack ate* in its corresponding set, since *Jack ate* specifies what the question fails to specify. On the side of confirmation questions, the incompletenesses include hitches and abuses. Felicitous assertions are free of these incompletenesses.

Now the reader will have noticed that my examples of sentence-types used to ask confirmation questions are not deformed, while the sentence-types used to ask open questions have undergone *wh*-movement or inversion. This, in English, is the noticeable syntactic distinction between sentence-types used to ask the two kinds of question; again, it cross-cuts the distinction between *wh*-questions and *yes-no* questions.

My treatment here has been necessarily rough. It will be the business of Chapter 3 to distinguish open questions from confirmation questions in more detail, and to identify various subspecies of each.

1.3 Grammar and use

I wish to conclude this preview by going over the same terrain—the distinction between open questions and confirmation questions—but this time at a slightly higher altitude, focusing on grammar and use.

When speaking, we perform a vast number of activities. Some of these activities are under our conscious command. Others of them are not. The simplest of our linguistic gestures reveals this duality. We often consciously decide which word to say. But, when saying the word 'bat' we seldom consciously decide to lower our tongues to make the vowel. Nevertheless, to say 'bat', we must lower our tongues. So not only is it true that some of our activities are conscious and some not, it also is true that some of our activities are forced to occur once an independent choice is made. To be sure, we can attend to at least some of our forced choices; we can observe our tongues lowering to make a vowel. But normally, the linguistic activities that are forced are beneath our notice. And, as against the activities that are normally beneath our notice, there are other activities that are beyond our notice. Our sequencing of words involves the application of syntactic knowledge, the application of the rules that determine well-formedness for the sentences of our languages. But we cannot make ourselves conscious of the application of this knowledge to the course of our speech. We can decide which word to say next, but we cannot consciously consult the rules of syntax. The most we can do is to deduce their nature through linguistic research.

In addition to grammatical knowledge, there is another sort of linguistic knowledge that is beyond our consciousness. Like our grammatical knowledge, its nature can only be deduced through study. Once we have decided what we want to say, there comes the question what words we wish to say it with. The distinction between these two decisions is complicated, but in the simplest declarative circumstances, we have on the one side the decision which proposition to express and on the other the decision which sentence-type to use to express it. The first decision is usually conscious; we usually consciously decide what to say. But the second choice is often not conscious. Knowing what we want to say, we normally quite unconsciously pick out a sentence-type that will serve to say it. There are times when we consciously agonize over wording, of course, but to a large extent, and in many respects, sentence-types are chosen unconsciously.[9]

There are rules of sentence choice. Grice (1975) discovered some of them; he proposed that the cooperative nature of language favors some sentence-types

---

[9] So my use of the word 'decide' should not be taken to imply that all of the considerations that go into the decision are, or could be made to be, conscious. In choosing A over B, it may be that the properties that make A seem desirable are unconsciously derived.

over others in the course of conversation. But there are many other kinds of rule of sentence choice, among them rules whose nature does not depend on the cooperative nature of language.

Grammar provides a definition of sentence-type. A syntax provides a definition of well-formedness for the sentence-types of a language, and a semantics provides the meanings of those sentences by composing the meanings of their parts. Both are parts of grammar; a semantics provides those aspects of meaning that are grammatically determined. The extent to which meaning is grammatically determined is debatable, but I think there is no one who really believes that there are no grammatically determined aspects of meaning. There are also rules of sentence choice, which state how a speaker decides which sentence-type to utter a token of. I have tried to use the terms syntax and semantics in ways that few, if not no one, would object to. But what I have said about use needs comment. I have been assuming that a significant consideration in the practice of talking is deciding which sentence to utter. If I wish to say something, I cast around for a sentence-type which, if a token of it were to be uttered in the current circumstance, would serve to express that thing I wish to say. There are indeed rules about this practice. They are not rules of grammar, but rather rules that state how to choose among the tools that grammar provides. They do not tell us what to say, rather they underlie our ability to decide what to say.

Rules of sentence choice are not the same kind of rules as rules of grammar. They are rules in a different sense. Rules of grammar, when broken, yield defective tools. Rules of sentence choice, when broken, yield defective applications of tools. By saying *We was robbed!*, I break a rule of agreement in standard English grammar. By saying *We was robbed!* to inform you that pigs fly, I break a rule of sentence choice: the sentence *We was robbed!* is not a tool that lends itself to that purpose, though some wild scenario might be set up in which that use of the sentence-type might succeed. Sometimes we are lax with our grammar, at other times lax with our usage. Sometimes, current circumstances do not require that we find a sentence-type that expresses exactly what we wish to get across. At other times, we must be more careful.

That I generally cannot use the sentence *We was robbed!* to inform you that pigs fly is an instance of the more general rule that if you intend to speak literally and directly and if you intend to be taken as meaning that P, you should choose a sentence that means that P. When we speak non-literally or indirectly we flout this rule, but that is the best evidence that we generally respect it. There is another rule of sentence choice which I have already touched on, and which will be discussed in more detail in Chapter 3. And that is that, if a speaker wishes to ask an open question, the speaker should select a 'deformed' sentence-type to do so. In the case of *wh*-questions, the *wh*-expression is fronted; in the case of *yes-no* questions the auxiliary verb is fronted. So sentence-types such as *Who are you talking to?* and *Did Bernini design that?* are used to ask open questions. And there is another rule of sentence choice that states that if a speaker wishes to ask a confirmation question, the speaker should select an 'undeformed' sentence-type to do so. So *You're talking to who?* and *Bernini designed that?* are used to ask confirmation questions. These are merely rules of sentence choice; there are circumstances under which one can get the same effect by using a structurally different tool. In fact, in circumstances of indirection, there are effects that can only be achieved by choosing a tool normally reserved for a distinct purpose. This is characteristic of rules of use, not rules of grammar.

The tools that English presents us with are structurally related to each other. *It's raining?* and *Is it raining?* are related by a syntactic rule, inversion, that moves the auxiliary verb 'is' to the beginning of the sentence. We have the option of using the moved or unmoved form, and I have suggested that, if we wish to ask an open question we use the moved form, while if we wish to ask a confirmation question we use the unmoved form. But is the syntactic movement itself optional, or is it obligatory? I am maintaining that syntax does not and should not contain morphemes such as 'Q' or 'Open Q', that would have the power of triggering inversion. Structures do not contain their uses. Sufficient for all purposes is to allow that inversion is optional, that its application reveals a kind of incompleteness, and then to state the rules for choosing the moved and unmoved forms. This is in contrast with some current styles of theorizing, including the minimalism initiated by Chomsky (1995), which hold that all syntactic movement is obligatory, that all movement is triggered by syntactic requirements. And that would lead to the view that there is something like a morpheme 'Open Q' that triggers obligatory movement. The syntactic account that I offer in Chapter 5 avoids all of that.

In sum, the type of questioning speech-act one wants to perform depends on the kind of ignorance one has, and the kind of sentence-type one utters depends on the kind of questioning speech-act one wants to perform. There are two sorts of ignorance that are matched by two sorts of speech-act that are matched by two sorts of sentence-type. One sort of ignorance consists in lacking an item or a predicate. If one is ignorant in this way, one should ask an open question, using a sentence-type that is incomplete. The other sort of ignorance consists in lacking the capacity to assert something. If one is lacking in this way, one should ask a confirmation question. There is a rule of sentence choice that states that one should use deformed sentence-types to ask open questions and undeformed sentence-types to ask confirmation questions; the distinction between open questions and confirmation questions cross-cuts the distinction between *yes-no* questions and *wh*-questions. The speaker of a question expects the hearer to believe that the reason for producing something incomplete is that something complete cannot be produced, the implication being that the hearer is meant to provide the completion. That is the convention of asking questions.[10]

1.4 Outline of what follows

I have described some of the grosser features of the terrain that I will be exploring. The ordering of topics moves from the general to the more specific. First we must agree on how to talk about talk. That is the business of Chapter 2. In Chapter 3, I consider a wide range of questioning speech-acts, aiming primarily to distinguish those that make use of deformed sentence-types from those that make use of undeformed sentence-types, the open questions from the confirmation questions. The distinction between the speech-acts using inverted sentence-types and those using *wh*-sentence-types is a secondary matter. Here I aim for completeness, but certainly fail, and for two reasons. One source of failure comes from the fact that whether or not an utterance succeeds as a questioning speech-act, and what kind of questioning speech-act it succeeds as being, depend on circumstance of use, and it is impossible to exhaust circumstances of use. Though one hopes that the speciation of questioning speech-acts is not as fine-grained as circumstance of use, it is not at all clear what the right size of grain should be. Secondly, there is no sharp boundary separating the questioning speech-acts from the rest, so even aiming for completeness must be misguided. Nevertheless I have managed to include quite a few cases, including some near the ill-defined boundary. In Chapter 4, I dispense with *yes-no* questions and with confirmation questions as well. What remains are open *wh*-questions, the better understood for having been introduced in contrast with the other kinds of question. It is in this area that the interaction between syntax, semantics, and use is the most intricate and the most robust. I first distinguish 'what' from 'which' semantically, developing an analysis from wider distinctions that separate quantifiers. That allows me to situate 'who' correctly. That done, I move from the simple cases, to consider multiple *wh*-questions, both those including multiple occurrences of 'who' and those including multiple occurrences of 'which'. This is a vast area, and the interactions between syntax and speech-act theory are extremely complex. There is much that I will leave untouched, including much of interest concerning adjunct-questions, such as *why*-questions, *where*-questions, *when*-questions, and the like. Nevertheless, by the end of the chapter, some syntactic generalizations are converged on. In Chapter 5, I present some syntactic proposals, these being designed so as to comport well with the semantic, syntactic, and speech-act generalizations achieved in the previous chapters, including a discussion of the syntactic incompleteness displayed by inversion and by *wh*-variables. As it happens, up to this point, the book was conceived backwards. The actual thinking-through of the material

---

[10] I wish to thank a reader for helpful comments concerning these general points.

proceeded backward from a very specific insight concerning the syntax and use of multiple questions which appears in Chapter 5, to successively more general topics concerning the nature of questioning, developed in the earlier chapters. In Chapter 6, I display the resulting theory, concentrating on a few hard and beautiful facts. At the end, analysis of *Who is who?* and *Which is which?* provides the opportunity to consider the question how ignorant a speaker may be when asking a question, as well as the nature of identity questions.

2

The Instrumental Model of Talking: How to Talk about Talk

2.1 The use and using of expression-types

My overall conception of talk is instrumental, grounded on the locution that we use language, and informed by common-sense considerations concerning how one goes about doing things with tools. We each know one or more languages, those languages contain sentences, and one of the things that we do with sentences is to ask questions with them. There are many kinds of question that we can ask, and the number of sentences available to us is practically limitless. Neither of these considerations seems to slow us down. Somehow, we decide what question we wish to ask and select a sentence, which, when uttered, will serve to ask it.

There are rules speakers follow when selecting a sentence-type to perform a speech-act. To investigate those rules, it is necessary to determine what speech-acts a sentence-type might be used to perform, and what aspects of sentence-types might make them good candidates for the performing of particular speech-acts. Some sentence-types, because they have the structures that they do, lend themselves to the performing of questioning speech-acts. And some questioning speech-acts, because of their nature, are most accurately performed using sentence-types of a particular structure. As already mentioned, undeformed sentence-types such as *It's raining?* and *You talked to who?* lend themselves to the asking of confirmation questions, while deformed sentence-types such as *Is it raining?* and *Who did you talk to?* lend themselves to the asking of open questions.

Conventional meaning (and conventional use) are functions of a sentence-type; reference and truth (and occasional use) are functions of the using of a sentence-type. Let me begin with these assumptions, which are, in part, due to Strawson (1950*a*). Sentence-types have conventional meanings; when conventionally used, they are used with their conventional meanings. Expressions other than sentence-types also have conventional meanings. Lexical items do. The expression 'cape' has the conventional meaning 'promontory of land'; it is conventionally used to mean that. There is a distinct but homophonous expression 'cape' that has the conventional meaning 'sleeveless cloak', and *it* is conventionally used to mean *that*.

A speaker must learn the conventional meanings of expression-types, both sentence-types and lexical items. The learning of the conventional meanings of the vocabulary of a language is, in one respect, a finite task: there is a finite number of items in the vocabulary of any language. To be sure, the learning of the conventional meaning of a vocabulary item is complicated, ongoing, and subject to error. One might, for example, mistakenly think that one conventional meaning of 'cape' is 'bay' since Cape Cod presents both a promontory and a bay. The Cape of Good Hope would then provide the corrective. And homophony itself is a serious problem; the learner must often decide, in a language such as English, whether she is confronting two occurrences of the same expression-type or not. The difficulties should not be underestimated. But the vocabulary at least has the advantage of being finite.

The learning of the conventional meanings of sentence-types is a different story. The number of sentence-types is infinite, yet sentence-types do have conventional meanings. Compositionality makes this possible. The conventional meanings of sentence-types are determined from the conventional meanings of the lexical items they contain, and the rules governing their combination. But what of conventional use? Over and above the rules determining the conventional meanings of sentence-types, there are rules that determine their conventional uses.[1] These rules fasten on generally defined structural properties of sentence-types and identify the conventional uses of sentence-types that have those structural properties. There are structural properties of certain sentence-types in virtue of which they are candidates for particular conventional uses.

Incomplete sentence-types are conventionally used to ask open questions. I am suggesting that there is a rule of sentence choice that fastens on structural incompleteness and says of those sentence-types with that property that they may be conventionally used to ask open questions. For that to be the case, structural incompleteness must be identifiable across the infinite range of sentence-types. That is possible because structural completeness can be finitely defined. The syntax of a natural language itself provides the grounds for a finite definition of syntactic incompleteness: in English, a sentence-type is syntactically incomplete if it presents an application of *wh*-movement or inversion. Since the syntax of natural language is recursively defined, it is possible to identify an unlimited number of instances in which either *wh*-movement or inversion apply.

In contrast, there is no structural property of sentence-types used to ask confirmation questions that signals that those sentence-types are conventionally used to ask confirmation questions. In particular, these sentence-types are not structurally incomplete; rather, the incompleteness inheres in the *using* of the sentence-types chosen for asking them, not in the sentence-types themselves. In

---

[1] Of course, if the doctrine were that conventional meaning *is* conventional use, this could not be said. I am distinguishing them, taking the conventional meaning of a sentence-type to be part of its grammatically determined structure.

John saw who? a *wh*-expression fills object position; in *It's raining?*, the glue is in place. These sentence-types are, in a way that I will explicate in Chapter 3, complete. Some might think that the contrast between *It's raining* and *It's raining?* is given, if not syntactically, at least phonetically, in terms of rising intonation, and might therefore claim that both open questions and confirmation questions owe their statuses *as* open questions and confirmation questions to grammatically determined properties of sentence-types after all. I will argue that this view is false to the facts, and that rising intonation, despite appearances, is not a grammatically determined property of sentence-types used to ask confirmation questions. There is no conventional meaning, or structural characteristic, determined of sentence-types, in virtue of which they are conventionally used to ask confirmation questions. In my view, the use of confirmation questions is not conventional but occasional, determined in the asking of them.

Confirmation questions are directed not toward the completion of sentence-types but toward the completion of utterances. To a great degree, they address the infelicities identified by Austin (1962). The sentence-types used to ask them are complete. But, in the using of them, the speaker presents himself as lacking the relevant required intentions or as being unable to avoid a hitch or a flaw. An utterance, in particular an assertive utterance, to be felicitous, must be accompanied by certain beliefs, and must be said completely. The absence of either of these constitutes an incompleteness in the assertive event.

Many of the sentence-types used to ask confirmation questions have other uses as well. Perhaps most noticeably, the sentence-types used to ask *yes-no* confirmation questions may also be used to make assertions. The question then comes whether declarative sentence-types have conventional meanings closely identified with their assertive use. If one group of sentence-types may be used both to ask confirmation questions and to make assertions, it may be doubted whether declarative sentence-types have assertive conventional meanings at all. Indeed, I do doubt this. Let us agree that the term 'declarative' should not suggest that there is some aspect of meaning in virtue of which a sentence-type, containing an expression or expressions with that meaning, is, or can be, used to make an assertion. Rather, declarative sentence-types are those sentence-types that are, or can be, conventionally used to make assertions. I can then theorize that in the asking of a confirmation question, one selects a declarative sentence-type, whose conventional use is assertive, in order to ask a question, the *occasional* use of which is confirmatory. On this account, occasional use and conventional use can coexist and yet diverge. Here, we have a sentence-type that has one conventional use, being used in an utterance with a distinct occasional use. I think that is probably the best way to express how at least some confirmation questions work. The occasional uses of confirmation questions depend on the (distinct) conventional uses of the sentence-types used to ask them. And, since matters of reference and truth arise in the using of sentences, not in their use, it follows that matters of truth and reference arise in the asking of confirmation questions in a way different from the way in which matters of truth and reference arise in the asking of open questions, a point that will be explored further in Chapter 3.

I assumed in the previous paragraph that one of the conventional uses of declarative sentence-types is to make assertions. And I suggested that one of their occasional uses is to ask confirmation questions. Are there other uses, either conventional or occasional, to which declarative sentence-types may be put? Certainly. Declarative sentence-types may be used to suppose. They may be used to propose courses of action and to express opinions. A speaker may use declarative sentence-types to perform a wide range of speech-acts. Which of these uses are conventional and which occasional is far from clear. One might wish to claim that the assertive speech-act is somehow primary, but that would have to be argued empirically. Here, apart from taking on some suggestions found in Austin (1953), I will not attempt an exploration of the assertive speech-acts.

A few words about terminological choices seem necessary at this point. Strawson (1950*a*), especially section II, although the source of much that I assume, comes to a somewhat different set of terminological choices from what I do. I agree with him that one should take seriously what it is 'natural' to say about using sentences and about uttering them. However, I have partially different views about what is natural, and have slightly different goals. It is central to Strawson's concerns to explicate the expression 'same use of a sentence', where the term 'sentence' may be replaced for clarity by 'sentence-type'. Suppose speakers A and B use sentence-type S at the same time to say something about the same person. Then, according to Strawson, they have made the same use of S. On the other hand, if A and B use the sentence-type S at the same time to say something about different people, they have made different uses of S. Because a sentence such as *I am hot*, even if used at the same time by A and B, says the same thing about *different* people (A and B), as Strawson wishes to speak, no two people can ever make the same use of the sentence *I am hot*.

How would this terminological decision play itself out in other domains? Suppose that I use wax to seal my letters, and that you use wax to seal yours. Extending Strawson's terminological proposal from the use of sentences to the use of wax, it would seem that we do not make the same use of wax. Just as, in the sentence case, you use the sentence-type *I am hot* to speak of yourself and I use the same sentence-type to speak of myself, so in this case you use wax to seal your envelopes and I use wax to seal mine. Now I think this is a very narrow restriction to place on the use of the expression 'same use'. A broader way to talk would be to say that we made the same uses both of wax and of the sentence *I am hot*: each of us to seal his letters, and each of us to say that he is hot, respectively. This broader usage would seem to be the usage of common talk. It is allowed on this broader usage that one sentence-type may be used to express distinct propositions, and further that, when this occurs, the uses of them may, nevertheless, be the same. Sameness of proposition does not follow from sameness of use. It serves Strawson's purposes to concentrate on the use of a sentence-type, as opposed to the using of a sentence-type. The use of a sentence-type is something it has even if it has never been used. The using of a sentence-type is an event which consists in the sentence-type being used. As I have said, I believe both notions are needed to account for questioning. The question for me is not only whether a sentence-type has a particular conventional use, but also whether a sentence-type, having the conventional use that it does, can have a certain occasional use, a matter of particular concern in the case of confirmation questions.

A final point on Strawson: he considers it natural to say that the same sentence is uttered on different occasions. For clarity, I have decided to exclude this way of speaking. I agree that this usage is common shorthand, as when I say that you and I own the same book if we own copies (tokens) of the same book (type), a reading that many expressions allow in many environments. Strictly speaking, though, a speaker uses types but never tokens and utters tokens but never types, a point I will return to. There are various questioning speech-acts, in the performing of which various tokens are uttered. And there are various sentence-types that are used when these speech-acts are performed.

In this chapter, I must bring use and grammar under one analytical vocabulary. Since Austin (1962), the things that we use sentences to perform have been called 'speech-acts'. The question before us is how speakers choose among sentence-types to perform speech-acts, and specifically questioning speech-acts. The domain of sentence-types and the domain of speech-acts have been explored, at least in part. On the side of sentence-types, linguistics provides us with an account of their syntactic structures, and there are various positions within linguistics as to how those structures are assigned meanings. On the side of speech-acts, we have the study of pragmatics. But I need to have a way to talk about talk that bridges the two domains, and unites their contributions. Here there is some work to do, for there is the tendency within each field to believe that all of language can be handled with the analytical tools available to just that field. To a significant extent, each field sees language in its own terms only. But there is a very clear connection between them, a connection which accepts that the two domains are distinct. That connection is that the objects that linguistics studies are the objects that speakers use, and the objects that speakers use are among the objects that pragmatics studies.

Those objects are sentence-types; when we talk, we use sentence-types. There is much within that formulation that demands clarification. One word to become clear about is the verb 'use', and another word to become clear about is the noun 'sentence'. We need a more general view of instrumentality, a more general conception of what using consists in. With that perspective, we can then discern how using sentences is like the using of other kinds of things, and how using sentences is a special kind of using. Regrettably, the verb 'use' has not received fair attention. But while the expression 'sentence-type' is a technical term, and can be awarded a regimented sense ad lib, the verbs 'use' and 'utter' apparently occur in discussions of these domains with their common-English senses. What are those senses? We should consider how common English deploys the verbs 'use' and 'utter' in general. Furthermore, in the case of sentence-types and sentence-tokens, we should consider common-English talk about types and their tokens. One question that arises here is whether, when talking of tool-using generally, we would commonly say that people use types or tokens. Admittedly, common speech is not the last word on the subject of sentence-use, or the type-token distinction (or anything else, for that matter). But, as Austin once quipped, common usage is the first word on this and other subjects, and it is in any event a good idea to keep tabs on common usage when prying into scientific matters, if only to guard against bringing in unnoticed assumptions.

So: Given the syntactic frame 'X uses Y in order to do Z', where in place of 'X' we may have the name of an agent, and in place of 'Z' we may have the name of an act, what may be replaced for 'Y'? A name of a tool. Now, how do we talk about tools? Do we, for example, say we use tokens, types, or some other thing entirely? And in the specific case in which, in place of 'X', we have the name of a speaker and, in place of 'Z', we have the name of a speech-act, with what may we replace 'Y'? These questions concern what used to be called the selectional restrictions of the verb 'use'. If 'use' were not so important a word, a word as important, in this area, as 'mean' and 'refer to' are in semantics, the interest of this topic would be lexicographical only. Here, however, getting clear on these points is central to settling theoretical terminology. Must we have a regimented sense for the verb 'use', or is its common sense adequate? To investigate this, we must consider common talk concerning instrumentality, and common talk concerning types and tokens.

2.1.1 Common talk of using types and tokens

Let's begin by considering common type-token talk about matters other than language use.[2] Take talk about books. I might say *You and I have read the same book*. There are two circumstances under which my statement might be true, either we both read the same physical item (I lent it to you when I finished), or we read different tokens of the same type (perhaps you, a paperback and I, a hardcover). Even, in the second case, if I read it in English and you read its translation in Russian, it would still be commonly said that we read the same book. (This point is underlined by the fact that, if you read *The Idiot* in Russian, and I read a *bad* translation in English, you could protest *It's not the same book!*) So there are circumstances in which, when speakers use the word 'same', they might either mean to reintroduce the same item or to say of an item that it belongs

---

[2] See also Fiengo 2003.

to the same type as another item does. I will call that the 'same-token/tokens-of-the-same-type' distinction. And the criteria for type-membership—for books at least—span translation. The same ambiguity arises in the use of demonstrative 'that'. Suppose you are reading *Moby-Dick*, and, pointing to it, I say *I've read that, too*. Here again I might be talking about the same item, or I might only be saying that I have read a different token of the same type (that again spans translation). The ambiguity is even more general. Suppose, pointing to an old VW, I remark, *I used to own that car*. I might mean that I once owned a token of the type that that car is also a token of, or I might mean that I once owned that very one (with cars, the question of translation does not arise). There are, to be sure, unambiguous cases. It is, a think, a great deal harder to find a tokens-of-the-same-type-use for *We have met the same man* or *I've met that man*. (Suppose, walking along, I spot a Lithuanian typographer with red hair, a man I've never met. However, happening to know several Lithuanian typographers with red hair, I say *I've met that man*. That seems wrong, though I have met that *type* of man, and in common talk we actually say *I've met that type*, or *I've met his type*.) But where the ambiguity exists, our uses of 'same' and demonstrative 'that' agree, in that no formal device need appear to mark the same-token/tokens-of-the-same-type distinction. If the potential ambiguity would be conversationally problematic, we take pains to avoid it. If one wishes to be clearly understood as speaking of the token, not the type, one can sometimes say *That very one*, although this provision is not always decisive. There are other tactics. Now the cases just discussed are interesting in and of themselves—it is not obvious, for example, how, by pointing at a book, and saying 'that book', one manages to drag the type of that book into the conversation. But, without explaining that, one thing we can conclude is that types do cut a figure in our common usage, though, since it is not commonly marked, it might escape our notice. And, specifically we can draw a conclusion about the verb 'use'. The same ambiguity arises when I say *I've used that tool* or *We've used the same tool*. The same-token/tokens-of-the-same-type distinction holds for objects of the verb 'use'.

There are constructions involving 'use' that seem to allow a third reading. Consider *I can't decide which tool to use*. Here, it might be that tokens do not figure in my decision at all. I might just be asking myself what kind of tool to use. *Should I use glue or nails?*, I might be wondering, without considering any particular glue or nails. On the other hand, in other conversational circumstances, I might be deciding among tokens, either tokens of the same type or tokens of different types: *Should I use this hammer or that hammer?*, *Should I use this hammer or that wrench?* So the statement *I can't decide which tool to use* is ambiguous between a type reading and a token reading. Another such case is *Beethoven used the cello in a characteristic way*. In some conversational circumstances, it would be clear that no particular cello is in point, and in other circumstances some cello would be in point. So we have observed that the English verb 'use' allows objects that denote tokens, tokens of the same type, and also allows objects that at least appear to denote types, tokens not being in point at all. Now at the very least we know that if we wish to say that we use sentence-types and not sentence-tokens, we cannot base our argument on any *general* prohibition in English against saying that we use tokens. We do, in some cases, commonly say that we use tokens; this reading is certainly prominent in *I used the hammer*. On the other hand, if we wish to say that we use types, there is support for that in common English as well.

Now we are ready to consider talk about talk. Suppose you say *It's raining*, and I say *It's raining*, and that we speak at the same time in the same place about the same weather. We say that we said the same thing, and we say that we used the same sentence. Now suppose you say *Il pleut* and I say *It's raining*, speaking at the same time in the same place about the same weather. Again we say that we said the same thing, but we do not say that we said (or used) the same sentence. So, in contrast with our talk of books, where translated versions can be called tokens of the same book, when we talk of sentences, a sentence of English and its translation into French are not called tokens of the same sentence, even though the two sentences can be used to say the same thing. We may conclude that there is a common-talk use of the expression 'saying the same thing' that involves the content of what is said; if two people say sentences that have the same content, whether they are sentences of different languages or not, then they say the same thing, in this sense of the expression. But the expressions 'saying the same sentence' and 'using the same sentence' cut finer.

Now consider 'utter'. What might we mean by saying: *A and B uttered the same sentence*? If talk about talk proceeds as talk about books and cars does, this statement should be true either when A and B uttered the same sentence-token or when A and B uttered distinct tokens of the same sentence-type—that type, as just pointed out, not spanning translational differences. But important divergences between talk about talk and talk about books and cars become visible here. The first is that, in the case of talk, it is just impossible for A and B to utter the same token. As already mentioned, it may be said, as Strawson does, that two people utter the same sentence and mean by that that they utter distinct tokens of the same sentence. But only in some exotic circumstance, one in which, say, A and B share brains and vocal tracts, only when A and B become the same person in the relevant ways, would it be right to say that A and B uttered the same sentence-token. And this just reveals that *distinct* people cannot utter the same sentence-token. (Of course, the same *written* tokens—signs, for example—may be used by different agents.) So it comes to this. When we say that A and B uttered the same sentence, we normally can only mean that they uttered distinct tokens of the same sentence-type, since we normally cannot mean that they uttered the same token. And this raises a related distinction between talk about using sentences and talk about using other tools. Normally, it is all right to say that A used a tool-token, and then that A, later, used that very tool-token again. We can say that of a particular hammer, but we cannot say that of a particular sentence-token. I cannot lend you the sentence-token that I have just uttered, nor can I utter a particular sentence-token repeatedly myself, as I can use other tool-tokens, such as hammers. Uttered sentence-tokens are fixed in their time of utterance, and fixed to a particular agent.

Tools such as hammers and saws have the following properties. First, different people may use the same tool. Secondly, tools such as hammers and saws may be used at different times: they are persistently available. Hand tools are not always in use; we take them up, use them, and lay them down. Now, if we ask ourselves what in language, sentence-types or sentence-tokens, have *these* properties of tools, the answer is clear that, at least as we commonly talk about these matters, only sentence-types, and never sentence-tokens, have this status. Different people may use the same sentence-type. And sentence-types are persistently available; we take them up, use them, and lay them down. For these reasons, then, it is consistent with common usage that, when talking of the use of sentences, we generally talk of using sentence-types.

But we *can* also say that we use sentence-tokens. I certainly did use the previous sentence-token to make a point. As I noted, the English verb 'use' allows both that we use types and that we use tokens, as well as different tokens of the same type. It is just that when we talk of sentence-use we generally talk of types. In response to potential ambiguity, I have endorsed the practice of saying that we use sentence-types and utter (or write) sentence-tokens. In this mildly regimented way of talking, one uses sentence-types, not sentence-tokens, and one utters sentence-tokens, not sentence-types. Admittedly, just as 'use' poaches in the domain reserved for 'utter', so 'utter' poaches in the domain reserved for 'use'. But I think it is clear enough which belongs on which side.

2.1.2 Personal tools: the things that linguists study

Commonly, talk about language is talk about sentence-types. We consider *the* sentence *Flying planes can be dangerous*, and we notice that *it* is ambiguous. We ask what the meaning of *the* word 'dicey' is, and so forth. And when linguists ask how many sentences French contains, *J'ai faim* counts as only one. The commonly expressed conception is that there are sentence-types, and linguistics follows this. Not only are sentence-types the things that speakers use, they are also the things that linguists study. Pragmatics is the study of the use of those things that linguistics studies the structures of. It remains to be made clear what role the term 'language' plays in all of this. As Chomsky has been right to emphasize,[3] we talk on the one hand as though there is this one thing English or this one thing Chinese, and we say that people either speak it or they do not. On the other hand, we know perfectly well that English and Chinese each vary, sometimes greatly,

---

[3] For example, see Chomsky 1980: 217ff.

depending on where they are spoken and by whom, and we are aware that natural languages change over time, sometimes slowly, but at other times quickly and radically. That we can assign a single name to something that changes, perhaps radically, over time is not something peculiar to naming languages—the same is true of naming people, or any living thing. But in talking about languages a danger does arise that does not arise in talking about people: the danger of inferring from the existence of the name 'English' that there is one thing English that does not change. Although they do have sociopolitical import, names such as 'English' or 'Chinese', do not refer to linguistically distinguished entities. This does not make the study of universal grammar impossible. Our talent for learning languages, as Chomsky also first emphasized, may be viewed as a function from our linguistic experience to the knowledge of language we acquire. To study universal grammar is to study that function. While that function may be the same for all of us, our linguistic experience is not—the upshot being that there may be no two people that have exactly the same knowledge of language.

Nevertheless, for convenience, people often assume that they speak the same language. Perhaps, by this, they only mean that they can understand each other when they speak, despite the differences that may or may not be noticeable to them. When we make this common assumption, we can go on to say that different people use the same sentence, meaning by that that they use distinct tokens of the same sentence-type, that type belonging to a hypostasized common language. This usage can of course be replaced by one in which it is said that each person uses his own sentence-types, those sentence-types sometimes coinciding. For the fact remains that there is my English now and your English now and, if they are sufficiently alike, we can understand each other. And that's about it. But if this is the truth, and all of it, there is something further about sentence-types that makes them different from tools such as hammers and saws, which, as I noted above, are tools that can be passed from one user to another. In the view just expressed, I have my sentence-type *Max left* and, if your knowledge of grammar is sufficiently like mine, you have your sentence-type *Max left*—but we need not say that there is one sentence-type *Max left* that I can use and then you can use, drawn from hypostasized English.[4] We need not say that there is a tool box of sentence-types apart from us that you and I can equally reach into so as to choose our tools. I have my tools, you have yours, if our knowledge of language is similar, many of our tools will coincide, but no tool of yours is the same thing as any tool of mine. So sentence-types, the things we use when we speak, are *personal* tools, tools available only to the individuals that use them.[5]

---

[4] We need not say it. But we commonly do say it, not caring about the question what ontological status the hypostasized language might have.

[5] On this, see also Fiengo and May 2006.

If sentence-types are personal tools, then they are in certain important respects unlike carpenters' tools, and more similar to parts of our bodies. We say we use our hands, feet, fingers, or shoulders to do things, and we also say that we use our depth perception, color vision, or hearing to do things. We quite generally say that we use our abilities. In these cases, we are clear that A cannot use B's depth perception, that A cannot use B's color vision. True, we can say that A used B's leg (to pry open a door) but then we speak of the leg as alienably possessed, not as inalienably possessed. But we cannot use another's faculties, and our sentence-types, our personal tools, are our inalienable possessions.[6] Clearly, to understand the common use of the verb 'use', one must consider tool use, but equally clearly, the term 'tool' does not comfortably encompass all of the things that are used. Here we hit the limit of the analogy of sentence-types with tools.[7]

To be sure, speakers may find that circumstances demand that they speak not using their own sentence-types, but sentence-types underwritten by prescriptive grammar. Or they may choose to use sentence-types characteristic of someone other than themselves. But in these cases, the choices are individual choices; speakers may choose to speak in a way that others say is proper, or in the dialect of others. Such choices can be risky, as we seldom use unfamiliar tools well.

Summing up, in talk about talk, the verb 'use' commonly takes objects that refer to sentence-types, these sentence-types being tools that are inalienably possessed. The sentence-types that we use are our own personal sentence-types, not sentence-types that belong to the language English or the language Chinese. And the sentence-types that linguists study are the personal sentence-types of individuals, not sentence-types that belong to the language English or the language Chinese.

---

[6] A reader notes that we could imagine a voice synthesizer of the type Stephen Hawking uses being shared by two agents who, on an occasion, produce the same sentence-token. Indeed we could; this example puts pressure on the expression 'same sentence-token'. There is a choice. If all that is required for sentence-token identity is that there be one acoustic (visual, etc.) event, actuated by however many intentions one pleases, then I accede to the example and the usage it suggests. If, on the other hand, part of a sentence-token is the intentional activation of it, then I think we ought to say in the synthesizer case that we have two sentence-tokens that happen to conflate physically. I like the second path because it squares with the intuition that, when the wave on the beach recedes and we read *God is dead* in the sand, we do not consider what we see a token of the sentence-type *God is dead*. We consider what we see an outrage of nature that looks for all the world *like* a token of the sentence-type *God is dead*. Even Russell, who wishes to define the spoken word 'dog' as 'a class of similar movements of the tongue, throat, and larynx', points out that 'we cannot do so without taking account of intentions': 'A German is apt to say "dok"; if we hear him say "De dok vaks hiss tail ven pleasst", we know that he has uttered an instance of the word "dog", though an Englishman who had made the same noise would have been uttering an instance of the word "dok"' (1940, 1962: 22).

[7] In analogizing language use with tool use, Wittgenstein (1958: §41) goes further than I would. He analogizes names without bearers to broken tools. In one way, this makes sense. Suppose a tool is broken in such a way that it cannot perform its assigned task. Then, if its assigned task is to refer to Pegasus, 'Pegasus' is broken. But do names have only one assigned task? Plainly empty names have some use, a point that Wittgenstein sees clearly. Perhaps he would say that no name is completely broken.

2.2 How we talk: uttering tokens of types and recognizing types of tokens

In each of us, knowledge of language comes in parts. One part consists of our knowledge of phonology, another of syntax, and another of semantics. Our knowledge is such that it provides for each sentence-type in our language what we know of it in phonological, syntactic, and semantic terms. Generally, on confronting sentence-tokens of a language we know, we recognize the sounds they are composed of, know the structures of the types they are tokens of, know what they mean, and so forth. Each of us has within us a working theory of sentence-types. Our ability to detect which sentence-type we are confronting a token of is so automatic and so fast that it normally escapes our notice. This is actually a remarkable ability. Although no two voices are quite the same, although there are variations in speed, frequency, and volume, we are able to tell whether distinct individuals have produced tokens of the same sentence. Of course, there are limits. Some speech is so faint that it cannot be heard, some so fast or slurred that it turns into mere noise. And there are dialects so removed from our own that we miss a great deal, while other dialects are close enough that we can adjust to them. But within such understandable limits, there is a wide and diverse range, within which we can identify tokens of the same type.

The phonetic representations that linguists produce reflect this. Those representations omit matters such as difference in speed, frequency, and volume. What is represented are those aspects of perceived speech that are linguistically significant. More precisely, phonetic representation includes all and only those aspects of a spoken linguistic token that are necessary and sufficient for that token's being a token of its (linguistic) type; there might be 'feature-detectors', devices in the business of detecting in and extracting from the speech signal the distinctive features that the phonetic elements of a language are composed of, as Eimas *et al.* (1971) suggest. That might not be the correct model of phonetic perception; there are other imaginable ways that the acoustic chaff might be excluded and the wheat retained. But there can be little doubt that part of our ability in speech perception consists in being able to recognize, among sometimes widely varying speech signals, tokens of the same type.

Spoken sentence-tokens and written sentence-tokens have no grammatical structure. If one views the sentence-token just prior to this one, one can observe that it is a pattern shaped of ink-marks less than ten inches long, less than half an inch in height, and black. All of these are properties that the sentence-type of which it is a token lacks, and no property of it is a syntactic property, nor are the ink marks phonetic or semantic in any way. If we ask what, if any, properties suggestive of the sentence-type the ink marks do have, the answer is that, given the conventions of English orthography, the ink marks, in virtue of their shape (and not, for example, their color), represent a pronunciation, a pronunciation of an English sentence. But that represented pronunciation has no audible properties. If you now read the first sentence of this paragraph aloud, you have produced another sentence-token, which does have a set of audible properties: it is in your voice, has a duration of so many seconds, and a particular distribution of frequencies and volume. We wish to say what is commonly said: that both the ink marks at the beginning of this paragraph and the sequence of sounds of your reading them just now are tokens of the same sentence-type. And these tokens are tokens of particular sentence-types in virtue of being occurrences of pronunciations (or occurrences of representations of pronunciations) of sentence-types. But those marks or those sounds certainly have no grammatical structure. We engage in writing natural language on the assumption that the addressee knows the instructions for assigning a pronunciation to the marks we make. We can create the tangible tokens of Braille, thereby communicating with a deaf and blind individual who knows no corresponding pronunciation. It is essential to sentence-tokens that they be perceivable.[8] This flushes out an important point about sentence-types, a point that has been tracking us silently. Generally, and I think surprisingly, when we talk of sentence-types, we mean pronunciation-types. Consider how linguists talk about ambiguity, saying, for example, that *the* sentence *Flying planes can be dangerous* is ambiguous. There is only one pronunciation-type in point, and plainly we must be talking about that, since once we assign the sentence *Flying planes can be dangerous* one or another of its possible syntactic structures, then we no longer have a sentence that is syntactically ambiguous. Of course we can also say that there are two sentences, individuated by meaning, that have the same pronunciation. But the odd fact is that we can speak of one sentence-type and by that just mean one pronunciation-type.

As would be expected, this is revealed in our uses of 'use' and 'utter'. If I know that A uttered *Flying planes can be dangerous* meaning one thing, and B uttered *Flying planes can be dangerous* meaning the other, I can say that A and B uttered the same sentence (with different meanings). This is the shorthand way of saying that A and B uttered tokens of the same pronunciation-type. The ambit of the verb 'utter' is restricted to matters of pronunciation only, a restriction it does not always respect, but which it tolerates well. Often, to say that A and B 'uttered the same sentence' is to say that A and B produced tokens of the same pronunciation-type, that type being a member of an assumed language common to them. (This last proviso serves to exclude the case in which John says *Peter leaped* and Hans says *Peter liebt*.[9] The two utterances may be phonetically alike, but they are tokens of types in different languages.) But we could never say in

---

[8] Perhaps better: A sentence-token is a perceived intentional act. See note 6 above. Thanks to a reader for some perceptive comments here.

[9] I wish to thank David Pereplyotchik and Richard Brown for discussion of this example.

this case that A and B *used* the same sentence. What this shows is that we neither use pronunciation-tokens nor pronunciation-types. As already pointed out, it is just impossible for two speakers to use (or utter) the same pronunciation token, what we now see is that we do not use pronunciations at all. And there is a further conclusion we may draw. While pronunciation-tokens, the things we utter, do not have syntactic structure or meanings, the types that they belong to, the things we use, do have syntactic structure and meanings. The reason we cannot say that A and B used the same sentence where both uttered *Flying planes can be dangerous* (with different meanings) is that the sentence-type that A used is different in structure (and meaning) from the sentence-type that B used.

We are now ready to lay out how we talk. First, the structure of the tools. A sentence-type is composed of at least the following: (i) a pronunciation-type, (ii) a syntactic structure, and (iii) whatever aspects of meaning are grammatically determined by the logical structure of the sentence-type.[10] A pronunciation-type is composed of just those features that a pronunciation-token must have to be a token of that type. When we are spoken to, when we confront a spoken sentence, we have the ability to determine which pronunciation-type it is a token of. Having determined that, we have the further ability to determine which sentence-type that pronunciation-type belongs to. That ability resides in our grammatical knowledge, applied to the case at hand. It is the business of a grammar to inform us which pronunciation-types are associated with which syntactic structures. Two sentence-types may contain the same pronunciation-type and distinct syntactic structures—this is the case of syntactic ambiguity. In the case of syntactically ambiguous sentences, there will be more than one sentence-type that the pronunciation-type belongs to. Grammar, when applied to the case, will tell us that. Choosing which sentence-type one has heard a token of may also depend on one's estimation of the current intentions of the speaker; sometimes we get this wrong. But often enough, once we have determined which sentence-type the pronunciation-type that we have heard a token of belongs to, we have determined which sentence-type we have heard a token of.

In the case of talking, if we decide to utter a particular pronunciation-token, we do so because it meets the definition provided by a particular pronunciation-type. We choose to utter a pronunciation-token that meets the definition of one pronunciation-type, and not some other, because that pronunciation-type belongs to a particular sentence-type. And we wish to utter a pronunciation-token that meets the definition of a pronunciation-type that belongs to that sentence-type, and not some other, because that sentence-type is the sentence-type that we wish to use. If we notice that the pronunciation-type a token of which we intend to utter belongs to more than one sentence-type, we try to judge whether the hearer will be able to decide, given his estimation of our current intentions, which sentence-type we are using. Sometimes, we get this wrong. And we choose

[10] See May 1985.

to utter a token of a type in part because that type has a structure that lends itself to the speech-act we have decided to perform.

Ideally, the relation between pronunciation-type and logical form would be one-to-one. And, also ideally, there would be no syntactic 'distance' between the structure interpreted in phonetic terms and the structure interpreted in logical terms. The first ideal is not realized in natural languages: there are both synonyms and homonyms. The second ideal falls to the fact that in natural languages, rules of syntax — movement rules in particular — intervene between pronounced sentences and interpreted ones, leading to a syntactic derivational distance between pronunciation and logical form. Perhaps there are languages that show no movement. But in languages that are not ideal as so defined — and English appears to be one of them — there arise conditions that, in various ways, limit the distance between pronunciation and logical form. There are, for example, cases in which more than one pronunciation might be derivationally paired with a logical form to be deployed. In some such cases, syntax provides only the *simplest* pronunciation. (The 'superiority effect', to be discussed in Chapter 5, is one instance of this.) Sentence-types containing different pronunciation-types but the same logical-form-types may have different uses, which rules of use must determine.

2.3 Further implications of the instrumental approach

2.3.1 The performative proposal again

On one account, the performative proposal states that some sentence-types express propositions that state what they are used for. According to this proposal, the sentence-type *Is it raining?* expresses what *I ask you whether it is raining* does. But the sentence-type *I ask you whether it is raining* may be used to express two different things. It may be used to assert (as in *I (always) ask you whether it is raining*), or it may be used to ask a question (as in *I (hereby) ask you whether it is raining*). But one non-Austinian version of the performative hypothesis goes further. It states that, when a sentence-type such as *I (hereby) ask you whether it is raining* is used to ask a question, it is also used to say something *true*, namely that I, in the event, ask you whether it is raining. I cannot accept this, nor can I accept that one may use *Is it raining?* to say something true. I also cannot accept that as a matter of conventional meaning or occasional meaning, *Is it raining?* is ever true. I follow Austin in these matters. But whatever one's stance here, it is plain that the performative proposal, understood in this way, cannot replace a theory of use.[11]

---

[11] On the idea that the phenomena that motivated Austin can be reduced to truth-conditional semantics, perhaps supplemented by a syntactic performative analysis, see Lemmon 1962, Sadock 1974, and especially Levinson 1983, sections 5.2–5.4.

To see this, consider the explicit performative sentence-type (i):

(i) I ask you whether pigs fly.

By uttering a token of (i)—under appropriate circumstances, sincerely, etc.—a speaker asks a question. Consider now the sentence-type (ii):

(ii) He asks you whether pigs fly.

If a new speaker utters a token of (ii) to the person that a token of (i) has been addressed to, the speaker's statement is true, and the speaker has failed to ask a question.

Now either (i) and (ii) have the same conventional meaning or they do not. Suppose they do. Then the fact that (ii) cannot be used to ask a question and (i) can be so used cannot be due to a difference in conventional meaning. So the contrast between (i) and (ii) must be due to something else. That something else is given by a theory of use, which states that (ii) cannot be used to ask a question and (i) can. So if (i) and (ii) have the same meaning, we must have a theory of use, distinct from a theory of meaning, in whose terms the difference between the uses of (i) and the uses of (ii) is stated.

Now suppose that (i) and (ii) do not have the same conventional meaning. Then surely that difference of meaning must serve to explain why (ii) cannot be used to ask a question and (i) can. The theory to be developed must state that, because (i) means what it does, it may be used to ask a question, and that, because (ii) means what it does, it may be used to make a statement, but not to ask a question. There are then two possibilities. Either we have a theory of use which is distinct from a theory of meaning or we have a theory of use which *is* a theory of meaning. In any case, we have a theory of use, the only question being what its relation is to a theory of meaning.[12]

If we wish to understand the speech-act of questioning, the problem is not how to tag sentence-types for use. The use of a sentence-type is not part of the structure of a sentence-type any more than the use of any tool is part of the structure of that tool: it makes no sense to say that the use of a fork is *in* the structure of a fork. It does make sense to say that because the structure of a fork is as it is, it can be used to perform a wide variety of activities, including picking up a bean, or puncturing small holes in a pie crust. It also makes sense to say that because chopsticks are structured as they are, they also may be used to pick up a bean, but not for puncturing small holes in a pie crust. And when talking about the use of language, the same considerations apply. The issue, rather, is which syntactic or semantic properties of sentence-types make them suitable for one task and not another.

---

[12] On either account, the verb 'ask' would have to be improved upon. We say we ask both open questions and confirmation questions, but these are distinct speech-acts. The prefix 'I ask you . . .' is too crude.

Knowledge of grammar must be separated from knowledge of how to talk. Knowledge of grammar consists in knowing the structures of the tools. How to use those tools, knowing how to talk, is a different matter. One may know the structure of a tool and yet not know how to use it, and one may know how to use a tool and yet not know its structure. It is traditional, and indeed common-sensical, to say that, when one is talking, one is both deciding what content to express ('what to say', in one narrow sense of the phrase) and also deciding what to do by saying something with that content (deciding whether to inform, warn, denounce, etc.). On the instrumental view of the distinction just made, a view according to which talking is tool-using, that distinction is the distinction between deciding what tool to use and deciding what to do with it. Since one can use the same tool to do different things, without altering the structure of the tool, the possibility is raised that two tokens of the same sentence-type might constitute the performings of different speech-acts. If talking turns out to be like *this*, decisions concerning what content to express are decisions concerning the structure of the tool used, and are distinct from decisions as to what to do with the tool chosen. In talking, a speaker decides what he wants to do by uttering something, and finds a sentence-type (there might be many to choose from), an uttered token of which would do the job.

So the instrumental approach to talking allows that different utterances might have the same content but differ as to what speech-act they are the performings of. An utterance of *I will return* might be a promise, a threat, or a prediction, and it seems reasonable to say that, as a matter of grammatically determined content (tool-structure), all these would be the same: the same tool may be used to do any of these things.

2.3.2 Form follows failure

What is it about the form of a sentence-type that makes it a suitable tool for a particular function? Does the rubric 'form follows function' apply? That question can be taken in different ways, and is taken in different ways in the many domains in which it has been raised. I think the central idea this rubric seeks to express is that the reason that something has the form that it does in some way derives from the fact that it is used to do a particular thing. The notion of 'reason' pertinent here is hard to pin down. We say, for example, that the reason that this sandpaper is smooth is that it has been already used; this causal use of 'reason' seems clear enough. The using has caused a change in structure: the form of the sandpaper is an effect of its having been used. But, speaking roughly and in a different sense, we also say that the reason that a hammer has claws is that it is used to pull out nails. Here we speak of the reason why the hammer is made that way. The reason that hammers are made with claws is so that they may be used to pull out nails, the reason in point being not why hammers have claws but why hammers are made with claws. So the form of hammers follows from the fact that they are made to be used to pull out nails. I think it is clear that 'form follows function' cannot apply to language in either of these senses, and if one considers the rubric as applying to 'evolutionary' changes in tool structure, then the rubric would appear to be false. Languages change and human artifacts change, but according to very different pressures from those that impose themselves on biological species or human artifacts. In the case of human artifacts, Petroski (1992) argues that form follows *failure*: the reason a paperclip has the form that it does is that *previous* designs for 'related' tools (the 'ancestors' of paperclips) failed in one way or another. And of course Darwin (1899) saw that the same is true of living organisms. They have the forms that they do because *previous* related organisms, with different forms, *failed* where the current ones succeeded. The forms we observe are those that remain when different forms have died off. Form is not determined by function; rather, dysfunctionality leads to failure. It seems to me that we see this clearly when we talk about the history of species or the history of technology, areas that we have some understanding of. So when we talk about more complex and elusive things such as language, things that we do not understand all that well, we should not start grasping at straws. The forms of sentence-types do not follow from their functions. Languages, sets of sentence-types, change for a multiplicity of reasons, but the well-worn rubric does not appear to tell us anything about why the sentence-types have the forms that they do nor the direction in which they might change.[13]

Sentence-types are in many ways different from artifacts or organisms. It is not clear that they change in anything like the same way that artifacts and organisms do. But it is equally clear that it makes no sense to say that the reason that the sentence-types *Sparrows are brown* or *Haste makes waste* have the forms that they do is that they are used to do particular things. Rather we say that the reason that we can use *Sparrows are brown* to inform someone that sparrows are brown is at least in part because it means that sparrows are brown, and the reason that we can use *Haste makes waste* to instruct someone to slow down is at least in part because it means that haste makes waste. Tools, because of their structures, are suitable for the performing of some tasks and not others. So it will be no part of what follows to suppose that a particular sentence-type has the form that it does because it is used to perform a particular speech-act, or that language has the form that it does (whatever that might mean) because it is used to communicate, or to do anything else.

To summarize, the instrumental approach to talk takes talking to be tool-using. The logic of tool-using, according to which different tools may be used to perform the same task, different tasks may be performed using the same tool, some tools may not be used to perform certain tasks, and other tools may be used to perform a great variety of tasks, applies to the using of sentences in much the same way

---

[13] It is a very different question how our species evolved in such a way as to have language. I assume this question has an answer, though we may never find out what it is.

as it does to the using of hammers. This complexity in the relationship between sentence-structure and use should by itself make us suspicious of any syntacticizing of use. Lastly, the instrumental approach denies the view that form follows function, since that view seems inapplicable to the use of language generally.

2.4 Knowing how to talk to others

An instrumental approach to talking requires that people, if they know how to talk, know how to decide what sentence-type to use, and know how to determine what speech-act can be performed by using a sentence-type. If they do not know how to do these things, they just do not know how to talk. On top of this, people make these decisions in what is, from any human perspective, an unlimited number of situations, and speakers have an unlimited number of (personal) tools at their disposal. So the choices that speakers make when talking are made from among an infinite set of tools. Here, as an instrumental activity, perhaps talking is unique: it is hard to think of another activity that is pursued using a limitless number of tools.

Knowledge of grammar consists in knowing linguistic legislation. This is the subject matter of linguistics. But knowing how to choose which sentence-type to use is not. And it is largely outside the reach of psycholinguistics also. People hear sentences, read them, interpret them, but the study of how people choose which sentence-type to use, the study of how people go about this aspect of talking, is in important respects beyond experimental control. The problem is that people frequently and unpredictably say what they want to. Now there are, to be sure, some important things that have been learned about the articulatory activities that go on during talking and the psychoacoustic activities that accompany them. And it is tempting to include the articulatory abilities of a speaker within a speaker's knowledge of how to talk. It seems unobjectionable to say, for example, that some people *know how* to make certain sounds in certain languages (some can make the French 'r'), and that other people do not. But this knowing-how is in important respects distinct from the knowing-how just considered: the knowing how to *decide* what sentence-type to use and what speech-act to perform. The latter knowledge is tactical in nature, subject to individual style, the basis of limitless creativity, part of a cooperative enterprise. Knowing how to make the sounds of a language, on the other hand, is not knowing how to *decide* anything; it is a different kind of knowing-how (though one that is necessary for accomplishing the other).

It will help to say a few obvious things about some simple cases. I have distinguished between knowing how to decide what sentence-type to use and knowing how to decide what speech-act to perform. If, for example, I wish to warn you that the bull is about to charge, I should select among sentence-types in part on the basis of content, and I should make that decision in deference to the fact that I wish to warn you that the bull is about to charge by uttering something with that chosen content. So, depending on how it is pronounced, the circumstances under which it is said, and so on, an utterance of *The bull is about to charge* might be either a warning or a statement of fact. Sometimes such things as intonation serve to remove possible ambiguity as to which speech-act is being performed. But when there is no danger of misidentifying which speech-act is being performed, intonational tricks are fairly widely *not* resorted to, a point that I will return to.

Conversation is cooperative tool-using, though there are limits to the analogy. We choose to use sentence-types that will further the cooperative enterprise, and we choose to understand sentence-types in such a way as to further the cooperative enterprise. It was Grice (1975) who first stressed that the process of holding a conversation is a cooperative activity, and that much can be learned about how a speaker decides what to say from recognizing that speakers believe themselves to be engaged in a cooperative activity. He argued that, in deciding what to say, a speaker has in view a wide variety of considerations that go well beyond the conventional meanings of the sentences used: he distinguished the conventional meaning of an utterance from that which is merely implicated, making it possible to strip away those aspects of meaning due to the cooperative nature of conversation, leaving the conventional meaning of the utterance open to view. Thus Grice identified an important set of factors that a speaker must consider when deciding what to say.

Take Grice's maxim of quantity. If one speaks the truth, but not the whole truth, false implicatures may arise. When choosing what to say, one must take account of this. One must know the conventional meanings of sentence-types, and be able to determine the implicatures that would arise from using them. The rules of sentence choice that I am interested in studying are different from this. They require sensitivity to correlations between the grammatical properties of sentence-types (including their syntactic properties) and the kinds of speech-act they might be useful for. I have noted that incomplete sentence-types, for example, are useful for the performing of open questions. Grice might say that, in many circumstances, the kind of sentence-type useful for the performing of an assertion is one that expresses the whole truth. But structurally very different sentence-types might express the same whole truth. Correctly, Grice's maxim of quantity would not distinguish between these sentence-types, though other maxims might. Grice's maxims do not pry into the structures of sentences as such. Furthermore, they are largely silent concerning the speech-acts sentences are used to perform. The rules of sentence choice that I am interested in do concern these two domains, and the relations between them.

I have suggested that the tools used for the asking of open questions are incomplete sentence-types. A speaker who wishes to know what John is doing has at her disposal a (personal) sentence-type which, when uttered, will do the job. By uttering *What is John doing?*, the speaker uses a sentence-type that is incomplete in a particular respect, and marked to reflect that fact. The sentence-type contains no expression following the verb 'doing', and that fact is overt. By using an incomplete sentence-type, the speaker indicates that she cannot complete the sentence-type that she has used. And the conventional reasoning that she is relying on, on the part of the hearer, is that the reason that the speaker has used an incomplete sentence-type is, first, that she cannot complete it, and secondly, that she wishes that the addressee complete it. So we have a property of a tool, an incomplete sentence-type, that makes it a natural tool to use to ask a particular kind of question. But form does not follow function: it would be wrong to say that the reason that sentence-types are incomplete is that they are used to ask open questions. Rather, some sentences are incomplete, which makes them handy to ask open questions. In these crucial respects, talk of using sentence-types and talk of using of hammers are the same.

2.5 The wielding of sentence-types

Wielding a sentence-type is acting, sometimes dramatically. Once we have chosen our lines, we must act them out. We dress them with intonation; we put on a pronunciation act. In addition, there are various gestures that we use when we wield sentence-types, many of them reflecting cultural tradition, and many others reflecting personal style. These styles allow analysis—a vast enterprise that is not my concern here. I wish only to place the contribution of a tool, its use, and the manner in which it is wielded on the table together, in order to sort them out. Here a central question involves the boundaries between grammar and the rest. The rules that tell us how to choose a sentence-type do not tell us what to say. They do tell us, once we have decided what to say, how to choose a tool to pull that off. There are rules about this practice. They are not rules of grammar, but rather rules that state how to choose among the tools that grammar provides. And once a sentence-type is chosen, the question comes how to wield it. And there are rules about that.

2.5.1 On the wielding of sentence-types when using them to ask questions

Speakers, when they set out to say something, choose among sentence-types, hoping to find one which, if used, will serve their purposes. And speakers, when they set out to say something, also choose which speech-act to perform. Those decisions are intertwined. But over and above these decisions, there are further choices that speakers face, choices that might roughly be characterized as matters of affect. To utter a particular word, we must make certain sounds; to utter 'bat', we must make the sound [b]. But when we utter a sentence, there are many aspects of pronunciation which are discretionary. If a speaker wishes to sound angry, sad, rushed, or the like, there are various phonetic effects that the speaker can avail himself of.

Apart from deformation, the mark of questions most often cited is intonation, a phonetic effect often called 'question intonation', and I wish to consider its status. Is question intonation more like pronouncing [b] or more like sounding angry? In other words, is question intonation the result of linguistic legislation, as much a part of grammatical knowledge as syntax proper? Or is there no linguistic legislation singling out question intonation, making it not a matter of grammatical knowledge at all? And whether it is or not, what is the relation between the intonational pattern of an utterance and the asking of a question?

In my view, 'question intonation' is not determined by grammatical rule. We know how to do a very great many things by using language that are not themselves the applications of knowledge of language. Let me put the point in instrumental terms. Speakers face the choice of what tool to use and what task to use it for. But they also face a choice as to how to wield the chosen tool for the chosen task. Different musicians wielding the same instrument may contrast sharply, and we speak of their techniques and their abilities in wielding their instruments. In some domains, technique is paramount, in others less so, but, when taking about cellists or plumbers, we normally distinguish decisions as to how to wield a chosen tool from decisions as to which tool to use and decisions as to what task to perform.

Certain intonational contours are indeed matters of grammatical form. Lexical stress, for example, is in part a matter of linguistic legislation in English: by phonological rule, the adjective 'content' is stressed on the second syllable and the noun 'content' on the first. Certainly to some degree sentential intonation is a matter of linguistic legislation. But I believe that to a large extent, choices of sentential-intonational and prosodic contours are not choices among sentence-types—not choices among different tools—but are, primarily, choices as to how a tool, once chosen, should be wielded.

Let us first ask: What kinds of things have intonational contours? Certainly utterances do; their intonational contours can be stated in acoustic terms to any degree of precision we desire. What might be doubted is whether (unuttered) sentence-types, the kinds of objects that syntacticians and semanticists are in the business of studying, have intonational contours.[14] To see this point, a few obvious facts should give the doubter pause. Plainly, we are highly skilled at creating effects using intonation, and the range of effects at our disposal is vast. We may manipulate prosody and intonation to express sarcasm, irony, puzzlement, wonder, awe, disdain, admiration, disgust, boredom, impatience, interest, gruffness, haughtiness, timidity, piety, credulity, disbelief, exasperation—this just the beginning of a very long list. We can combine these.

[14] See Liberman and Sag 1974.

Consider the various intonations we might employ when uttering *To be is to be the value of a variable* with pious wonder, haughty exasperation, gruff sarcasm, and so on. When we talk we are constantly pulling off effects such as these. Now three reactions force themselves upon us. One is the pretty clear perception that nobody in the phonology business would want to say that there are intonational or prosodic contour rules that, applying in the phonological component to sentence-types, place boredom contours on them, to take one example. No phonologist *has* said such a thing, so far as I know. The second is the feeling that, if we were able to sluice off from the pronunciations of sentences the kinds of intonational effects just alluded to, there might not, intonationally speaking, be anything of much interest left. The doubt confronts us whether there is much of anything invariant in all of the various intonations that a sentence-type may display. And the third comes from the observation that the sentences that we are really interested in talking about are not said in isolation. They are said after other things have been said, and in preparation for saying other things. As is well known, the intonational contours of sentences are sensitive to these facts.

Let's digress for a moment to consider the classic treatment on this topic. In *The Sound Pattern of English* (1968, hereafter *SPE*), Chomsky and Halle began a generative tradition on this point by saying that sentence-types do have intonational contours, and have them as a matter of obligatory rule. According to *SPE*, there are rules of sentence intonation that apply to surface structures, syntactic descriptions of sentence-types. "Once the speaker has selected a sentence with a particular syntactic structure and certain lexical items (largely or completely unmarked for stress, as we shall see), the choice of stress contour is not a matter subject to further independent decision" (*SPE*: 25). This approach faces descriptive difficulties and is restricted to a few rather simple cases, as *SPE* freely admitted. I have no problem with that. The question I wish to raise is whether the stress contour and intonation observed in an utterance are, generally speaking, functions of the sentence-type used or functions of the using of the sentence-type. I think it is fairly plain that while certain aspects of stress-contour are determined by linguistic legislation, a great deal depends on matters of affect. *SPE*'s rules provide the intonational contours of uncontrastive, unhedged, unexpressive, emotively bland declarative sentences used to make statements, the sorts of pronunciations one hears in language labs produced by people listening to tapes. They are not, specifically, in the business of stating those intonational contours that utterances display in various circumstances of utterance. If it is possible to sluice off the kinds of intonational effects I have been alluding to and have anything left, then to that extent it might make sense to say that sentence-types have intonational contours. But question-intonation will not appear among those intonational contours left. Question-intonation is a function of the using of a sentence not of a sentence-type.

How does the contribution of rising intonation in questions compare to the contribution of inversion, which certainly is a property of sentence-types? In the case of inversion, we have simply the circumstance in which inversion has applied and the circumstance in which inversion has not applied. Only those two circumstances exist, and they are exclusive of one another. The same would be true of intonation if there were a grammatical property rightly called 'question intonation', an intonation restricted to sentences used to ask questions. And, since these two distinctions would crosscut each other, there would then be four kinds of sentence-type to deal with, and question-intonation would be comparable to inversion. But things are not that way at all.

When we know a language and wield its sentence-types, we surely have knowledge of the effects of various intonation patterns we may choose. I can say *Nice haircut!* with an intonation that indicates to you that I am complimenting you, or with an intonation that indicates to you that I am being sarcastic. I can also say *Nice haircut!* with a smile or with a frown, not changing the intonation pattern—and each of these would indicate to you my different intentions. Knowledge of what intonational contours mean is like knowledge of what smiles mean—they can inform us concerning an agent's intentions; we can employ them to make our intentions known. We can smile for the sake of doing it, but otherwise smiles (and intonation contours) accompany other of our acts.

Again, is there grammatically determined question-intonation? The most important observation to make is that there is *not* a correspondence between things said with rising intonation and things said to ask a question. Many questions are uttered with flat intonation, or with intonation patterns characteristic of assertions. *Where are you?* and *I love you* can have similar (non-rising) intonation patterns. On the other hand, many things uttered with rising intonation are in fact *not* questions. This lack of correspondence by itself suggests that rising intonation is not part of the sentence-type, but rather is part of the wielding of the sentence-type to produce some desired effect. I would venture that, by and large, 'rising intonation' indicates an invitation for conversational turn-taking. But while this may be a natural accompaniment to the asking of questions which demand responses, the effect is by no means a requirement. So what *are* the requirements to ask a question? I am claiming that, to ask a question, whether an open question or a confirmation question, a speaker should present himself as lacking something. The lacks are different, and are signaled differently, in the two cases. In either case, a speaker succeeds in presenting himself as lacking if the hearer concludes that he is lacking from how he presents himself. And a speaker succeeds in presenting himself as lacking in a particular respect if the hearer concludes that he is lacking in that respect from how he presents himself. When a speaker is asking an open question, the lack is syntactically marked. But when he is asking a confirmation question, the lack is often not syntactically marked. As noted above, many of the sentence-types used to make statements are also used to ask confirmation questions. So if a speaker wishes to ask a confirmation question, the speaker should take care that he not be taken to be making a statement. One way to do that is to wield the sentence-type with rising intonation. But that is not always necessary, since the speaker may find himself in a circumstance in which he could only sensibly be taken to be asking a question, not making a statement. In that sort of circumstance, a speaker can choose to utter a sentence that contains no formal marking of questionhood and no special intonation, yet still succeed in asking a question. In short, in a circumstance in which a speaker can rely on being taken to be asking a question, that speaker may find that he can successfully ask a question without either using a sentence-type marked for the purpose, or wielding it with rising intonation.

If one listens to conversation with this possibility in mind, it is astonishing how frequently this actually occurs. In print, it is perhaps most easily 'heard' by imagining an interrogation scenario, such as the following: *You were in Central Park. Yes. You wanted to make a statement. No. You had always hated pigeons. No. You poisoned the bird seed. No. You waited for your chance. No.* Plainly, the interrogator can, in this circumstance, assume that what he says will be taken as the asking of a confirmation question, and, since he can assume this, he need not make it clear that he is asking a question by wielding the chosen sentence-types in an intonationally special way. And, as mentioned, the same thing occurs commonly in normal conversation. The intonations of the questions asked may be the same as the intonations would be if the same sentence-types were used to make statements. So there are clear cases where non-rising intonation accompanies non-inverted questions.

Now take the observation the other way around. Are there speech-acts other than the asking of a question that can be performed when uttering sentences with rising intonation? Indeed there are. The easiest example is one of the most common utterances: *Hello?* said when answering the telephone is clearly not a question. Another example that comes to mind is the often stereotyped teenage girl who wields virtually *all* of her sentence-types with a rising intonation pattern, with the purpose not of questioning, but of ensuring that her conversational partner continues to stay involved. As with the courtroom example, such intonation occurs not just with this particular stereotype, but commonly in normal conversations, should anyone care to listen for it. I have noticed that people often use rising intonation when introducing an anecdote, as a way of 'setting the stage', as with: *So I was in the frozen food aisle?* or: *When I was in graduate school?* While I have here followed the convention of some authors who use 'question marks' to indicate rising intonation here, clearly these last two are not questions. The speakers display no ignorance, the sentence-types display no lack of any type. They cannot be answered by *Yes* or *No*, or with any information. The only possible response is something like *Uh-huh*, an indicator of a turn being taken.

When considering inverted sentence-types such as *Is it raining?*, wielded with rising intonation, we might conclude that one can only say such a thing so as to ask a question, but that may be not because of the rising intonation but because of the inversion, which can be a good indicator of questionhood by itself. If we turn to *It's raining?* with rising intonation, we note that, if it is given falling intonation, it could only be used to ask a question if it could not be mistaken as assertion. Interrogation, as we just saw, is one of many circumstances in which this can be pulled off. That said, rising intonation on uninverted sentence-tokens can be a good indicator of questionhood.

2.6 Conclusion

We use sentence-types, we utter tokens of them, and we wield them in various ways. The using of sentence-types is like the using of other kinds of tools, but there are significant differences. Perhaps most important is the fact that sentence-types are personal tools. We have the tools we do because of the grammar we know. There is no other set of tools at our disposal that is infinite, no other set that is systematically defined. In that way the tools of language are unique. The analogy of tools is helpful, however; in many respects the using of sentence-types follows the 'logic' of using generally. This is particularly seen in the relation between form and function. Furthermore, sentence-types are the things that linguists study and that speakers make use of. They constitute the point of contact between linguistics and pragmatics. That said, we may now consider in detail the various uses to which complete and incomplete sentence-types may be put when performing the questioning speech-acts.

3

Open Questions, Confirmation Questions, and how to Choose which Sentence-type to Use when Asking them

3.1 Two kinds of incompleteness

3.1.1 Preliminaries

As I have said, ignorance is a lack, and natural languages provide a way to address it. Languages contain sentences that, when used, allow us to display what lacks we have. When we ask questions, we utter such sentences and, in so doing, display the lacks that we wish to relieve ourselves of.

There are two kinds of incompleteness. Incompleteness may be conventional, and reside in the form used, or occasional, and reside in the using of the form. These two kinds of incompleteness separate two kinds of speech-act. The former incompleteness is characteristic of sentence-types used to ask open questions; the second kind of incompleteness is characteristic of the asking of confirmation questions.

In this chapter, I will be investigating the speciation of the questioning speech-acts, placing open questions and confirmation questions in opposition. Parallel to this opposition within the class of speech-acts, there is a syntactic opposition more basic than the familiar syntactic distinction between *yes-no* questions and *wh*-questions. Open questions are asked by using deformed sentence-types, while confirmation questions are asked by using undeformed sentence-types. There are many kinds of open question, and many kinds of confirmation question, and the business of this chapter is to distinguish among them. The overall aim is to reveal the act of questioning.

Having decided which question to ask, we face the choice as to which sentence-type to use to ask it. We must, for example, calculate whether the person being questioned will be able to discern the lack that we represent ourselves as having. Sometimes we miscalculate, speak too indirectly, and are misunderstood. Since people differ in their powers of discernment, and we know that they do, part of our calculation involves estimating the powers of the addressee. Laying aside such considerations, we may assume that the person being questioned knows the various ways in which we might be ignorant, and the rules for displaying those kinds of ignorance, given the tools available. In English, there are inverted sentence-types and *wh*-moved sentence-types, and these two display their formal incompletenesses unmistakably. In the proposition expressed by the open question *Who are you talking to?*, there is no person talked to. If one knows the grammar of English, and the rules for using the sentence-types of the language, one knows what lacks those sentence-types are capable of expressing.

The incompleteness of questions, whether open questions or confirmation questions, stands in opposition to the completeness of their corresponding assertions. Assertions provide the standard of completeness. Where questions may be incomplete in one of two different ways, assertions within the answer set must be complete in both of them. Asserting is an activity that has parts. Felicitous asserting is the complete uttering of a complete sentence-type, together with the appropriate array of beliefs and intentions. If there is incompleteness in the using of a sentence-type or incompleteness in the sentence-type used, then, in one way or the other, assertion fails.

When asserting, one uses a complete sentence-type, but what happens when the act of using a complete sentence-type is itself incomplete? The act of asserting, to be complete, should be accompanied by certain beliefs. As Austin put it, "the procedure [of performing a particular speech-act] is designed for use by persons having certain thoughts" (1962: 39). The procedure of making assertions is designed for use by persons who have the beliefs expressed by making those assertions. But suppose that a speaker sets out to make an assertion without having the requisite beliefs. Austin held that this always leads to one or another kind of 'misfire' or abuse of the procedure (lying and overstatement being prominent examples).

But there is something rather similar which is, in fact, not an abuse but rather an indication that another speech-act, not assertion, is taking place. One may use a complete sentence-type without having the beliefs requisite for underwriting that assertion, just in case, when doing so, it is clear that one does not intend to be taken as having those beliefs. Abuses cannot be abuses if they are admitted to from the outset. If I engage in the procedure of making an assertion, but at the same time let on that I do not have the requisite beliefs for making that assertion, then I have not made an assertion, as that term is normally used—I have not affirmed anything, since my addressee knows that I lack the grounds that would underwrite affirmation. My act, as viewed against the standard of assertion, is incomplete. What have I done, then? I may have been offering a wild guess. *Bernini designed that?*, said while looking at a fountain in Rome, is an example. Unlike asserting, the speech-act procedure of wild guessing does not require the accompaniment of certain beliefs. I might have some grounds for belief, having read that Bernini did design some of the fountains in Rome, but not grounds sufficient, in current conditions, for licensing the assertion that Bernini designed that particular fountain. For now the point is only that, in the case of confirmation *yes-no* questions, incompleteness can reside in the fact that, while complete sentence-types are used, their using is incomplete, lacking the conventional license of assertion. They are complete in form but lacking in the using of them. The point of using a sentence-type that meets the formal standard for completeness of assertion while presenting oneself as not having license for assertion is to display that very lack, inviting the interlocutor to provide that license, the grounds that would underwrite assertion. In that way, when one says *Bernini designed that?*, one uses a sentence-type commonly used for an assertion, but succeeds in asking a question. So incompleteness in the tool used and incompleteness in the using of a tool, where, in both cases, assertion is the standard of completeness, characterize open questions and confirmation questions, respectively.

3.1.2 On what the questioner presents himself as lacking and as not lacking

Open questions have received much more attention than confirmation questions, and, since these two types stand in direct contrast with each other, the result is that both kinds of question have been misunderstood. As I have just said, the distinction between them involves what lack the speaker presents himself as having. A speaker, in asking an open *wh*-question, may present himself either as lacking an item (a thing-in-the-world) or as lacking a bit of language. That is, a questioner may present himself as not knowing what item, or what bit of language, rightly fills the incompleteness in the sentence-type he is offering a token of. Similarly, a speaker, in asking an open *yes-no* question, presents himself as not knowing whether the predicate he presents ought rightly to be applied to an item (the sentence-type lacks what I have called 'the glue'). Nevertheless, when asking a question, there is much that a speaker must present himself as knowing, as well. If, seeing you on the telephone, I ask *Who are you talking to?* I present myself as having the belief that there is someone that you are talking to. So quite generally a person who asks a question not only presents himself as not knowing certain things, but also presents himself as believing certain things.

When contrasting types of question, one must consider what the speaker presents himself as knowing and what the speaker presents himself as not knowing. A speaker who asks an open question presents himself as being incapable, in a particular way, of completing a proposition. In the case of *Who are you talking to?* the speaker presents himself as being unable to produce the person you are talking to. On the other hand, the speaker of *Who are you talking to?* limits the range of satisfactory answers to those people you might be talking to, presenting himself as believing that the answer is to be found among those people. The speaker presupposes that there is someone you are talking to, but does not assert that there is someone you are talking to. This is the way *Who are you talking to?*

differs from *You are talking to someone.*[1] The proposition expressed by *Who are you talking to?* is incomplete, lacking a person talked to. No assertion could express the content of such a question, since assertions, to be felicitous, must be complete. By using a sentence-type that expresses an incomplete proposition, the speaker presents himself as having no way to complete that proposition. As we would normally say, in that respect, the question he asks is open.

In contrast, the asker of a confirmation question presents herself as being unable to *complete her speech-act* to the standard given by assertion. I have given an example— *Bernini designed that?*— in which the incompleteness resides in the requisite beliefs of the speaker, but there are other ways in which a questioning speech-act might be incomplete. The speaker might utter an uncompleted sentence-type. Suppose someone says *You just talked to . . . ?* (It sometimes helps an utterance like this along by making a rolling motion with one's hand where the dots appear, a gesture which, like intonation or eyebrow lifts, falls into the bag of tricks we use to wield our tools.) By uttering something that one does not complete, one indicates that one cannot complete it, and, in this case, thereby asks the hearer to complete the sentence, to say who was just talked to. Now some might object that sentences such as *You just talked to . . . ?* are simply ungrammatical, to be ruled out syntactically, and to be dismissed from consideration. Whether such sentence-types are ungrammatical or not (a sterile question really), anyone who is curious about how we actually talk will observe that such uncompleted sentence-types are a common choice when asking a certain kind of question. This last fact is interesting.

In particular, certain uses of *You just talked to . . . ?* are comparable to certain uses of the so-called 'echo question'. Suppose there is a lot of background noise, and I hear you say *I just talked to (mumble).* I may say either *You just talked to . . . ?* (perhaps while cupping my hand around my ear), or *You just talked to who?* (perhaps with emphasis on the 'who'), and, in either case, in doing so, indicate that I cannot complete what I have said to form an assertion. This suggests that, where a speaker deploys a *wh*-expression in a confirmation question, he indicates that he cannot complete his sentence at that point.

3.1.3 The rule of choice

The rule of sentence choice says that deformed sentence-types are used to ask open questions and that undeformed sentence-types are used to ask confirmation questions. The incompletenesses are different in kind: deformity indicates formal incompleteness while non-deformity indicates incompleteness in the speech-act. Rules of sentence choice do not have the same status as the rules of grammar; rules of sentence choice define our practices, while rules of grammar

---

[1] But see Section 4.3.2, where the use of indefinites to ask questions is discussed.

define the structures of the tools we use in practice. Breaking rules of use has consequences different from breaking rules of form. Speakers may—and often do—intentionally flout rules of use so as to gain certain effects, while no such effects derive from breaking rules of form. We will be concerning ourselves with both kinds of rule, and considering not only questioning but answering as well. A speaker, when questioning, displays ignorance with the intent that the hearer recognize that ignorance, and take action to relieve it. The action of a hearer responding appropriately to such a display is called answering. It can be a good strategy, when analyzing questioning behavior, to examine answering behavior, because if a satisfactory answer can be isolated, we may be able to infer what ignorance the questioner intended to be taken as having. By isolating perfectly responsive answers, we may determine what the questioner was angling for.

3.1.4 On the incompleteness of open *yes-no* questions and the absence of 'the glue'

I have anticipated my views concerning the status of *wh*-expressions in confirmation *wh*-questions: a speaker uses such an expression to flag the position in his utterance that he cannot complete. Is any position flagged in an open *yes-no* question such as *Is Jack fat?*

If, as I have proposed, formal incompleteness is characteristic of sentence-types used to ask open questions, it follows not only that *wh*-questions are formally incomplete, but that *yes-no* questions are as well. I suggested in Chapter 1 that, although *Is Jack fat?* may seem complete, it formally lacks what I called 'the glue'. Let me expand on that. There once was a view that pretty much all words are names, and in particular that subjects and predicates are both names. But then the question arose what relates these names. Since sentences seem not to be mere lists of names, the reasoning went, there must be some third thing that unifies the parts of a sentence. Aristotle had it that the copula is that third thing; the copula refers to nothing, but "implies a copulation or synthesis, which we can hardly conceive of apart from the things thus combined" (1973: 121). Frege, on the other hand, held that "statements . . . can be imagined to be split up into two parts, one complete in itself, and the other in need of supplementation, or 'unsaturated'—it contains an empty place; only when this place is filled up with a proper name, or with an expression that replaces a proper name, does a complete sense appear" (Frege 1891: 31, and elsewhere). While for Aristotle the copula was the glue, for Frege, saturation was the glue (or the gluing): the unsaturated concept-word, a predicate, is saturated by an object-word. There are other proposals concerning the nature of the glue, including that in Austin 1953, which I will consider in a moment. But on all such accounts, sentence-types used to make statements contain the glue; what is distinctive, I am claiming, about inverted sentence-types such as *Is Jack fat?* is that they lack it. When someone utters *Is Jack fat?*, the sentence-type used is incomplete in that it is not part of what is expressed that the predicate 'fat' applies to Jack. So a speaker of English, if he wishes to bring into question whether a predicate applies to an item, may choose an inverted sentence-type, a sentence-type in which part of the predicate-expression has been moved. That is a way that English has of signaling that the glue is missing. In this respect, of course, assertions are complete. No matter how it is used, the sentence-type *Jack is fat* presents subject and the predicate as glued together.[2]

This is not the only view of predication. Predication may also be analyzed as a speech-act one performs in acts of asserting (Searle 1969). If my claim about sentence-types used to ask *yes-no* questions is that they, like *wh*-questions, are grammatically incomplete, I am, of course, committed to saying that the glue is present in sentence-types used to make assertions. The glue is a matter of grammar, not of use. So while it is perfectly fine to say, as Searle does, that, when asserting, speakers refer to items and predicate predicates of them, I do not follow him in saying that only in virtue of performing a predicative speech-act does predication arise. For the glue—the enabler of predication—is part of the sentence-types we use when we make assertions. We use sentence-types in which predication obtains, since the parts of these sentence-types are glued together.

Austin (1953) has a very different take on these matters. He holds that the truth of a sentence such as *Jack is fat* requires that Jack belong to a type that *matches* the sense of the predicate 'fat', although Austin would have preferred to say 'satisfactoriness' where I have just said 'truth'. On this view, satisfactoriness is symmetrical. The asymmetric matching of type to sense, or sense to type, is Austin's glue.[3] Now Austin explicitly refrains from saying what types and senses are, but supposing they were considered to be sets of individuals, he would then be proposing to cash in predication in terms of set-equivalence, not set-membership. Given a sentence in which the glue is missing, the Austinian view would be that sentence-types in which the glue is missing fail to express whether the type of the subject matches the sense of the predicate.

Suppose that *Jack is fat* is false. Austin would say that in that event Jack fails to belong to a type that matches the sense of 'fat'. Following him, I would say that in *Is Jack fat?*, it is not said whether Jack belongs to a type that matches the sense of 'fat'. The matching-to is the glue, and the glue is missing. Now the relation of matching is given very special treatment by Austin; I will consider this point in more detail below.[4] But here it may be noted that matching, as a treatment

---

[2] As mentioned in Chapter 1, accounts of the glue vary as to whether it connects bits of language or an object and a bit of language. Also, as a matter of terminology, Frege applied the term '(un)saturated' both to expressions and to their denotations. Following Furth (1967), I apply the term '(in)complete' to expression-types and '(un)saturated' to their denotations.

[3] Symmetric match of type and sense yields satisfactoriness, but match may be achieved either by matching sense to type or by matching type to sense, an asymmetric relation depending on onus of match.

[4] In Section 4.6, and especially Chapter 6.

of predication, allows a straightforward treatment of a certain distinction among the uses of questions. Suppose it were asked whether Jack is fat. There are two distinguishable circumstances in which this might be done. If the type that Jack belongs to is taken for granted, the question might be whether the sense of 'fat' is such that it matches it. In Austin's terminology, the 'onus of match' then falls on the sense of the predicate. On the other hand, if the sense of 'fat' is taken for granted, the question might be whether Jack is of a type that matches *it*. Open *yes-no* questions in fact display this ambiguity. The question *Is Jack fat?* might be directed toward asking whether it is fat that Jack is or toward asking whether Jack is such that he is fat. And those are different questions. The truth conditions of the sentences used to answer them positively are identical, but they are different questions.[5] One need not adopt Austin's proposal concerning match to explain the distinct uses of *Is Jack fat?* just described. I will take up Austin's analysis of these matters again in later chapters; here I wish only to point out that the observed distinction does follow directly from his proposal.

Collecting the points just made, it can be seen that sentence-types used to ask open *yes-no* questions are incomplete in a way that their corresponding answers, uninverted sentence-types, are not. And, again, it is natural that the incompleteness of sentence-types used to ask questions should be assessed with respect to sentence-types used to make assertions, and not, say, sentence-types used to make promises or to issue threats. For assertions are the answers to questions. They, and not promises or threats, are the kinds of things that express what questions are in the business of asking for. By asking a question, one displays a lack, a lack that can be relieved by the making of an assertion.

3.1.5 An alternate account of open *yes-no* questions

My account is in contrast with any account which has it that to ask a *yes-no* question is the same as to ask whether a particular proposition is true. It has been suggested that a *yes-no* question (vacuously) presupposes the disjunction of its positive and negative answers.[6] It has also been suggested that a *yes-no* question refers to its answers, or perhaps only to its true answer.[7] I am not engaging these views here; they should be taken as purely semantic proposals. However, if accepted, they might lead to the view that to ask a *yes-no* question is the same as to ask whether one of the presuppositions or referents of the question is true. That would be a mistake.

---

[5] Perhaps an assertive case will help. As this is written, there is doubt as to the truth of the sentence: *The facts on the ground in Iraq constitute civil war.* But there are two possible sources for doubt. One could be clear about the sense of the predicate 'constitute civil war', but unclear about the facts on the ground in Iraq. Or one could be clear about the facts on the ground in Iraq, but unclear about the sense of the predicate 'constitute civil war'. It is difficult to see how one could worry about the truth of the sentence if one had doubt on both sides.

[6] See Katz 1972.

[7] See Hamblin 1976 for the former view and Karttunen 1977 for the latter.

Plainly if Jack is fat, it is true that Jack is fat, and vice versa. Equally plainly, the (correct) answers to *Is Jack fat?* and *Is it true that Jack is fat?* will always coincide. But truth conditions, and answerhood conditions, are crude tests in this context, and not revealing here. It is more relevant to ask under what conditions we ask each of them. Now according to the view that to ask *Is Jack fat?* is really to ask *Is it true that Jack is fat?*, it follows that to ask *Is it true that Jack is fat?* is really to ask *Is it true that it is true that Jack is fat?*, and so on. And I think that at least one eyebrow should be raised at this point, since (really) asking whether it is true that it is true that P is a preposterous thing to ask, whatever the circumstances. That aside, there are real differences between asking *Is Jack fat?* and asking *Is it true that Jack is fat?* On the view that I am defending, in the first the speaker uses a sentence-type that lacks the glue between the predicate 'fat' and the subject Jack, while in the second the speaker uses a sentence-type that lacks the glue between the predicate 'true' and the proposition denoted by the *that*-clause 'that Jack is fat'. What difference does that make?

To see the difference, imagine that during a movie, I turn to you and say *Do you like it?* No problem there. Now suppose instead that I had said *Is it true that you like it?* Very odd. This second question would be more natural in another circumstance: if, for example, I had heard that you like it, and wanted to verify what I had heard. In that circumstance I could ask the former question as well. My question does not have to be directed toward what I have been informed of. But if I have no basis for believing that you like it, if I have heard nothing, it is certainly odd to ask *Is it true that you like it?*

The point is echoed in assertion. The assertions *It's raining* and *It's true that it's raining* share truth conditions. But suppose you walk in, not having seen me all day. It is reasonable for you to say *It's raining*, but it would be quite odd for you to say *It's true that it's raining*. The latter sentence-type does have uses, though, and, again, these are instructive. Suppose I say *I want to go for a walk*, and you reply *It's raining*. I can now continue with *It's true that it's raining, but I want to go anyway*. By saying this, I concede agreement with what you have said. I can also use 'it's-true-that' sentences to show only partial agreement—for example, if you say *She knows a lot of interesting people*, I can respond *It's true she knows a lot of people*, conceding that she knows many people but not that they are interesting. This all goes back to a dispute between Austin (1950) and Strawson (1950*b*) concerning what the adjective 'true' may rightly be ascribed to, part of the question being whether 'P' and 'It is true that P' come to the same thing. Strawson said that they do, and Austin said that they do not. I have just used the sort of argument that leads me to side with Austin. Strawson sided with Frege; in 'Thought' Frege says: "It is also worth noting that the sentence 'I smell the scent of violets' has the same content as 'It is true that I smell the scent of violets'" (Beaney 1997: 328). I follow Austin in thinking that the contents of the two are different but that their truth conditions are the same. The point here is that we certainly can assert both, and ask both, and we are careful which we do. The more general point is that, if one holds that to ask a *yes-no* question is just to ask whether a certain proposition (or statement) is true, this distinction is missed. I conclude that *Is it raining?* and *Is it true that it is raining?* are distinct sentence-types used for distinct purposes. The first asks whether it is raining. The second asks whether the proposition that it is raining is true. Nothing is gained, and much is falsified, by analyzing one in terms of the other.

3.1.6 Other uses of incomplete sentence-types

My general view is that the asking of questions is the display of incompleteness. But although many displays of incompleteness can only be taken as the asking of questions, not every display of incompleteness is the asking of a question. One and the same sentence-type can in some circumstances serve to ask a question, and in others serve to make a statement. Many sentence-types are multi-purpose. If I say *I don't know your name*, I will, in some circumstances, present myself not only as lacking your name, but also as asking you to tell me what it is. In other circumstances, I will not be understood as asking you to tell me what it is. One can display an incompleteness without intending to be taken as wanting it filled.

The view that sentence-types in which inversion has applied lack the glue allows a fresh approach to some old problems. I have based my analysis of questions on the idea that ignorance is a lack and that, when speaking, one chooses a sentence-type that is incomplete in a way corresponding to the lack one currently has. But lacks give rise to other attitudes than those we normally associate with questioning, such as puzzlement and curiosity. Lacks also can give rise to desire. Sometimes, when we lack something, we desire that thing, and, as it turns out, we can use inverted sentence-types to express not only curiosity or puzzlement, but desire as well.

There is, for example, the case in which an inverted sentence-type is used not to ask a question but to make a request. If I say *Would you pass the salt?*, I may not be asking you whether you would pass the salt or not, I may be requesting that you pass the salt. The speaker of *Would you pass the salt?* takes up the subject-phrase 'you' and the predicate 'would pass the salt', and places them in a glueless sentence-type, in which no saturation is denoted. If, in the current circumstance, I know that I will be taken not to be asking a question but rather be taken as expressing an attitude—which is, in effect, an attitude toward a lack of saturation, the desire that the lack be removed—I may safely come forward with the glueless sentence-type to make a request. In that way, instead of asking whether you fall under the predicate 'would pass the salt', I express my desire that you pass the salt. To be understood to be making a request is to be understood, in effect, as desiring that an object have a property.[8]

---

[8] For a different account in terms of indirect speech-acts, see Searle 1975 and Brown and Levinson 1978, 1987: 132ff.

Again, consider someone saying *Is she ever smart!* The speaker again takes up subject and predicate, and places them in a glueless sentence-type. But here the attitude expressed can be surprise, or wonderment. One holds subject and predicate apart, so to speak, and, in uttering a token of a sentence-type in which this is the case, expresses wonderment that completing the predicate with that subject yields truth. One may find the jigsaw-puzzle piece that one has been looking for, and know that it fits, be impressed by the intricacy of the fit, and so on, before one actually puts the piece in its place. This last case extends to examples involving *wh*-expressions such as *How handsome you are!* and *What wonders I saw!* In these sentences, the glue is present, but they display incompletenesses at the sites of the traces of the *wh*-expressions. Wonderment is expressed that that degree of handsomeness is the degree of handsomeness you have and that those wonders were wonders that I saw. Under this approach, the attitudes of desire and surprise are not part of the grammatically determined meanings of sentence-types. Those attitudes are expressed through the wielding of incomplete sentence-types. It is no accident that not only asking questions, but also making requests and exclaiming, involve deformed sentence-types. The reason is that these speech-acts all are naturally performed by displaying lacks, for which incomplete sentence-types are well suited.[9]

3.2 Confirming beliefs (the epistemological setting)

In the case of open questions, the sense of 'open' I intend is non-technical; we commonly consider a question open if we have no preconceptions, at least within some important range, as to how it might be answered. In the case of asking an open *yes-no* question, such as *Will the Yankees win?*, we present ourselves as believing that the game might go either way; in the case of asking an open *wh*-question, such as *Who is the president of Italy?*, we present ourselves as believing that there is a significant range of values (people) that might satisfy the propositional function in question (being the president of Italy). In general, questions are asked so as to 'close' points in question, and this is a second piece of common terminology I wish to rely on. When a person considers a point in question closed, he considers that that point is no longer *in* question, or, from the other perspective, he considers that there is no longer any question *about* it. The question is settled. To close a point in question, a speaker attempts to *acquire* a belief concerning the point in question, a belief which, if accepted, will serve to close the point in question.

Some might be tempted to restrict the term 'question' to the open case, and so distinguish two speech-acts types: asking a question and confirming a belief.

---

[9] I reject the view that questions should be analyzed as requests for information, but a full exposition would require an analysis of requests and imperatives, a task I hope to return to. For the alternative, see Hare 1949, Hintikka 1974, and, for discussion, Levinson 1983: 275.

Common usage, when applied to our behavior, goes against this, however, and I think that in this case common usage is more revealing. The application of the term 'question' under consideration here is within the class of speech-acts, not the class of grammatical forms. The term 'question' applies, or fails to apply, to a speech-act on the basis of what kind of speech-act it is, not on the basis of what form of sentence is used to perform it. And, by taking the term 'question' to apply both to the open and confirmation kinds, both ends of the dimension of uncertainty that provide an impetus for the asking of questions are nicely included. The common sense of the verb 'question' is labile in this way. On the acquisition (open) side, we question people for information. When questioning them, we question who did it, what happened, whether it is worth it, why we should take it seriously. On the confirmation side, by questioning, we express uncertainty or doubt so as to achieve certainty and clarity. We question a person's competence, the wisdom of a course of action, the need for candor, the criteria for success, and so on, and, when we do these things, we are not simply in the business of seeking information. We are in the business of clarifying, setting things straight, getting it right, probing for error, evaluating the evidence, establishing more firmly. Thus, whether we are acquiring or confirming beliefs, we question, and I will use the term in this Janus-faced and totally natural way. And I will say that, when we seek to acquire beliefs, we ask open questions, and that, when we seek to establish beliefs more firmly, we ask confirmation questions.

It should be understood that there are many reasons a speaker might have for choosing to confirm a belief concerning a point in question, instead of asking an open question to close it. There might be evidence supporting the belief, but not evidence sufficient to close the point in question, and the speaker's interest would be whether the belief is correct. Or the belief might follow from other, perhaps more general, considerations, and those more general considerations might figure in the speaker's interests. Or the speaker might know that the answer has already been provided, that the point in question has already *been* closed, but not herself know the answer, or at least not completely. These and other possibilities will be discussed below. Similarly, there are many reasons that a speaker might have for choosing to ask an open question. It is impossible to catalogue all of these reasons on either side, but there are regularities.

A speaker who considers a point in question to be open *should* ask an open question, while a speaker who intends to confirm a belief concerning a point in question *should* ask a confirmation question. This 'should' points to the consideration that, if the asking of an open question is the performing of a different kind of speech-act from the asking of a confirmation question, and the difference between them is discernible, then a person asking an open question will be *taken* to believe that the point in question is open, while a person asking a confirmation question will be *taken* to be in the business of confirming a belief. A person asking an open question presents himself as believing that the point in question is open, while a person asking a confirmation question presents himself as uncertain whether a particular belief is, or should be, held. At least this is how the contrast plays out between open *yes-no* questions and confirmation *yes-no* questions. These are different ways to present oneself, and one should not misrepresent oneself. The fact that people do, of course, often intentionally misrepresent themselves again illustrates the difference between pragmatic and grammatical rules. In the following sections we will see different examples of the effects of presenting and misrepresenting alike.

3.2.1 On the uses of confirmation *yes-no* questions

By asking a confirmation *yes-no* question, a speaker presents himself as lacking a belief sufficiently strong to warrant assertion. Often, that is done so as to prod the hearer into confirming the belief. But, as we have already seen, confirmation questions may be asked with other ends in mind. This section will explore some of these possibilities.

When asserting, a speaker intends to be taken as believing what she says. On hearing someone assert something, we infer that he believes it. Of course it does happen that people say things that they do not believe. They might be lying, overstating, or understating. Even putting lying aside, we often question whether a speaker has warrant for what he says. Suppose a beginning chemistry student asks: *Gold is an element?* and the professor responds: *Gold is an element.* The student has presented himself as lacking a belief strong enough to license the assertion, while the professor has presented herself as having a belief strong enough to license asserting that gold is an element.

Now take the reverse case. Suppose the beginning student asserts: *Brass is an element,* and the professor responds: *Brass is an element?* The professor's sentence-type might be wielded in various ways. In perhaps the most straightforward wielding of this sentence-type, the professor presents herself as lacking a belief strong enough to license the very assertion that the student has just made. Thus the professor's utterance serves as a corrective, provided the student defers. In another way of wielding this sentence-type, the response might go: *Brass is an element?! Amazing! And gold is an alloy?* Here we have surprise with sarcasm. The relation between disbelief and surprise (and the parallel contrast between non-acceptance and astonishment) are considered below. The point to see here is that the sentence-type *Brass is an element?* can be wielded in such a way as to present oneself as not having a belief of sufficient strength to assert that brass is an element, that being because one knows full well that brass is not an element.

One may even ask a confirmation question to confirm a belief concerning someone else's belief. Suppose I have reason to believe that you believe that the milk is spoiled; you might, for example, have made a certain expression after having tasted your coffee. But suppose that your facial expression is not sufficient, in my opinion, to confirm my belief that you believe that the milk is spoiled. I can present myself as seeking to confirm my belief concerning your belief by asking a confirmation question, such as: *You believe the milk is spoiled?* But the question may be asked more tersely. Suppose your expression is enough to suggest to me that you believe that the milk is spoiled. To confirm that, I might ask: *The milk is spoiled?* Note that, by asking that, I need not be confirming my belief that the milk is spoiled. For example, suppose I know that there is buttermilk in your coffee, that you have never before tasted buttermilk, and that the buttermilk is not spoiled. Plainly, then, by saying *The milk is spoiled?* I do not seek to confirm my own belief, since I do not believe that the milk is spoiled. But I might want to find out whether you believe it is spoiled. So the belief that I seek to confirm is my belief that you believe that the milk is spoiled.

All of this is to be distinguished from asking either the open question *Do you believe that the milk is spoiled?*, where the point in question is whether the addressee believes that the milk is spoiled, or the open question *Is the milk spoiled?*, where the point in question is whether the milk is spoiled. This last may not be asked in the buttermilk scenario. It also may not be used to confirm the belief that the milk is spoiled or the belief that the addressee believes that the milk is spoiled. And this is because open questions are not used to confirm beliefs at all.

3.2.2 On when to ask confirmation questions, and how to respond to them

Let us return to the simplest kinds of confirmation question in which the speaker has a belief that P, but a belief not strong enough to warrant the assertion that P. What are bases for belief? What constitutes sufficient basis can vary by individual. Some bases are stronger than others; some just barely give us license. We sometimes say that our only basis for belief is hope. In such cases, the speaker seeks to confirm a belief on the hope that it is right: at least sometimes, asking a confirmation question is a stab in the dark. Perhaps the speaker hopes desperately that Paul will win, and hopes that the addressee believes that Paul will win on the basis of some facts that he might have, but has no substantive reason to believe that Paul will win, no grounds for belief that would survive careful scrutiny. Such a speaker, by asking *Paul will win?* hopes to confirm his desperate belief. So here the speaker presents himself as trying to confirm a belief, which is based merely on his hope that Paul will win.

Sometimes the basis for belief is not a matter of hope, but of evidence. Suppose you walk in, drenched, water pouring off of you, umbrella in hand, with galoshes and a slicker on. Suppose, based on this, I form the belief that it very likely is raining. I may now ask *It's raining?* and when I ask that, it is not so as to ask the open question whether it is raining, but to ask a confirmation question so as to confirm my belief that it is raining, since I have, on the evidence, formed the belief that it is raining. But here a nagging doubt might arise in the minds of certain semanticists, in particular those who get all solemn at the mention of certainty and truth. Their doubt would be: How *sure* should a speaker be of his belief before asking a confirmation question? How *in the dark* need a speaker be concerning the point in question before asking an open question? And if one cannot specify that degree of certainty that would underwrite the asking of a confirmation question instead of an open one, is not the distinction between open questions and confirmation questions itself in doubt?

Although these may seem like deep and dangerous questions, they are not. Let me deflate the worry. Suppose we ask how careful one should be when crossing the street. Some might piously proclaim that one should be *very* careful, specify some angelic measure of carefulness, and turn an intolerant eye on those who fail to respect the strictures lain down. But who cares about such arbitrary strictures? The fact is that level of care in crossing the street depends on the individual, and what circumstances that individual considers himself to be in. There is no interesting general answer to the more humble question of how careful people *are* when they cross the street. And the same holds for the choice between open questions and confirmation questions. Asking out of the blue, the timid will prefer an open question where the presumptuous might prefer a confirmation question. To make sure they've got something obvious right, the insecure may ask many confirmation questions, while those who jump to conclusions may ask none in the face of doubt. And so forth. The choice between asking open questions and confirmation questions does not depend on some *objective* standard of certainty to justify the asking of confirmation questions. The distinction exists and the option between them is a matter of temperament and style.

Sometimes, we ask confirmation questions when we really should ask open questions and vice versa, not because we wish to deceive, but because we simply pick up the wrong tool. That should not be surprising; other times we pick up the right tool but wield it badly, or incorrectly. Some of these mistakes we call speech errors. When we are in the throes of conversation, sometimes we do not go to the trouble to find the right tool, at other times we fail to appreciate what we have set out to do. When we are in haste, we settle for anything that will do the job. These considerations make it difficult to lay down absolute rules concerning this kind of behavior. But there certainly are rules of tool choice.

Let's return to the circumstance in which you have just arrived drenched, in which I ask the confirmation question *It's raining?* This might seem to be a pretty lame conversational move. *Of course* it is raining, why would one need confirmation for that? But lame or not, there is a clear difference between asking the confirmation question *It's raining?* and asking the open question *Is it raining?* under the same circumstances. For to ask *Is it raining?* is to present oneself as having no clear basis for deciding the question, which, in the case at hand, would mean that the speaker is presenting himself as not being able to interpret the obvious data as providing such a basis, data that would lead any sensible person to bet the farm that it *is* raining. It is one thing to ask a confirmation question when one clearly has it right, that just shows (perhaps excessive) caution. But it is quite another thing to ask an open question when there are clear data before one's nose that form a basis for deciding the point in question. That is to be dense. Notice that here, as before, it is a matter of temperament and style what it is to be dense or to be overly cautious in these particular ways. In other circumstances, it might be in a speaker's interest *falsely* to present himself as dense, or *falsely* to present himself as overly cautious. Such a speaker might even rely on an addressee's realizing that he is misrepresenting himself so as to achieve some other effect. All sorts of effects can trace their sources to the decision whether to ask a confirmation question or an open one.

Considering a variant on the raining case involving a third party shows the clear distinctions that we would expect under this analysis. Suppose I see Fred walk in drenched. I can ask him the uninverted confirmation question *It's raining?*, so as to confirm my belief that it is raining. But suppose that when Fred walks in, drenched as before, I am on the phone with you, and suppose further that I do not know whether you think it is raining or not, and that I have told you nothing about Fred's appearance, and have no other reason to believe that you think it is raining. Suppose then I say to you *It's raining?* To this you might respond *What makes you think that?*, or *What makes you think that I think that?*—a good indication that I have been taken to be asking a confirmation question. To you on the other end of the telephone, the confirmation question is decidedly odd. Since you have not seen the evidence I have seen, you can respond in no other way. If instead, under the same circumstances, I ask you the open question *Is it raining?*, then I present myself (misleadingly) as considering the matter open, although you will most likely find the question perfectly natural. Apparently, once I have the evidence, there is no simple way of asking you about the rain that would not be untoward in one way or another.

A last point about answering that further reveals the difference between confirmation questions and their open counterparts. Take the case in which the speaker asks a confirmation question seeking merely to confirm his belief that it is raining. The speaker thereby reveals that he has some basis to believe that it is raining and wishes to confirm it. The speaker may ask *It's raining?* and the hearer might answer *Yes*. In this case, however, the hearer has another option—the answer could be *Right*. 'Right' is not a literal answer to the question; by saying *Right*, the hearer directly gives approval to the belief the questioner sought to confirm. He can also disconfirm that belief by saying *Wrong (I fell in the pool)*. But notice that if the circumstances were different and the questioner considered the question open whether it is raining or not, and asked the open question *Is it raining?*, the hearer can answer neither *Right* or *Wrong*. And that is because by asking an open question one does not present oneself as having a view on the point in question.

3.3 Sarcasm and irony

Once sarcasm and irony get into the mix, a speaker pretending to be clueless is knowing and a speaker pretending to be stupid is wise. By wielding open questions and confirmation questions in certain ways, these effects and many others can be achieved. Here are a few cases.

3.3.1 Accusation

Suppose, confronting a burglar cracking my safe, I say *Are you supposed to be doing that?* I have uttered an inverted sentence-token, and uttered it with an intonation characteristic of questions. But have I asked a question? If so, I have asked an open question; presenting myself as considering the question open whether the burglar is supposed to be doing that. By doing so, I misrepresent myself: I am not so dense as to consider the question open whether I should be robbed. But the misrepresentation is calculated: the burglar will surely realize that I am not as dense as I am presenting myself to be, that I do not really consider it to be an open question whether he is supposed to be breaking into my safe. But have I asked a question? The short answer is No, but that is not the end of the matter. For, by saying what I have said, I intend first to be taken as having asked a question and then to be taken as not having asked a question. For, by my being understood to be asking a question, a chain of reasoning is begun that terminates with the conclusion that I should not have been understood to have been asking a question. That is one of the ways of sarcasm.

It is also one of the ways of irony. Saying the question ironically, I again present myself as considering the question open whether the burglar is supposed to be breaking open my safe. And again I misrepresent myself. But if I also present myself in a sharp and aggressive way, the burglar must conclude that I emphatically do not consider it an open question whether he should be robbing me. Again, by being understood to be asking a question, I educe the conclusion that I am not asking a question. That is the way of irony.

But suppose that, in the given circumstance, I had chosen to ask the burglar not an open question but a confirmation question. Suppose I had said *You're supposed to be doing that?* Here I might be presenting myself as seeking to confirm my belief that the burglar believes that he is supposed to be doing that, as with the case of the buttermilk. I have, thereby, presented myself as believing that the burglar is a moral ignoramus. And so the effect in this case is to insult. If the belief that I seek to confirm is my own, then I present myself as trying to get the burglar to confirm my belief that he is supposed to be cracking my safe. In this case, I present myself as trying to get it confirmed that I believe something, which, if I did believe it, would indicate that I am some sort of ignoramus. And, in the ways of irony and sarcasm, the effect is to come off as a wise guy. In either case, I misrepresent myself, and the misrepresentations are calculated to achieve different effects.[10]

But what speech-act was I performing? In all of these cases, the burglar knows that I am not asking a question with the goal of receiving an answer as to whether he is supposed to be cracking my safe, and knows that I am not trying to confirm my belief that he is. He understands that I have no doubt on any of that. However, by saying what I did, I did do something else. I confronted the burglar with my belief that he is cracking my safe, thus achieving the effect of accusation. It is easy to see this when considering how the burglar might respond. The response might be *Yes, you're right, you caught me red-handed*, where the burglar admits that the accusation is just. But that response is not a literal answer to the original question; it is a response to the speech-act accusation, an accusation that also could have been issued more straightforwardly by uttering *You're burgling my safe!* which is not a question at all. And similarly, and for the same reasons, it is in bounds for the burglar to protest his innocence by uttering *You're wrong, I'm just oiling the hinges*, again not answering the question, but responding to the accusation.

3.3.2 Politeness

I have claimed that by saying *Would you pass me the salt?* a speaker may express a desire, an attitude toward a lack. The object of desire is, in effect, the absence of saturation, revealed by inversion. The speaker is not asking a question, but making a request. When questioning, a speaker indicates that he is not able to complete a sentence-type or to complete a speech-act. In that way, he asks that they be completed. In the case of requests, a speaker indicates an attitude toward an incompleteness, a desire, and in that way requests that the desire be satisfied. Much has been written about the relationship between questions and requests, especially under the rubric of 'indirect speech-acts'.[11] Here I will restrict myself to drawing out the implications of the theory I am advancing.

There are various 'polite' forms having different effects. By uttering *Could you pass me the salt?*, the speaker expresses an attitude toward your not saturating the predicate 'could pass me the salt'. It is generally agreed that, in many circumstances, this is a politer form of speech than *Will you pass me the salt?* Expressing a desire concerning a *possible* future event contrasts with expressing a desire toward a future event. The first desire is less presumptuous. What is the explanation for this? One popular suggestion is that the speaker is asking whether the addressee is able to pass the salt, assuming that the addressee will reason that

---

[10] The ways of irony and sarcasm are complex, and there is a very large literature concerning them, which I must pass by here. I would only recommend a suggestive, but neglected, tabular comparison of irony, sarcasm, wit, satire, etc. in the 'humour' entry of Fowler 1926.

[11] For an excellent discussion, see Levinson 1983: 263ff.

the speaker is not actually asking whether the addressee can do this.[12] Of course the speaker believes that the addressee can do this, so the addressee should reason that the speaker must be doing something else. And the something else must be to request the salt. One would have to tell similar stories for *Would you pass me the salt?*, and so forth, and it is not clear whether ability is always, or ever, in point. But however these details are overcome, it is not clear in this popular sort of theory how one reasons from the assumption that the speaker is not asking a question to the conclusion that the speaker is making a request. How are these speech-acts related, on this view?

In the account given here, the relation is to be found in incompleteness. A request is the expression of an attitude toward a lack, a question expresses the lack itself. The politeness associated with *Will you pass the salt?* derives from the fact that the speaker, in using this incomplete (glueless) sentence-type, removes any presumption that the addressee will do this. It is an open question whether the addressee will pass the salt. The further politeness associated with *Could you pass me the salt?* derives from the fact that the speaker, in using this incomplete sentence-type, removes any presumption that the addressee could do this. It is an open question whether it is even possible for the addressee to pass the salt. This is why saying the uninverted, confirmation question *You could pass me the salt?* lacks politeness, and why some wieldings of it might even be taken to be offensive. Here, the presumption is that the addressee could pass the salt, since, in saying it, the speaker presents himself as seeking to confirm the belief that the addressee could pass the salt. Of course the addressee has not yet passed the salt, though able to. So confirming what is obvious, that the addressee is able to pass the salt, points toward some other explanation for the salt not being passed, the implications being potentially offensive.

3.4 Rhetorical open questions and rhetorical confirmation questions

A rhetorical question is one that does not demand an answer, a question asked not so as to obtain information, but so as to produce some other effect. A rhetorical question may perfectly well *have* an answer, of course, it is just that a rhetorical question is not asked so as to demand an answer, not asked so as to close a point in question. It is essential in asking a rhetorical question to make sure that one is not understood to be asking for an answer. Some rhetorical questions are safer than others; there are some sentence-types that are standardly used to ask rhetorical questions, examples being *Is the Pope Catholic?* and *How many angels can dance on the head of a pin?* The less formulaic rhetorical questions must be

[12] See Searle 1975 and Levinson 1983, section 5.5. On politeness generally, see Brown and Levinson 1978, 1987.

handled more carefully. In general, there are two kinds of question that a speaker can ask that will normally be understood as rhetorical: those that have no answer, and those whose answers are so well known or obvious that it would be insulting or untoward to ask them so as to get answers. Since one would not normally want answers to unanswerable questions and insultingly obvious questions, one would usually be understood as speaking rhetorically. In general, one who asks a rhetorical question intends to be taken as not wanting an answer.

There are both open and confirmation rhetorical questions. Our appreciation of rhetorical questions has been skewed by the fact that only open rhetorical questions have been attended to. Let's start with rhetorical questions used so as to imply that they have no satisfactory answers. The speaker of a rhetorical open question uses a sentence-type that is formally incomplete, while intending not to be taken as wanting it to be completed. The speaker of a rhetorical confirmation question fails, in one way or the other, to perform a speech-act complete to the standard of assertion, while intending not to be taken as wanting it completed.

On the *wh*-question side, I can, so as to indicate that there was nothing that I could do, ask the open question *What could I do?* Here I use a sentence-type that expresses a proposition that lacks a thing done. If I rightly gauge the circumstances of utterance to be such that I will be taken as asking a question that does not have a satisfactory answer, I may succeed in implying that there was nothing that I could have done. Another almost formulaic case is *Who cares?*

While rhetorical open *wh*-questions are very common, the rhetorical use of confirmation *wh*-questions is more limited. Suppose my car has broken down, I am late, and you complain. Feeling unfairly criticized, I might respond *I could do what? Build an airplane?*, suggesting one of a presumably large number of unsatisfactory completions. To ask *I could do what?* is to ask my interlocutor to finish the speech-act I have partially performed, my intention being to indicate that there is no satisfactory completion. If I rightly gauge the circumstances of utterance to be such that I am taken as speaking rhetorically, I succeed in implying that my utterance cannot be satisfactorily completed: there was nothing that I could do to prevent my tardiness.

On the *yes-no* question side, I might, in exasperation, ask the rhetorical open question *Is this lecture going to end?* All lectures do end, of course, so by using a sentence-type expressing a proposition that lacks the glue between subject and predicate, while gauging the circumstances of utterance correctly, I succeed in implying that there is no knowing whether the predicate 'going to end' should be applied to the lecture.

On the other hand, if I utter the rhetorical confirmation question *This lecture is going to end?* I imply that I lack a belief strong enough to allow me to affirm that the lecture is going to end. In what circumstances might this be useful? Perhaps, during the lecture, you whisper to me that we should get a drink after the lecture, and I respond *This lecture is going to end?* If I gauge the circumstances of utterance to be such that you will not take me to be demanding that your belief be confirmed, I succeed in implying that your belief is not so obvious to me.

Now consider questions whose answers are so obvious or well known that they could only normally be asked rhetorically. Suppose you ask *Will the Yankees win?* and I answer *Is the Pope Catholic?* Here I use a sentence-type that expresses a proposition in which the glue is missing. But of course the predicate 'Catholic' so obviously applies to the Pope that I succeed in implying that the same obviousness must apply to the question you asked me: *of course* the predicate 'will win' applies to the Yankees. Now imagine that I had instead responded *The Pope is Catholic?* The uninverted confirmation question works far less well. Under this analysis, it is clear why this is so. By uttering *The Pope is Catholic?*, I intend to be taken as not having a belief sufficiently strong to license the assertion that the Pope is Catholic. To pull this off as a rhetorical confirmation question, the circumstances of utterance must be such that I will be taken to imply that I seek confirmation for the well-known fact that the Pope is Catholic. This is by itself fine, but the effect achieved does not have any analogy to your original question about the Yankees, and so my utterance falls flat. On the other hand, had you originally said *The Yankees will win?*, responding *The Pope is Catholic?* would have worked well.

The point of asking a rhetorical question depends on circumstance, and it is not possible to survey each circumstance. But we have reached some tentative generalizations. There are rhetorical questions whose answers are so obvious or well known that one who asks them must be up to something else. And there are rhetorical questions in which the speaker intends to be taken as implying that they have no answer at all. The speaker can use a sentence-type that he intends to be taken as expressing an uncompleteable proposition (the open-question case), or a speaker can, in one way or another, present himself as incapable of completing an assertive speech-act (the confirmation-question case). The point of offering a sentence-type that expresses an incomplete proposition is to indicate that the proposition is uncompleteable. The point of performing a speech-act that is not underwritten by the requisite beliefs is to indicate that the speech-act cannot be completed in a satisfactory way, the utterance is insupportable.

The effects that can be achieved through speaking are practically limitless; the limits are determined by our abilities to compute the implications of what is said. Individuals vary in this respect, and there are, in addition, personal and cultural norms governing such things as degree of directness. But we each are presented with tools that can be wielded so as to request, insult, accuse, crack wise, and so on. We do with them what we can. In this section, only some of the possible questioning speech-acts have been surveyed, hopefully giving a sense of the vastness of the terrain, as well as giving the underappreciated confirmation questions their due. I now turn to another class of questions that stand in contrast with open questions, questions that I call 'closed'.

3.5 Closed questions

3.5.1 Questions asked using negative sentence-types

There is a substantial difference between open questions and confirmation questions regarding the use of the negative, a fact that serves as further motivation for distinguishing them. In the case of confirmation *yes-no* questions, if a speaker wishes to confirm a belief, a belief that he would express by uttering the positive sentence-token *P*, the speaker may utter *P?*, and, if a speaker wishes to confirm a belief that he would express by uttering the negative sentence-token *Not-P*, the speaker may utter: *Not-P?* In both cases, the uninverted form is used. If I wish to confirm the belief that it is raining, I may say *It's raining?* If I wish to confirm the belief that it is not raining, I may say *It's not raining?*, the negative finding its role within the content of the belief that the speaker seeks to confirm. Since the belief the speaker seeks to confirm might be either one expressed in the negative or one *not* expressed in the negative, the presence of the negative is unexceptional.

In open questions, things are different. Recall that in an open *yes-no* question, the speaker presents himself as having no basis for determining whether P, presenting himself as holding that P and not-P are equally possible. Now, notice that if I have been in all day, and have not heard a weather report, and you telephone, I may ask the open question *Is it raining?* but I cannot ask *Isn't it raining?* While confirmation questions may be asked using sentences in the positive or the negative, it appears that open questions may only be asked in the positive. In the case just given, that may seem to be a natural result, another bit of linguistic markedness making itself felt. However, things are considerably more complex, since negative inverted sentence-types can, it turns out, be used to ask questions in other circumstances.

Before we examine those complexities, there is a prior issue: How can a negative sentence-type, at least for our purposes, be recognized? For guidance, consider the distinction between asking *Isn't Max reliable?* and asking *Is Max not reliable?* This last is ambiguous. On one understanding, the 'not' constituent-negates 'reliable', and, in that circumstance, we do not, as I wish to use the term, have a negative sentence-type used to ask a question. We have, rather, a positive sentence-type used to ask a question, one very close in meaning to *Is Max unreliable?* There is a simple test for this: one may only append 'or not' to the end of a question when a positive sentence-type is used to ask it. And, when 'not' constituent-negates 'reliable', it is possible to append 'or not' to yield the possible, though clumsy, *Is Max not reliable, or not?* On the other understanding of *Is Max not reliable?*, and on the only understanding of *Isn't Max reliable?*, however, this is not allowed. The 'not' of a negative sentence-type used to ask a question must be sentential in its scope: like positive statements, positive questions may *contain* constituents that are negated, but they are not *themselves* negated. Consideration of sentence-types in which 'not' has sentential scope reveals that these negative sentence-types are used in pursuit of what I will call the 'eliminative tactic'.

3.5.2 The eliminative tactic

What is the status of the negative in inverted negative sentence-types used to ask questions? What work does it do? Let's take a case. Suppose it is ninety-five degrees and someone sees you with a sweater on. She might say *Aren't you hot?* In the given circumstance, this question seems natural. But what sort of question is it, and what does its speaker ask in uttering it? The speaker has a basis for the belief that you are hot: people are generally hot at ninety-five degrees. And the speaker has a basis for the belief that you are not hot: despite the circumstances, you are wearing a sweater. So, there are conflicting bases for belief.

We have seen that not all questions are asked so as to close a point in question. Rhetorical questions are not. But for those that are, we have so far only considered cases in which a speaker either has some basis for closing a point in question, or does not. Now we confront a circumstance, which is common enough, in which a speaker finds herself with conflicting bases for belief. There are two subcases to consider. In one subcase, the speaker considers the conflicting bases to be, for current purposes, of equal weight. In the other subcase, the speaker considers one of the bases to outweigh the other. We will see that a speaker in the first circumstance asks a positive open question; the equally weighing bases 'cancel each other out', and the case is no different from one in which she considers herself to have no bases at all. Adjusting terminology on this point, an open question can now be more appropriately defined as one asked by a speaker who considers herself to have no *outweighing* basis for deciding it. The second subcase, in which a speaker considers herself to have conflicting bases, one outweighing the other, is more interesting. It is in that circumstance that the speaker may use an inverted negative sentence-type, asking what I have termed a 'closed' question.

In asking a closed question, speakers adopt the eliminative tactic, a brief outline of which follows. Suppose there is a point in question. That point may be pursued (eliminatively) by bringing a further point into question, which is whether the outweighed basis for deciding the original point in question is sufficiently strong to prevent the speaker's closing the original point. The reason the negative sentence-type is useful here is that the polarity of the further question will be the reverse of the polarity of the original question, since the further question takes as *its* point in question not whether the bases supporting a particular answer to the original point in question are to be accepted, but rather whether the bases *contravening* support of a particular answer to the original point in question are to be accepted. That is, where the original point in question is whether P, and the outweighing bases support P, the further point brought into question becomes whether not-P. In pursuing the original point in question by raising a further point, the speaker attempts to eliminate the counterexamples, so as to pave the way for acceptance of the outweighing bases as sufficient for closing the original point in question. This is why I call this the 'eliminative tactic'. For illustration, let's return to the example where you are asked *Aren't you hot?* In this case, the original point in question would be whether it is the case that you are hot; the outweighing basis being the ninety-five degree temperature. The further point in question would be whether you are *not* hot, the outweighed basis being the wearing of the sweater.

Like open questions, closed questions are asked using deformed sentence-types. To accommodate closed questions, our generalizations of sentence choice may be adjusted as follows:

(1) To ask a confirmation question, use an undeformed sentence-type.
(2) To ask an open or closed question, use a deformed sentence-type.
    (a) To ask an open question, use a positive sentence-type.
    (b) To ask a closed question, use a negative sentence-type.

Let's examine these last in turn. (2a) states that, when a speaker considers there to be no outweighing bases, and seeks to ask an open question, the positive form must be chosen. That is the case, already mentioned, of asking *Is it raining?*, but not *Isn't it raining?*, when a speaker has no idea of what the weather is. When a speaker does have an opinion as to the weather, to ask a closed question, a negative form *must* be used. To ask *Isn't it raining?* is to pursue the eliminative tactic, seeking finally to close on the conclusion that it *is* raining. But by asking the positive *Is it raining?* a speaker *cannot* be pursuing the eliminative tactic; he cannot be seeking to close on the conclusion that it is *not* raining. He may only be asking a positive open question. Thus (2b) complements (2a).

The eliminative tactic just outlined is a little bit of natural-language scientific practice. By implementing it, we pursue the truth in a way that is so natural that it might be mistakenly thought to be grammaticized. Let's further explore the factual terrain. It is clear that the question whether the outweighed bases are sufficient to block acceptance of the theory supported by the outweighing evidence certainly could *itself* be debatable. In many circumstances, even a small bit of counterevidence can block at least full acceptance of a highly supported theory. It depends what kind of theory is in question, and what kinds of criteria for acceptance are in force. And it depends very crucially on the individuals involved: some leap to conclusions where others are more cautious. As we saw when considering the decision whether to ask an open question or a confirmation question, there is no interesting answer to the question under what epistemic circumstances the eliminative tactic *should* be pursued. The eliminative tactic is available, different speakers pursue it in different circumstances, and that is the (descriptive) end of the matter.

As already mentioned, in pursuing the eliminative tactic, only inverted sentence-types may be used. A speaker *cannot* pursue the eliminative tactic by asking an undeformed confirmation question, even when the sentence-type used is negative. To see this, consider what the upshot of asking a confirmation question in pursuit of the eliminative tactic would be. Suppose a speaker considers that the outweighing bases support that it is raining, and that the outweighed bases support that it is not raining. In particular, suppose that it was not raining when I came in, but I now see you walk in with a wet umbrella. By asking you a confirmation question, would I be able to pursue the eliminative tactic? I cannot say *It's not raining?*, since by saying that I would be taken as trying to confirm my belief that it is not raining, a belief I did have, but am now leaning against. And I cannot be seeking to confirm the evidence of your wet umbrella, since that is evidence that it *is* raining. Nor, in pursuit of the eliminative tactic, can I say *It's raining?* since that only goes to confirm the evidence of your wet umbrella. To be sure, if you answer *Yes, it is,* I have more evidence against my former belief that it is not raining, but not through pursuit of the eliminative tactic, a point I will return to.[13]

By asking a closed question, a speaker reveals what she believes concerning the original point in question. It will help to reconsider the matter of the heat versus the sweater. Recall that the conflicting bases are the fact that the addressee is wearing a sweater and the fact that it is ninety-five degrees. Suppose the speaker takes the basis provided by the outside temperature as outweighing the basis provided by the wearing of the sweater. For such a speaker, the puzzling part is the wearing of the sweater. Such a speaker, taking the evidence of the sweater as the outweighed basis, may ask the closed negative question *Aren't you hot?*—this is the question already considered that I said seemed natural in the circumstance. The question asks whether the addressee is not hot. On the other hand, another speaker might decide that the evidence provided by the wearing of the sweater outweighs the evidence provided by the outside temperature. Perhaps there is reason to doubt the accuracy of the thermometer, and so for this speaker, the ninety-five degree reading is the puzzling part. If such a speaker, taking the evidence of the temperature reading as the outweighed basis, asks a question to decide the point, he must ask the open positive question *Are you hot?*, since the temperature is what provides the evidence that the addressee is hot. The question asks whether the addressee is hot. (And, of course, the speaker might consider the temperature and the sweater as equally strong but conflicting bases for deciding the point in question, and here, if the speaker asks a question, the speaker must ask a positive open question.) But the point I wish to focus on now is this. Consider what the speaker reveals herself to believe in the first case. By asking *Aren't you hot?* the speaker reveals that she considers the outweighing evidence to be that you *are* hot, since her question is posed so as to address the outweighed basis for believing that you are *not* hot. So this question, which,

---

[13] If I believe that it is raining, and you say *I'm going out to play baseball,* I may respond *It's not raining?!* The belief being confirmed is my newly acquired belief that it is not raining, a belief based on your decision to go out. I express surprise, since I had thought otherwise. See Section 3.6.2.

in virtue of its structure, can only be asked in pursuit of the eliminative tactic, reveals how the speaker is leaning concerning the original point in question, and therefore also may serve to imply other opinions the questioner holds: that your attire is inappropriate, perhaps. In the second case, however, this is not so. The question asked is open, and, merely by asking an open question, a speaker does not present himself as leaning one way or the other, as having any opinion.

Finally, consider the negative confirmation question *You're not hot?* This question takes the fact that you are wearing a sweater as the basis for holding the belief that you are not hot. So a speaker asking *You're not hot?* would be presenting himself as seeking to confirm the belief that you are not hot. As in the case of the spoiled milk, that belief might be the belief of the speaker, but it also might be the belief of the addressee, in which case it might not be the case that the speaker believes that the addressee is not hot.

Can one ask a closed question without having conflicting bases for belief? Not straightforwardly, I believe. Suppose you know that it is raining and know that the addressee knows that it is raining, and it develops that the addressee wants nevertheless to go out so as to avoid some responsibility. Then you might ask *Isn't it raining?* You have asked the closed question even though you are certain that it is raining. The closed question succeeds in this case, through misrepresentation. Although you have no conflicting bases, you make as if to believe, and as if to believe that the addressee might believe, that it is not raining but also while presenting yourself as leaning toward the belief that it *is* raining. The effect is to point out that the addressee is going out even though it is raining. Such pointed closed question cases can thus be used as an indirect way of expressing disapproval or criticism of another's behavior.

3.5.3 Tag questions

There is an important, and quite lovely, restriction on the applications of generalizations (2a) and (2b) in the previous section. Tag questions are also closed questions and are also used to pursue the eliminative tactic. They, however, unlike the full questions under consideration above, may appear in both the positive and negative forms, that choice being a function of the polarity of the sentences expressing the original points in question. Full open questions are positive, and full closed questions are negative, but tag questions, all of which are closed, may be positive or negative. The switch in polarity found in tag questions is a reflex of the fact that what the eliminative tactic aims to eliminate is the opposite of the proposition that enjoys the outweighing support; as a result we see both negative tags like *It's hot, isn't it?* along with positive tags like *It isn't hot, is it?* This syntactic reflex of the tactic is so regular that it has traditionally led students of the topic to the view that tag questions derive their structure by linguistic rule. The tag question transformation was an early instantiation of this approach. Now I believe that it is a mistake to encode polarity switch into the syntactic legislation of English, as the tag question transformation, or its modern descendants, would require. The reason is that, next to tags that show polarity switch, such as *You're going to beat me up, aren't you?*, there are others that do not, such as *You're going to beat me up, are you?*, which will be discussed further in the next section. Of course these two are intoned quite differently, at least in many circumstances, but, also of course, they are used to do very different things as well. My point is that, if syntax just provides the tags, leaving their polarity free, it need do no more. Rules of sentence choice specify, for each sentence-type, what it may be used for. Those in which there is a shift of polarity are used in pursuit of the eliminative tactic; these sentence-types I will continue to call 'tag questions'. Those in which there is no shift in polarity are used more aggressively; these I will call 'tag challenges'.[14]

First, we must ask why tag questions, which are closed, can be either positive or negative, when full closed questions are restricted to the negative. Why are tag questions closed? When I say *It's hot, isn't it?*, I first assert it is hot, and then ask the question . . . *isn't it?* Clearly the tag question must not be understood as open, since to ask an open question on a point that I have just committed on would be self-impeaching. If I am willing to assert that P, I cannot in the same breath go on to ask the open question whether not-P. And if I am willing to ask the open question whether not-P, I cannot just have asserted P. And all of this is true, *mutatis mutandis*, with the polarities reversed, were I to say *It isn't hot, is it?* So tag questions are not, and cannot be, open questions. They can, however, be used as closed questions; it is not self-impeaching, having asserted P, to ask whether not-P as a closed question: this merely brings the further point in question whether not-P, presenting it as having outweighed bases. This is indeed the same eliminative strategy seen with full closed questions. However, with full questions the eliminative tactic can only be pursued with a negative sentence-type, since positive sentence-types are used for open questions. With tag questions, the eliminative tactic can be pursued with both positive and negative sentence-types, since there is no mistaking a positive tag for an open question. Thus, positive closed questions are allowed precisely in the circumstance in which they cannot be understood as open. Among the full questions, we have both open and closed types, the first positive, the second negative. Among tag questions, we have only closed types, but they may be positive or negative.

3.5.4 Confidence and its lack: two examples of wielding tag questions

In the wielding of tag questions, English allows some subtlety. A speaker may indicate, by asking a closed tag question, either that she is confident that the

---

[14] Note that what I call tag challenges, Napoli (1993) calls 'belligerent' tag questions.

point in question is settled, or that she is not confident that the point in question is settled. Intonation is one method by which this is done. One may say *It's hot, isn't it?* with falling or rising intonation on the tag; if it is falling, the speaker presents herself as confident that the question whether it is hot is settled, if rising not confident that the question is settled.

Take these options in turn. Suppose a speaker says *It's hot, isn't it?* with falling intonation. By asserting *It's hot,* the speaker presents herself as believing that it is hot. By continuing with the closed tag question, . . . *isn't it (hot)?,* the speaker asks whether the addressee would say the opposite. This has the effect of eliciting agreement. By stating that P and asking the addressee whether he has reason to believe that not-P, the speaker presents herself as assuming that the addressee will agree with her that P. On the other hand, by saying *It's hot, isn't it?* with rising intonation, the speaker presents herself as not completely confident that the point in question is settled, not completely prepared to assert that it is hot. Perhaps the speaker has merely the expectation that it is hot: the soup has been on the stove long enough that, in normal circumstances, it should be hot. Or perhaps the speaker has a lot at stake that it be hot, but no evidence at all whether it is, in fact, hot: having just served the unknown soup to future in-laws, perhaps. Then the sentence *It's hot, isn't it?* might be said in trepidation. So in this case the speaker indicates lack of certainty that P and asks the addressee whether he has reason to believe that not-P.

Let me restate these points in terms of the lack that the user of a tag question expresses. The speaker who asks a tag question uses a sentence-type that expresses a proposition that lacks the glue, and which, were the glue to be provided, would express the negative of the proposition previously expressed. There are different ways such a sentence-type may be wielded corresponding to belief-states the speaker might be in. On one wielding, confidence is expressed; on another, its lack. The tag questioner may assert P with confidence, yet go on to ask whether the addressee would say the opposite. Or the tag questioner may assert P with no confidence, and go on to ask whether the addressee would say the opposite. The former is confident that the addressee will agree that there is no cause to say the opposite. The latter is not, allowing that the addressee might have cause to say the opposite.

3.6 The speciation of challenges

3.6.1 Tag challenges

If one wishes to perform the eliminative tactic with a tag question, one must choose a sentence-type in which both polarity shift and inversion obtain, since these are the forms of sentence used to ask closed questions. Tag challenges are distinct from tag questions in that they show no polarity shift; but like tag questions we find both positive and negative forms; alongside *Oh, so you're the Queen of Sheba, are you?*, there is also *So you aren't required to take logic, aren't you?*[15]

Are tag challenges open or closed? I will argue that they are open. Recall the reasoning that tag questions cannot be open, since a speaker would be impeaching himself by making an assertion and then presenting himself as considering it an open question whether the polar opposite is true. A speaker can, however, be pursuing the eliminative tactic without impeaching himself, so therefore tag questions must be closed.

In contrast with tag questions, tag challenges show no polarity shift. Therefore they cannot be used in pursuit of the eliminative tactic, since instead of examining a further point, the tag challenge re-examines the original point in question. Therefore the tag challenge must be open. But if a tag challenge is open, does the speaker impeach himself? In fact, no. Consider what the speaker is doing when he says *Oh, so you're the Queen of Sheba, are you?* The speaker is certainly not asserting that the addressee is the Queen of Sheba; in fact the point of the utterance is to say that the speaker believes no such thing. With the tag challenge, the speaker goes on to ask the open question whether what was just said is true. By making as if to assert that P, and then asking whether-P, the speaker immediately calls into question what has just been mouthed. The speaker does this without impeaching himself, because he intends the belief expressed to be attributed to someone other than himself. In this case, the speaker is presenting how (he believes) the addressee is representing himself, as can be seen from the fact that tag challenges fail to hit their target if the addressee is not representing himself in the manner in question, in this case, as the Queen of Sheba. By expressing how the addressee is representing himself and then asking the open question whether that self-representation is genuine, the speaker expresses non-acceptance. And that is to challenge the representation.

3.6.2 Non-acceptance and disbelief; astonishment and surprise

Unlike tag questions, tag challenges can stand on their own if said in direct response. Suppose you say *I'm the king of the castle!* and I respond (perhaps in a grave tone of voice) *Are you?* I have presented myself as considering it an open question whether you are the king of the castle. Since you have just committed yourself on a point that I have immediately called into question, I indicate that I do not accept what you said. There is, however, another way to pronounce the response, which might be punctuated *Are you?! (Wow!)*—and here

---

[15] These cases are to be distinguished from the sequence of a confirmation question and a (positive) open question, such as *It's hot, is it?*, said with a steadily rising intonation. This locution is common at least in the form of British English used by BBC interviewers, but not in American English, and I will not treat it here.

astonishment is expressed. Astonishment, as I am using the term, is expressed when one represents oneself as reporting that nothing had been further from one's mind. So depending on how they are wielded, (open) tag challenges may express non-acceptance or astonishment.

Suppose, when you say *I'm the king of the castle*, I choose instead to respond with the uninverted form *You are?* Since this uninverted type of direct response always stands on its own, never as a tag, I will call such responses confirmation challenges. As with its open counterpart, variations in tone and stress allow speakers to wield the confirmation challenge in different ways. Similar to the tag challenge, the confirmation challenge might be directed at how the addressee has represented himself or at the speaker's own grounds for believing what the addressee has said. In the latter case, *You are?* expresses surprise. Surprise, as I am using the term, is expressed when one represents oneself as having thought otherwise. In the former case, *You are?* expresses disbelief. You have asserted that you are king of the castle. And now I ask you to confirm that you believe that you are king of the castle. Note that, by seeking to confirm your belief, I am not actually disagreeing with you as to whether you are king of the castle, but questioning your belief that you are. It is at this point that non-acceptance and disbelief separate. These must be distinguished, since there is the possibility that you really *are* the king of the castle, that you believe that you are *not* the king of the castle, and that you nevertheless dishonestly but accurately assert *I'm the king of the castle!* In such a case, in uttering the confirmation question *You are?* seeking to confirm your belief that you are the king of the castle, I challenge your honesty, not your veracity. So, depending on how they are wielded, confirmation challenges may express disbelief or surprise.

What is the relationship between non-acceptance and astonishment? And, what is the relationship between disbelief and surprise? Furthermore, what is the relationship between the distinction between non-acceptance and astonishment on the one hand, and disbelief and surprise on the other? For clarity, let me repeat each of the four terms in the precise senses I have used them:

One does *not accept* something when one does not think that.

One *disbelieves* something when one thinks otherwise.

One is *astonished* at something when one never would have thought that.

One is *surprised* at something when one has thought otherwise.

As I have defined the terms, disbelief and surprise are felt when there is conflict with what has been assumed, and non-acceptance and astonishment are felt when nothing one way or the other has been assumed. This is the distinction between having negative expectations and having no expectations. And since, in the case of disbelief and surprise, there is conflict between what has been said and what has been assumed, it is natural that disbelief and surprise would be expressed through the asking of a confirmation question. And equally since, in the case of

Table 3.1. The speciation of challenges (said in response to *I'm the king of the castle*)

	(Open) tag challenges, example: *Are you?*	Confirmation challenges, example: *You are?*
	Nothing assumed, no expectations	Conflict with what is assumed
Questioning addressee's grounds	non-acceptance	disbelief
Questioning own grounds	astonishment	surprise

non-acceptance and astonishment, there has been no assumption one way or the other at all, it follows that non-acceptance and astonishment would be expressed through the asking of an open question. As a result, uninverted forms, those used to ask confirmation questions, are the sentence-types used to express either disbelief or surprise, while the inverted forms, those used to ask open questions, are used to express either non-acceptance or astonishment. This is summarized in Table 3.1.

Let's digress for a few moments to consider these distinctions and the facts that underlie them. Untangling the uses of questions to express such things as non-acceptance, disbelief, astonishment, or surprise is a murky business, but, now that I have discussed part of that terrain, it is possible that some would complain that I am making it far too clear-cut, that the distinctions are not as sharp as I have claimed. To offset that criticism, let me introduce some murk. If I introduce just enough of it, the reader will, I hope, complain that things must be more clear-cut than I am making them out to be, and the proper balance will have been achieved.

To begin with, there is a natural tendency to say such things as *Unbelievable!* or *Incredible!* even when we perfectly well believe what we have heard, but are either astonished or surprised by it. This seems to indicate that, in common English, what is surprising or astonishing is *hard* to believe, and that, when we say *Unbelievable!* in such circumstances, we exaggerate; we often *do* believe it, but it is *hard* to believe, and we are not actually in a state of disbelief (or non-acceptance), but in a state of astonishment (or surprise). This kind of exaggeration can be felt in the use of questions as well. Suppose you say *The New York Post has just published a slanted editorial!*, and I respond *It has?! What a surprise!* A sarcastic intonation helps this reading along. Here, overtly, I register surprise, and I do that so as to bring to mind that I am not at all surprised to learn that the New York Post has published a slanted editorial. I make as if to confirm an unexpected belief, a belief that in fact is not unexpected at all. Suppose, on the other hand, I react to your news by saying: *Has it?! Gadzooks! Who would have thought?* The wide-eyed wonderment of a simpleton may be an effective accompaniment in making this response. Here I overtly express astonishment when I feel that there is nothing in the least bit astonishing about it; I make as if nothing had been further from my mind, when in fact I've thought that all along. It should be clear that, in these kinds of performances, the distinction between astonishment and surprise, as well as sarcasm and false wonderment, can be mixed and confounded in all sorts of ways. It is natural that this sort of looseness would be found in these circumstances, since here, by posing *Has it?* and *It has?* as questions, the speaker intends it to become clear that he is not posing them so as to receive answers at all. So there are certainly circumstances in which the distinctions I have drawn are not directly in point, and are just used for effect. In such cases, we do not always distinguish surprise from astonishment or disbelief from non-acceptance, at least not very carefully.

Furthermore, the truth is that we do not, and in many circumstances cannot, really distinguish those beliefs we have never considered before from those beliefs that we have turned against. Sometimes, when we address a belief, we realize we have never considered it before. Suppose you are told *Pigs can't eat pumpkins.* Unless you have raised livestock, that is probably a new one on you, not a belief that you have turned against. But suppose you are told *Pigs can't play basketball.* Is that a new one on you, or one you have turned against? Certainly there are things that you believe about pigs that entail that pigs cannot play basketball. In contrast, you really never may have considered the difficulty pigs might have eating uncut pumpkins given the shapes of their snouts. So the distinction between beliefs we have never considered and beliefs that we have turned against can, in practice, be unclear. That lack of clarity makes it difficult in many cases to distinguish non-acceptance from disbelief. We can, furthermore, express either one, and add in either astonishment or surprise to boot, by saying *I can't believe my ears!* All that said, just because there are gray cats, it does not follow that we cannot tell white ones from black ones. There are clear cases.

Returning to the speciation of challenges, let's examine the same ground in the negative. As we have seen, a speaker may express non-acceptance by asking an (open) tag challenge or disbelief by asking a confirmation challenge. Whereas a positive statement may be non-accepted by asking its positive, inverted, open question counterpart, one may show non-acceptance of a negative statement by uttering its negative, inverted, open question counterpart. If you say *I'm not responsible!* I can show non-acceptance by saying *Aren't you?* (Recall that unlike tag challenges, the polarity-reversing tag questions cannot stand on their own. So when the polarity is reversed the responses fail: to the utterance *I'm not responsible!* the response *Are you?* fails, and to the utterance *I'm responsible,* the response *Aren't you?* fails as well.) By asking the open question *Aren't you?* in response to *I'm not responsible!*, a speaker can show non-acceptance since to ask such a question indicates that that speaker does not consider the point in question settled. Furthermore, a speaker can be a pest about it, and continue with *Aren't you? Aren't you?*, varying the intonation in ominous ways, and thus shade over into accusation, where here no *answer* is demanded, only defense being called for. But things need not go that far, and in those cases, only non-acceptance is registered. Similarly, a speaker may register disbelief of a negative statement by asking a confirmation challenge in the negative. If you say *I'm not guilty!* I may express disbelief by saying *You aren't?* By expressing disbelief, I seek to confirm your belief. And since you have just affirmed that very belief, trying to get you to confirm your belief is tantamount to saying that you did not say what you believed. Both astonishment and surprise can also be displayed with the negative, when instead of the addressee, it is the speaker's own grounds that are being questioned. When you say *I'm not responsible!* and I respond *Aren't you?*, I can be expressing astonishment—I never would have thought that you were not responsible. Similarly, when you say *I'm not guilty!* and I respond *You aren't?*, I can be expressing surprise because I had thought you were guilty. And so we see the same four-way speciation of challenges in the negative that we do in the positive.

3.7 Kinds of *wh*-questions

Let's turn to those questioning speech-acts in which *wh*-expressions appear. I have argued that, in the case of *yes-no* questions, the speaker decides whether to use an inverted sentence-type or an uninverted sentence-type on the basis of whether the speaker intends to ask an open question or a confirmation question. As with the choice between the inverted and uninverted forms in the case of *yes-no* questions, the speaker faces a choice, in the case of *wh*-questions, between forms in which *wh*-movement has applied and forms in which it has not. And there is a syntactic interaction between inversion and *wh*-movement: where, in matrix sentences, *wh*-movement has applied, inversion must apply as well (the possible exception being the case in which the subject has *wh*-moved). For reasons that will be discussed in Chapter 5, the speaker does not have the option to utter *Who John was talking to?* There is, however, a choice that speakers face between saying *Who was John talking to?* and saying *John was talking to who?* The facts indicate that the *wh*-moved form is used to ask open questions and the un-*wh*-moved form is used to ask confirmation questions. The choice between forms of *wh*-question parallels the choice between forms of *yes-no* questions: to ask an open question, the deformed sentence-type is chosen, while to ask a confirmation question, the undeformed sentence-type is used.

Recall that open questions express propositions that are incomplete in one way or another, while in the case of confirmation questions, the incompleteness resides either in the preparatory conditions for the utterance, or in the utterance itself. In both open and confirmation questions, the standard of completeness is given by the corresponding assertion. In the case of confirmation *wh*-questions, the presence of a *wh*-expression 'in situ' indicates a position in the utterance that the speaker presents himself as being unable to fill satisfactorily. In the following sections, I will explore some of the reasons why a speaker might be unable to complete an utterance in this sense.

3.7.1 Repeat questions

In linguistics, it has been common to call sentence-types that contain *wh*-expressions *in situ* 'echo' questions. It turns out, however, that there are various speech-acts that such sentence-types may be used to perform, only some of them having anything to do with echoing. Since, in linguistics at least, terminological mistakes have proven themselves to be irremediable, I will simply avoid the term.

Suppose you say something but I do not quite hear you. You say, for example, *I just talked with (mumble)*. I can respond with the confirmation question *You just talked to who?* By using the undeformed sentence-type, I present myself as being unable to complete the utterance in a satisfactory way. It is important to see that, when I ask *You just talked to who?*, I am not asking you whom you talked to. What I am asking is that you repeat what you have said. If you repeat what you have said, I will of course know whom you said you talked to, but that is different from asking you whom you talked to. The question asks that you produce a bit of language, a repetition of the bit of language that I did not hear. I call this kind of question a 'repeat question'. That we have requested that a bit of *language* be repeated can be directly appreciated when one considers the example *I just rafted down the Mononga(mumble)*, in which I cannot hear the last part of the last word. In this case, I may ask *You just rafted down the Monongawhat?*, and you may perfectly well respond *hela*. The missing few syllables of the name of the Monongahela River do not constitute a morpheme, so far as I know, let alone correspond to anything in the world, so plainly my question does not ask what is such that you just rafted down the Mononga it. Note that to ask for this bit of language, the *wh*-expression must remain *in situ*; there is no *What did you just raft down the Mononga?*, since words are syntactic islands.

While repeat questions ask for bits of language, it can often happen that the questioner's interest resides not so much in the unheard bit of language but in the item it denotes. If you say *I was just reading Tully*, and, not hearing your last word, I respond *You were just reading who?*, you may, in many circumstances, reply *I was just reading Cicero*. If you calculate that my interest is in the item and not in the bit of language denoting it, you have been responsive to my interests. Perhaps I should have asked an open question in that case, but failed to use the most appropriate tool. Also, if one does not hear what was said, one may ask an open question so as to find out what was said. One may ask, for example, *What did you say?* And, if one hears only a part of what was said, one may, instead of saying *You talked to who?*, say *Who did you talk to?* (it helps to stress the 'who' in a particular way). But this last, as I am using the term, is not a repeat question, but rather an open question asking whom you talked to. There is a way to appreciate the difference. A speaker may say, with the same force, either *Who did you talk to?* or *Who did you say you talked to?* if she had heard the addressee say *I talked to (mumble)*, but the repeat confirmation question *You said you talked to who?* is only comfortably asked in response to *I said I talked to (mumble)*.

3.7.2 How the challenge distinctions fare in using *wh*-questions

Suppose that you say something and I hear you all right, but I question what you have told me. Suppose you say *I just bought a horse*. As with tag challenges, I can respond by uttering *What did you just buy?*, registering non-acceptance or astonishment, depending on how the sentence-type is wielded. On the other hand, suppose I respond *You just bought what?* Here, in using an undeformed confirmation question, I register either disbelief or surprise. The four-way distinction in speech-acts holds. As I have already discussed, we do not always respect the divide between the epistemological side and the emotional one, nor do we always clearly distinguish those beliefs we have never considered from those that contradict what we have considered. Nevertheless, when we are careful about these matters, we are careful in the ways indicated; and, if we find ourselves in a position to honor these distinctions, they are formally available, as the following examples illustrate.

The difference between the speech-acts performed is, as before, a matter of wielding. On the open-question side, the non-acceptance case, *What did you just buy?*, is straightforward. By presenting myself as considering it an open question what you bought when I have just heard you assert what was bought, I register the fact that I do not accept your grounds for what you have said. The astonishment case runs parallel to this; here I question my own grounds, registering the fact that I do not 'believe my ears'. As before, a speaker may indicate non-acceptance versus astonishment through facial expression, gesture, or difference in pronunciation—all of these being a matter of wielding.

On the confirmation side, if I respond to your saying *I just bought a horse* by using the undeformed *You just bought what?*, I present myself as being unable to complete my utterance in a satisfactory way. Assuming it is wielded in such a way that it is clear that a repeat question is not being asked, I may instead indicate disbelief or surprise. In the former case, I am questioning your grounds: I might know that what you *actually* bought was a donkey, and that you are nevertheless claiming to have bought a horse. I indicate that to complete my utterance in the way you did would not be satisfactory. And that is to register disbelief. On the other hand, surprise is registered in a different circumstance: *You just bought what? I thought you were going to buy a donkey!* Here, as before, I question my own grounds, implying that I cannot believe my ears.

3.7.3 Quiz questions

To quiz someone, one asks a question, sometimes many. The sentence-types used to quiz people may be deformed or undeformed. I will use the term 'quiz question' to denote either sort; quiz questions may be open questions or confirmation questions. With this type, the undeformed cases have received more attention, and the term 'quiz question' has mostly stuck to them. Typical examples are: *Syntactic Structures was written by what linguist?* and *Fidel Castro is president of which Caribbean country?*

The first thing to appreciate about quiz questions is that their primary use seems to be in quiz shows and games involving quizzing. Of course it is a matter of format, not grammar, whether a quiz-show host chooses to ask a quiz question using the uninverted form. To the extent that quiz questions are asked in common talk, they bring with them the feel of the quiz-show format, the speaker taking on the role of emcee, putting the addressee in the role of contestant. Under some circumstances, that can be abrasive, so many of us do not normally do it—restricting such questions to game situations where the clear purpose is to have fun.

The second thing to understand about quiz questions is that the people that ask them know the answers to them, or at least have immediate and independent access to the answers, which comes to the same thing. And there is a further twist to this. Searle, who calls them 'exam questions', divides the terrain as follows: "there are two kinds of questions, (a) real questions, (b) exam questions. In real questions S wants to know (find out) the answer; in exam questions, S wants to know if H knows" (1969: 66). In this formulation, I think Searle gives quiz questions too much prominence. The primary distinction within the species of questions is between open questions and confirmation questions, quiz questions being just one version of each, having a limited use on each side. He is certainly right, however, to say that the asker of a quiz question poses it not so as to find out its answer but so as to find out whether his addressee knows its answer.[16] The further point is that the reason that the quizmaster can, on hearing the answer to his quiz question, determine whether the addressee knows the answer to that question is that the questioner knows the answer himself.

I have said that ignorance is a lack and that the sentence-types that we use to ask questions display what lacks we have. Quiz questions teach us that one may use a sentence-type that displays a lack without having that lack. Normally, of

---

[16] A reader suggests that, like normal open questions, open quiz questions are requests that the hearer supply certain information, and that they therefore should be considered to be the same sort of speech-act, differing only in the purpose for eliciting the information. Of course, very broadly, they are the same; they are both kinds of question. But there are sharp differences. A normal open question gets its point from a desire to find out certain information. A quiz question gets its point from a desire to find out whether the addressee knows the answer, another kind of information. Now if the contestants were angelic truth-tellers, they could simply answer *Yes* or *No* to any *wh*-quiz question, thereby indicating whether they know the answer. This would work in a quiz show in heaven. But a normal, non-quiz, open *wh*-question could never be answered *Yes* or *No*, even by angels. These two types of question not only differ in the purpose for eliciting information, they also fundamentally differ in the kind of information the speaker seeks to elicit.

course, this is deceitful: if one asks a question, one implies that one does not know its answer. But in the context of the quiz-show, it is understood that the emcee is not asking his questions out of curiosity, so there is no deceit involved. Both open and confirmation questions can fill the quizmaster's needs. By asking *What two metals is brass an alloy of?* the emcee uses a sentence-type that is incomplete in comparison with a sentence-type used to make an assertive answer. By asking *Brass is an alloy of what two metals?* the emcee performs a speech-act that is incomplete when compared with assertion. In either case, it is the contestant's job to supply the completion.

3.7.4 *Wh-the-hell* questions

To finish off, we have a case from the open side of the ledger. The treatment of *wh-the-hell* questions has generally been taken to depend on discourse structure, the idea being that, in contrast with *which*-questions, which are D-linked, *wh-the-hell* questions are not D-linked (Pesetsky 1987). In consequence, one may say *What the hell are you doing?* but not *Which the hell are you doing?* Now, in the name of good conversation, I oppose this proposal concerning discourse structure—a discussion that must wait until 'which' is discussed. But some small points for now, which will be expanded upon in the next chapter.

The first is that *wh-the-hell* questions are open questions, never confirmation questions. *What the hell are you doing?* is a perfectly fine thing to ask, but *You are doing what the hell?* is not. '*Wh*-the-hell' is not the only expression that marks this kind of question; there is also '*wh*-in-the-world', '*wh*-in-the-name-of-all-that's-holy', and others. The continuations after the *wh*-expressions serve to emphasize, simply in virtue of what they mean, that the range of items from which the answer is to be selected is maximally large and perhaps limitless. That being so, *wh-the-hell* questions suit themselves to a certain sarcastic effect: *What the hell are you doing?* is effectively said by someone who knows very well what the addressee is doing. And they lend themselves to being asked rhetorically: *What the hell could I do?* serves to emphasize the point that among some vast array of options there was nothing I could do.

The reason that *wh-the-hell* questions cannot be confirmation questions is that confirmation speaks not to the wide range of items that might complete the proposition but to the range of possible completions of the speech-act. Again, it must be remembered that to ask *You are doing what?* as a repeat question, to take one case, is not to ask what the addressee is doing. Rather it is to ask that the speech-act be completed, the standard of completion provided by the answering assertion. One may perform a variety of questioning speech-acts using a sentence-type containing '*wh*-the-hell'; the point just is that '*wh*-the-hell' binds variables ranging over things-in-the-world, not bits of language, so all of them must be open questions.

3.8 Closing remarks

I have argued that incomplete sentence-types are well suited to the asking of open questions, and that one may ask a different kind of question, a confirmation question, by incompletely using a sentence-type. Obviously, and to repeat, it does not in the least follow that only these two activities constitute the asking of questions nor that only the asking of questions may be accomplished by doing these two things. Again, we would not fall into these kinds of errors when talking about hammers, which we understand perfectly well, so there is no need to fall into these errors when talking about language, where there is much that remains mysterious. It can certainly be said that, just as hammers are well suited for the driving in of nails, so too incomplete sentence-types, and incompletely used sentence-types, are well suited for the asking of questions. In saying this, we do not deny what we all know perfectly well, that there are other ways to drive in a nail and other ways to ask a question.

As a final illustration, suppose, pointing to the cat stretching to get something under the stove, I say: *A.J. wants something*. If you think that I do not know what A.J. wants, and if you think I want to know what A.J. wants, you can take me as having asked what A.J. wants, and respond *Yes, the wine cork*. Have I asked you what A.J. wants? Have I uttered a question? Here, at least in this circumstance, I see nothing wrong with saying that I've asked you what A.J. wants. To continue the point, suppose instead I say *Is there something A.J. wants?* Here I certainly have not merely asked you a *yes-no* question, since it is plain that A.J. wants something, and that being so, it would be silly for me merely to be asking you whether he does. So I've got as close as can be to asking *What does A.J. want?* There are all kinds of lacks that sentence-types can manifest and these other sorts of deficit might play into the asking of questions as well, a point I will return to in Chapter 5. Sometimes use of grammatically indefinite expressions implies that one cannot use definite ones (a point that Grice noticed), and the effect of questioning is thereby achieved. And it is suggestive, but beyond the scope of this investigation, that there are, in some languages, close formal ties between the indefinite forms and the 'question-word' forms.

4

Quantifiers, *Wh*-expressions, and Manners of Interpretation

4.1 The manners of interpretation of 'each' and 'every'

For the remainder of this book, the focus is on open *wh*-questions. In this chapter, the meanings of quantifiers and *wh*-expressions will be my main topic, though it will be necessary also to consider the internal syntax of these expressions. I will examine various *wh*-expressions, and place them in contrast with the quantificational expressions of English, in particular 'each' and 'every'. In the course of this, I will distinguish quantificational force from what I will call 'manner'. Quantificational force is that aspect of a quantificational expression that states how many items must satisfy the following propositional function to yield truth. 'All' requires that all must, 'some' requires that some must, and '47' requires that forty-seven must. The English quantificational expressions 'each' and 'every', although the same in quantificational force as 'all', differ from each other in manner of interpretation. They differ in how the truth conditions of the sentences that contain them are derived. I will argue that 'which' and 'what', though they lack quantificational force, differ in manner in the way that 'each' and 'every' do. I will then go on to argue that, in consequence of their meanings, 'which' differs from 'what' and other *wh*-expressions both in its syntactic distribution and in terms of which questioning speech-acts sentence-types containing it may be used to perform. Since the semantic point is key, I will begin with it, deriving the implications for syntax and use at the end of the chapter. The development of the syntactic points will be the topic of Chapter 5.

4.1.1 Individualizing and Totalizing: the different manners of 'each' and 'every'

Natural language quantification is a good deal more subtle than standard treatments give it credit for. That is because, standardly, differences in quantificational behavior are restricted to differences in quantificational force and quantificational scope. The English expressions 'all', 'each', 'every', as well as a wide variety of expressions that contain universal quantifiers as parts of their logical structures, have the same force; they are all represented, at least in part, as '∀'. That being so, distinctions in behavior among the English universal quantifiers, when they are detected, can only be stated in terms of differences of quantificational scope, which might suggest that the lexical distinctions that English marks among the universal quantifiers always encode scope. But that is factually incorrect. One cannot read relative quantificational scope from the spellings of the universal quantifiers; 'all', 'each', and 'every' do not wear their relative scopes on their sleeves. An alternative would be that English contains a logically pointless system of synonyms. But this idea is both unattractive and dubious. Are these words really synonymous? Semantic comparison is complicated by syntactic differences. Not all syntactic environments allow substitution of one quantifier for another. We say *Each dog barks* and *Every dog barks*, but *All dog barks* is not allowed, suggesting that 'all' differs from 'each' and 'every' in terms of grammatical number. But 'each' and 'every' also contrast: we say *Each of the dogs barks* but not *Every of the dogs barks*. There are many idiosyncrasies in English; not all languages have forms that mark the distinctions that English marks, and within the recorded history of English there has been considerable variation in the meanings of the quantifiers. Nevertheless, we can, in English as it stands today, straightforwardly compare *Each dog barks* with *Every dog barks*, and, when we do, we find that while the quantifiers are the same in quantificational force, they differ in manner of interpretation.

In the interpretation of sentences containing restricted universal quantification, sentences whose logical forms are standardly written as $\forall$ x: Ψx [Φx], there are two distinguishable manners by which one may proceed: by Totalizing and by Individualizing, the terms due to Curme (1935). If we suppose the variables in the formula to range over items, the question comes by what procedure it is determined whether the items in U, the universe of discourse, are such that they support the truth of the formula. It may be said that, if truth is all that is at issue, any procedure will do, the only requirement being that it allow it to be told whether all Ψs are Φ. That is right, of course. But sometimes more than truth is at issue. Sometimes the manner by which truth is arrived at is at issue. That is the case here, I believe. I will reflect these manners in logical notation; the Totalizing 'every' will be represented as $\forall$T, and the Individualizing 'each' will be represented as $\forall$I. This means that difference in manner will be represented logically even though this difference never distinguishes truth from falsehood.[1] I will say more about this below, but I should first clarify the distinction between Totalizing and Individualizing.

Given an expression of the form '$\forall$Tx: Ψx [Φx]', Totalizing proceeds by first forming up the totality of Ψs occurring in U, the currently relevant context, and then determining, for the totality of Ψs, whether its members are Φ. More precisely:

[1] Except in opaque contexts, as will be seen directly.

Form the Totality of Ψ in U (i.e. that set containing all items in U that are Ψ, and no item in U that is not Ψ).

Determine whether the Totality of Ψ in U is Φ.

If the Totality of Ψ in U is Φ, then '$\forall$Tx: Ψx [Φx]' is true, otherwise false.

Individualizing, operating on an expression of the form '$\forall$Ix: Ψx [Φx]', proceeds differently:

Select an item in U, determine whether it is Ψ, and then, if it is Ψ, determine whether it is Φ.

Repeat this procedure until U is exhausted.

If all the Ψs in U are Φ, then '$\forall$Ix: Ψx [Φx]' is true, otherwise false.

It will be noticed that the last lines in these procedures do not quite match. To bring them into line, it must be said that the Totality of Ψ in U is Φ if and only if all the Ψs in U are Φ. Predicates may distribute into a Totality. That stipulation made, the truth conditions of formulas of the form '$\forall$Tx: Ψx [Φx]' and formulas of the form '$\forall$Ix: Ψx [Φx]' are the same; there can be no circumstance in which a sentence whose logical form is '$\forall$Tx: Ψx [Mx]' will come out true where a sentence whose logical form is '$\forall$Ix: Ψx [Mx]' will come out false, or vice versa. On the other hand, the prior lines in these procedures express distinct manners by which the truth conditions are derived. There is an important point to note. It is standard to hold that the interpretations of universal quantifiers, and indeed of quantifiers generally, exhaust the domains they range over, and in the case of Individualizing manner this is always so. We will see, however, that there are, in the practical use of language, circumstances in which Totalizing is not exhaustive, and that there are other manners of interpretation, of other quantifiers, that are not exhaustive either.

English makes use of both Individualizing and Totalizing manners, and sometimes overtly marks the difference. The interpretation of sentences such as *Every cat is fat* proceeds in the Totalizing manner, while the interpretation of *Each cat is fat* proceeds in the Individualizing manner. Before arguing this empirically, it will help to discuss manner in more general terms. I believe that the difference of manner of interpretation just sketched in the natural language treatment of quantification is in many ways comparable to a difference that Frege (1892) suggested might hold between distinct but coreferent expressions, such as 'Cicero' and 'Tully'. My view is that it would be just as wrong to conflate 'every' and 'each' representationally, as it would be to conflate 'Cicero' and 'Tully' representationally. If we do not allow distinct but coreferent terms, we will not allow true $A = B$, a form of sentence that natural language allows. For parallel reasons, we must not conflate the representations of quantifiers that are the same in force but distinct in manner, or 'mode of derivation'. Since force and manner make separate semantic contributions, they must be distinguished in logical representation. Frege (1892) held that, apart from the expression itself, and the item it refers to, there is a third thing, which is the way in which that expression refers to that item. I am suggesting that, in the case of quantifiers, apart from the quantifier-expression itself, and that part of the truth conditions of the entire sentence that it participates in deriving, there is a third thing, which is the way in which those truth conditions are derived. There is a conceptual affinity between the treatment of quantifiers that I am proposing and the separation that Frege made between expressions, their referents, and their modes of presentation.

In Frege's account, modes of presentation serve to solve certain semantic difficulties, among them the problem that, in some contexts, Leibniz's law appears not to hold. In transparent contexts, substituting 'Tully' for the coreferent expression 'Cicero' does not alter truth-value—the statements *Cicero denounced Catiline* and *Tully denounced Catiline* differ, but not in truth-value. However, such a difference can arise in opaque contexts—the statement *Joe believes that Cicero denounced Catiline* might be true while the statement *Joe believes that Tully denounced Catiline* is false. Frege's idea was that, in *that*-clauses, the expressions 'Cicero' and 'Tully' refer not to their customary referents, which are the same, but to their modes of presentation, which differ. Thus substitution is not, in this case, substitution of one expression with another coreferent to it, and, despite appearances, Leibniz's law holds after all. Many have found the idea that expressions can refer to their own modes of presentation hard to swallow, but, as it happens, there are various ways of implementing Frege's idea that do not depend on the proposal that expressions may sometimes refer to their own modes of presentation. One can disagree as to the status of modes of presentation and yet agree on the larger architecture of Frege's proposal. Centrally, my claim is simply that, in the case of quantificational expressions, manners may differ while truth conditions do not, and that these quantificational modes of derivation may, in some circumstances, contribute to the propositional content of a sentence.

There is another aspect to the comparison. If there were no distinction between 'Cicero' and 'Tully', a speaker would have no basis for deciding which to use. But on a Fregean account, since 'Cicero' and 'Tully' differ in meaning, the sentences *Cicero denounced Catiline* and *Tully denounced Catiline* express distinct thoughts, and it might be in the speaker's interest to express one thought and not the other. Similarly, if there were no distinction between 'every' and 'each', a speaker would have no basis for deciding between them, but, once it is seen that they differ in manner of interpretation, it can also be seen that a speaker does have a basis for deciding which to use. For example, a speaker might choose to use 'every' instead of 'each' if the totality of items under current consideration were in point, since the Totalizing manner of interpretation involves the forming up of the totality of items in the relevant domain. The Individualizing manner of interpretation associated with 'each' does not involve the forming up of such a totality, but rather the 'double-testing' of each item in the domain. Therefore, if a totality is in point over and above the items that constitute it, 'every' will be the quantifier of choice, while if the items themselves are in point over and above any grouping they might together constitute, 'each' will be the quantifier of choice. I will first illustrate this difference in transparent contexts.

4.1.2 'Each' and 'every' contrasted in transparent contexts

There are some preliminary matters involving the presuppositions and conversational implicatures that utterances containing 'each' and 'every' enjoin. Suppose, watching a ship go down, you ask: *Was each/every man saved?* I could answer: *Each/every man was saved, but in fact there was only one man aboard.* But it would be odd to answer: *Each/every man was saved, but in fact there was no one aboard.* This suggests that the occurrences of 'each' and 'every' in these questions introduce a presupposition that there is at least one item in the domain over which the variable they bind ranges (in this case, any and all men on board before the ship went down), and that they also introduce the conversational implicature that there is more than one item in the domain. It is this conversational implicature that is cancelled by the second clause in the first answer. In contrast with 'each' and 'every', it would be odd (or, perhaps, pedantic) to answer the question *Were all the men saved?* by saying either: *All the men were saved, but in fact there was only one man aboard* or by saying: *All the men were saved, but in fact there was no one aboard.* So, in contrast with 'each' and 'every', the expression 'all the men' (as well as 'the men all' as in *The men all were saved* or *The men were all saved*) normally introduces the presupposition that there was more than one man on board before the ship went down. It seems reasonable to assume that, formally speaking, the presupposition derives from the presence of the plural form in the examples involving 'all', which is not present in the examples involving 'each' and 'every'.

But 'each N' and 'every N', alike in contrasting with 'all the N' in these respects, differ from each other in other ways. First, consider the fact that 'every' is not comfortably used when talking about small numbers of individuals. Given a chessboard on which only two knights appear, we prefer to say *Each knight is pinned* to *Every knight is pinned* (though for some speakers, 'both' is preferred to 'each' when only two items are involved). To be sure, if both knights are pinned, statements containing 'each' or 'every' express the same truth. Why do we prefer to express that truth in the Individualizing manner? As already suggested, a speaker chooses to use Totalizing 'every' when the totality of items is in point over and above the items themselves. As we will see, a variety of circumstances affect this choice, but if the number of items is *very* small, the items become prominent as individuals, and the speaker will choose the Individualizing 'each' instead of the Totalizing 'every'. To take another case, if I brag *Every student I've ever had has done well*, and you subsequently learn that I have had only two or three students, you may rightly feel misled. Use of the Totalizing 'every' seems gratuitous and hyperbolic in such a case, which would not be the case with 'each'.

Secondly, and on the opposite side, consider the contrast between *You have every prospect of success* as against the rather odd *You have each prospect of success*. The former may be sincerely asserted by someone who is confident only that there is no bar to success, by someone who does not intend to, and perhaps knows he could not, list (Individualize) the prospects of success. On the other hand, the speaker of the latter would be Individualizing, in particular Individualizing prospects of success—an odd thing to do, for, after all, what exactly *is* a prospect of success? In this latter case, it would seem perfectly in line for someone to ask the speaker for a list of these prospects, a challenge in no way prompted by the former statement. I suspect that there is a fairly simple reason why one does not speak of counting prospects of success. The term 'prospect' contrasts with the term 'limitation', and, between the two, 'limitation' wears the pants. What we call a 'prospect' is an absence of a limitation (prospects are not opportunities), and we more happily count limitations than absences. Thus we can both Individualize and Totalize limitations, but only Totalize prospects. And when we Totalize prospects, as in *You have every prospect of success*, or when we Totalize 'reasons to believe' or 'rights to be angry', as in *I have every reason to believe you* or *You have every right to be angry*, there is, as before, a certain hyperbolic air, a hint of baseless grandiosity, whose presence may be explained by the fact that these are examples of Totalizing that cannot be independently defended by Individualizing.

When I introduced the procedure of Totalizing, I said that it is not always exhaustive. These are the cases I had in mind. As just noted, when I say *You have every prospect of success* or *I have every reason to believe you* I stand only on my belief that nothing will prevent your success or that nothing stands in the way of my believing you. The totality of prospects and the totality of reasons have not been arrived at by exhausting the prospects or reasons in U, and determining whether they meet one criterion or another. Rather, they have been arrived at by paring away their complements. The Totalizing manner of interpretation of 'every' in these examples is, in this sense, not exhaustive. Perhaps at least some generic sentences that contain 'every' should be analyzed in this way. Given the meanings of the words involved, I can see that nothing married could be a bachelor. Then my license for asserting *Every bachelor is unmarried* is not that I have exhausted the domain of bachelors and found that each is unmarried. Rather, my license for asserting *Every bachelor is unmarried* consists in my having realized, concerning the totality of bachelors, that no married person could belong to it. In contrast, *Each bachelor is unmarried* seems to commit me to exhausting the relevant domain, and so is not the way the generic proposition that bachelors are unmarried would normally be expressed.

A third case where Totalizing is preferred: Suppose, desperate for money, Ralph says to Norton *Give me every dollar you've got!* What is important to Ralph is the totality of money, that he get all he can, not the dollars as individuals. It is not that Ralph wants each dollar individually, it is rather that Ralph wants money. For this reason, it would be wrong for him to use 'each'. This observation allows us to be a little more precise concerning how a speaker decides whether to use 'every' or 'each'. One crucial consideration, highlighted here, is whether a speaker believes that a totality is in point over and above the individuals that comprise it. One of the various circumstances under which a speaker might believe this is when there are, for current purposes, no relevant differences between the individuals that comprise the relevant totality. As far as Ralph's current interests are concerned, one dollar bill is as good as another; the dollars are of no interest as individuals. Thus, when the items are, for current intents and purposes, *undiscriminated*, a speaker will choose Totalizing. Of course, differences among dollar bills *can* be of current interest; to indicate his collecting habits a speaker might need to Individualize and say *I retain each dollar whose serial number is prime*. While in Ralph's case, the dollars are undiscriminated, in the prior cases, such as *You have every prospect of success*, the prospects are not only undiscriminated, but *indiscriminable*. Thus a speaker may consider a totality to be in point, given current interests, either when the individuals that comprise it are indiscriminable, or, if discriminable, then undiscriminated, given current interests.

Fourthly, consider a standard group portrait of the nine members of the United States Supreme Court, and consider whether we say of it *This is a picture of every member of the Supreme Court*, or *This is a picture of each member of the Supreme Court*. It seems clear that the former is preferred; the interpretation of *This is a picture of every member of the Supreme Court* proceeds in the Totalizing manner, and this is appropriate to the case since, in a *group* picture, the totality of Supreme Court justices is exactly what is in point. Consider how the Individualizing manner of interpreting *This is a picture of each member of the Supreme Court* proceeds. For each person, it is to be determined whether he or she is a member of the Supreme Court, and then, if that person is a member, whether the picture is a picture of him or her. It is this last part that is odd. It is odd for the same reason that it would be odd to say, of the group picture, *This is a picture of Justice Breyer*. This statement carries the implicature that it is not a picture of anyone else, and, under the Individualizing manner of interpretation associated with *This is a picture of each member of the Supreme Court*, this inappropriate implicature can be felt as well. Note that we can say, of the group picture, *This picture contains an image of each member of the Supreme Court* just as we can also say *This picture contains an image of Justice Breyer*. In both cases, the offending implicature does not arise.

Fifthly, support for the suggested distinction between 'each' and 'every' comes from statements conjoining them. In the statement *Each and every man was saved*, what is added, over and above saying *Each man was saved*, or saying *Every man was saved*? By saying 'each and every' together, items in the same range are both Individualized and Totalized. Curme (1935) proposed that, in virtue of this, the conjoined statement is 'strengthened'. But strengthened in what way? Fleshing out Curme's suggestion, I have proposed that the distinction between Individualizing and Totalizing should be thought of as a distinction in mode of presentation.

Just as, in the Fregean view, different modes of presentation may determine
the same referent, so too may distinct manners, Individualizing and Totalizing,
determine the same truth conditions. Thus, a sentence of the form 'each and
every N . . .' contains two quantifiers that have distinct modes of presentation
and that determine the same truth conditions. This is in line with the intuition
that sentences of the form 'each and every N . . .' do strike us as emphatic rather
than redundant. On the analysis suggested here, there is no redundancy since, in
spite of there being sameness of truth conditions, there is difference in mode of
presentation. We find this sort of thing in other areas; we say, for example, *One
and the same expression may be used in different ways*, or *Two is the one and only
even prime*. Taken all together, these considerations support the conclusion that
'each' and 'every' differ in a way distinct from quantificational force.

Lastly, before continuing to the next section, there is a possible confusion that
I would like to head off. The distinction between Totalizing and Individualizing
should not be confounded with the distinction between the collective and
distributive readings of sentences, or of the expressions that they contain. The
point to focus on is that the distinction between Totalizing and Individualizing
does not affect the truth conditions of sentences in transparent contexts, whereas
the distinction between the collective and distributive readings of sentences
does affect the truth conditions of sentences in transparent contexts. The truth
conditions of the collective *Seven men lifted the piano* are distinct from the truth
conditions of the distributive *Seven men lifted the piano*. In the former case,
one cooperative lifting is required; in the latter case, seven solo liftings. The
circumstance that makes the distributive reading of *Seven men lifted the piano*
true is not one that makes the collective reading of *Seven men lifted the piano* true.
Furthermore, if a collective predicate is selected, there is no contrast between *Each
man gathered*, and *Every man gathered*. Neither may be used to depict a normal
gathering of men. And lastly, *Each man lifted the piano* and *Every man lifted the
piano* are both easily taken as distributive (as opposed to *Everyone lifted the piano*,
which leans toward the collective reading). Unlike the collective/distributive
distinction, distinctions of manner, being differences in mode of derivation, have
truth-conditional consequences only in opaque contexts.

4.1.3 'Each' and 'every' contrasted in opaque contexts

It is possible for a person to have all the supporting facts, yet not draw the
generalization that they support. Other times, we hold beliefs even though
we lack all of the supporting facts. Sometimes we are poised between the
two, flickering between cluelessness and baselessness. When we are careful to
distinguish between these two states, we say that we can either have the belief
that each A is B without drawing the generalization that every A is B, or that we
can have the belief that every A is B without having the supporting belief that
each A is B.

To be sure, we do not always speak as strictly as this way of putting it suggests; the distinction between cluelessness and baselessness is not often in point, and, when it is not, we can slip to either side. But we can, when we wish, speak strictly and, when we do, we speak in the way that I have suggested. Consider Max's beliefs concerning the sand on the beach. He might, having a firm grasp of the local geological conditions, believe that *every* grain of sand on the beach is quartz. This belief would be deduced from other beliefs, not induced from the inspection of each grain. For a belief of this sort, we use 'every'. On the other hand, Max might, having inspected all of the grains, have come to believe that *each* grain is quartz, yet not have derived the generalization that every grain is quartz.[2]

If Max is clueless, it is perfectly reasonable to say: *Max believes that each grain of sand on the beach is quartz, but does not believe that every grain of sand on the beach is quartz.* And, if Max is baseless, it is reasonable to say: *Max believes that every grain of sand on the beach is quartz, but does not believe that each grain of sand on the beach is quartz.* As I mentioned before, some might analyze these cases as showing that 'each' and 'every' should be distinguished scopally. In particular, it might be suggested that the former be analyzed as: *Max believes of each grain of sand on the beach that it is quartz, but does not believe that every grain of sand on the beach is quartz.* But this is not the understanding of the sentence that I wish to focus on. It helps to consider *Max is aware of the belief that each grain of sand on the beach is quartz, but is not aware of the belief that every grain of sand on the beach is quartz,* which has a perfectly consistent interpretation.

There has been some slowness to see this point about 'each' and 'every', and I think this stems from not assessing the relevant sentences correctly. We know quite well that the truth conditions of *Every grain of sand on the beach is quartz,* and *Each grain of sand on the beach is quartz* are the same, and when these sentences are embedded under 'believe' we hasten to the conclusion that 'that every grain of sand on the beach is quartz' and 'that each grain of sand on the beach is quartz' denote the same beliefs. That is the mistake; the truth conditions of these sentences when unembedded are not all that might be in point. Notice that we do not make this mistake when we consider the belief that Cicero was an orator and the belief that Tully was an orator. That is because we can easily imagine someone not knowing that Cicero is Tully. The problem with the quantificational example is that it is a little harder to imagine that someone could be so baseless, or so clueless, as not to realize that the manners of interpretation for 'each' and 'every', in the case at hand, lead to the same truth conditions, and so the conclusion is reached that belief of one 'immediately' leads to belief of the other. Only once we imagine that one might be baseless or clueless do we see that substitution of one quantifier for the other does not always go through.

---

[2] I am imagining that Max believes that there are no unexamined grains, believes that each grain is quartz, but is so clueless that he does not draw the generalization that every grain is quartz. Again, the scope of 'each' must be kept narrow to isolate the 'de dicto' reading I am pointing to.

To take another case, consider the belief that every spider has eight legs. One way to come to this belief is to learn that arachnids have eight legs and that spiders are arachnids, and then to deduce that spiders have eight legs. But now consider the belief that each spider has eight legs. One might be wary of this belief, knowing that some spiders, in the normal course of events, lose legs. Sometimes we are tolerant of exceptions, unless, because of their number or gravity, they threaten the generalization. In those cases we express the generalization by Totalizing. When, on the other hand, any exception has importance, and we wish to say that none exists, we Individualize.

Totalizing and Individualizing correspond to two ways that beliefs can be acquired, the two manners of derivation corresponding to two manners of investigation. Because they do correspond in this way, we can use them in contrast when the two manners of investigation are in point. But these correspondences should not blind us to the fact that the realities of natural language, and the realities of investigation that they speak of, are more complex than this. The central point here is that, in opaque contexts, the quantifiers 'each' and 'every' are not intersubstitutable. And that is because, though they are the same in force, they differ in manner of interpretation—a fact that makes itself felt in opaque contexts, just as in the case of coreferent names that differ in mode of representation.[3]

4.2 The manners and structures of 'which N' and 'what N'

4.2.1 The grammatical number of the restriction

I have observed that, in the case of 'each N' and 'every N', the restricting noun must be in the singular form, while in the case of 'which N' and 'what N' the restriction may appear in the singular or the plural. The reason for this appears to be that the lexical requirements concerning the number of the restriction reside in that part of the lexical structures of 'each N' and 'every N' that involves quantificational force, not manner. Since 'each N' and 'every N' have (universal) quantificational force, it would then follow that they may impose the requirement that their restrictions have a particular grammatical

---

[3] Consider the problem of contingent universal propositions, as Russell (1918) faced it. It might be thought that we can know the truth of contingent universal propositions solely by examining instances. But that cannot be: we also must know *another* contingent universal proposition, namely, the proposition that we have examined all the instances. As Pears puts it: "you look round a room and observe that each person whom you see is reading *The New Yorker*; you then claim to know without inference that you have seen everybody in the room, and so, given your observation, that all the people in the room are reading *The New Yorker*. The trouble about such claims to knowledge is, as Russell says, that they are often very shaky" (1967: 261). The semantic points I am advancing touch only the vocabulary in which the problem is expressed, but it is important to separate these matters from the rest of this rich area.

number: singular count. ('All', in contrast, requires a plural or singular mass restriction: *All roads lead to Rome* and *All bronze is beautiful* are allowed, but *All road leads to Rome* is not.)[4] It then follows that, since 'what N' and 'which N' lack quantificational force, there can be no requirement concerning the number of the restriction. This explains why both the singular forms *What newspaper do you prefer?* and *Which newspaper do you prefer?* are possible, as well as the plural forms *What newspapers do you prefer?* and *Which newspapers do you prefer?* So restrictions on the grammatical number of the restricting noun derive from certain assumptions concerning lexical syntax and differences between quantifiers and *wh*-expressions in that regard—specifically the fact that *wh*-expressions lack quantificational force.

But what difference is indicated by using 'what singular-N' as against 'what plural-N' or by using 'which singular-N' as against 'which plural-N'? What differences of meaning or use accompany the distinction in grammatical number? Clearly, to ask *What drug do you take?* is not the same question as *What drugs do you take?* The first presupposes that there is only one drug that you take, the second presupposes that you take more. Those presuppositions are grammatically triggered. The (rough) representation 'what x: drug x . . .' indicates that the variable ranges over individual drugs, and the representation 'what x: drugs x . . .' indicates that the variable ranges over pluralities. To answer a question containing the former, one drug should be produced; to answer a question containing the second, more than one. Since these are the kinds of answers that the forms of the questions ask for, one would of course only use those forms if one had—or wanted to present oneself as having—the requisite beliefs. In this way, the presuppositions are derived.[5] The analysis of the use and structure of 'which drug' and 'which drugs' proceeds in an analogous way, and extends to the case of multiple questions. The question *Which patient takes which drug?* seeks answers in the form of ordered pairs each consisting of a single patient and a single drug. The question *Which patient takes which drugs?* seeks answers in the form of ordered pairs each consisting of a single patient and more than one drug. In both cases, each ordered pair is a chapter in the complete answer, but nothing in the question presupposes how many chapters the complete answer has. This shows that English syntactically registers the singular/plural distinction on individual expressions, but not on pairings of expressions. It is not surprising then that *Which patient left?* presupposes that a single patient left, but that *Which*

---

[4] Finer lexical differences between 'each' and 'every' on the one hand and 'all' on the other determine whether a singular or plural restriction is required.

[5] The status of presuppositions in questions is too vast a topic to enter into here. On one side, we have the proposal of Belnap and Steele that "[a] question, Q, presupposes a statement, A, if and only if, the truth of A is a logically necessary condition for there being some true answer to Q" (1976: 5). On the other, we might identify the presupposition of a question as being a belief that a speaker ought to have when deploying a sentence-type to ask a question. The structure of the sentence-type deployed would be sensitive to that belief. I would seek to develop the latter view, convinced as I am by points originally made in Stalnaker 1974.

patient takes which drug? does not presuppose that only one patient takes drugs. In the first case, the answer is a patient; in the second case, the answer is one or more pairings. (Multiple questions will be discussed more in Section 4.5 and in the following chapters.)

4.2.2 The Individualizing manner of 'which N', and the Totalizing manner of 'what N'

Like 'each' and 'every', the *wh*-expressions 'which' and 'what' exhibit manner. The Individualizing manner of 'which' and the Totalizing manner of 'what' can be observed by constructing cases parallel to the 'each' and 'every' cases in the previous section. First, contrast *Which prospect of success do you have?*, *Which reason do you have for thinking that?*, and *Which right do you have to be angry?*, with *What prospect of success do you have?*, *What reason do you have for thinking that?*, and *What right do you have to be angry?* The 'what' cases sound more natural than the 'which' cases because, when we use 'what', we Totalize, not Individualize, the items under discussion. As already mentioned, prospects of success, and reasons and rights, as conceived of here, are undiscriminated and perhaps indiscriminable, so they are not fit for Individualizing.

Next, suppose we are again concerned about two knights on a chessboard. We prefer asking *Which knight is pinned?* over *What knight is pinned?* As with the parallel 'each' and 'every' example, when the numbers are small, we prefer Individualizing to Totalizing. As another example, suppose a chase is on, and at a fork in the road, the pursuer asks *Which way did he go?* That is preferable to saying *What way did he go?* When there are only two possibilities, those individual routes are paramount. We can see here the point of contact between the Individualizing 'which' and its use to express choice. When choice is the paramount concern, as it is in the chase example, use of 'which' is preferred. Choice consists in distinguishing among individuals, and Individualizing manner is preferred in expressing it. When choice is not the paramount concern, use of 'what' is fine. Suppose I know you intend to take a drive, but I have no idea where you are going. In this case, very likely the question does not arise which route you might choose. Then *What road will you take?* sounds fine, at least in the circumstance in which I intend to be taken as thinking that there are many roads you might take to wherever you are going. We will see that 'what' and 'which' differ in other ways; these examples show that they differ in manner.

4.2.3 Argument and predicate occurrences; covert and absent restrictions

In the cases already discussed, 'which' and 'what' appear with an overt restriction indicated by the following noun. But there is a worry concerning 'which' and 'what' when they appear without overt nominal restrictions. In these cases, an issue arises: is there a syntactically represented but phonologically empty (covert) restriction, or is the restriction understood in the context of utterance without syntactic support? In this issue, 'who' would not figure, since while there are structures of the form 'which N' and 'what N', there is no 'who N'. 'Who', as well as 'which N' and 'what N', may appear with (adjoined) prepositional-phrase restrictions, as in *Who in the legal profession is honest?*, but there is no 'who lawyer'. So the issue is, when 'which' and 'what' appear without overt restriction, are 'which' and 'what' (covertly) syntactically parallel to 'which N' and 'what N', or are they syntactically parallel to 'who', which allows no accompanying 'N' at all?

Another question intersects this one. Some *wh*-expressions cover the entire position of an argument and other *wh*-expressions cover the entire position of a predicate—at least before they are moved. There are contrasts here; while 'what N' and 'which N' may appear in either position, 'who' may only appear in argument positions. So the question comes whether the source-position of the *wh*-expression determines whether it has, or does not have, a nominal restriction.[6]

Consider, for example, *Which might that be?* and *Which tool might that be?*, in which 'which' and 'which N' are in predicate positions. To both questions, it is perfectly accurate to respond *An adz*, provided that, in the former case, it is plain that tools are in point. Similarly, compare *What might that be?* with *What tool might that be?* To both questions, it is again perfectly accurate to respond *An adz*, the answer denoting a property subordinate to the property of being a tool. On the argument side, consider *Which are you reading?* and *Which book are you reading?* To both, it is accurate to respond *Moby-Dick*, again provided that it is understood that books are in point. And to both *What are you reading?* and *What book are you reading?*, it is also accurate to respond *Moby-Dick*. This shows that both predicate and argument positions can be covered by both 'what' and 'which', and 'what N' and 'which N'. Nevertheless, there are complexities. Compare *What might that be?* with *What book might that be?* One might answer the first by saying *A novel*, but it is hard, I think, to answer *A novel* to the second. *Moby-Dick*, on the other hand, seems a fine answer to both. Though a novel is a kind of book, the question *What book might that be?* is taken as asking for a particular book, not a kind of book. And the question *What might that be?* can be taken more broadly, to be asking what, from all of the things it could be, that thing is.

But, to go back to the first issue, when 'which' and 'what' appear without overt restrictions, is a covert restriction present? Should *Which might that be?* and *What might that be?* be analyzed as [which Ø [that might be__]] and [what Ø [that might be__]], where 'Ø' is a phonologically empty syntactic occurrence of a noun? When restrictions are understood but not spoken, are they *merely*

---

[6] Predicate examples involving 'be' must be treated with care, since English contains both the copular 'be', which precedes predicates, and the equative 'be', which relates arguments. I return to this topic in Section 6.6.

understood, or do 'which' and 'what' always precede 'Ø'? There is evidence that 'which' and 'what' differ in this regard: 'which' is always followed by a noun whether it is spoken or not, while 'what' is only followed by a noun when it is spoken. Therefore, I propose that, in the predicate case, *Which might that be?* and *What might that be?* are to be analyzed as [which Ø [that might be__]] and as [what [that might be__]], respectively. In the argument case, *Which are you reading?* and *What are you reading?* are to be analyzed as [which Ø [you are reading__]] and as [what [you are reading__]], respectively. When the noun is overt, however, as in *Which book are you reading?* and *What book are you reading?*, the analyses are parallel: [which book [you are reading__]] and [what book [you are reading__]]. 'What' optionally allows a following noun, while 'which' requires a following noun that may or may not be pronounced. Importantly, it follows that, from the perspective of subcategorization, there will be two words 'what' and only one word 'which'.

One indication that we have two words 'what'—both 'what' and 'what N'—is that *What is that?* cannot mean *What person is that?* Both are grammatical and both have their uses, but *What is that?* never asks only for humans. (Of course, *What is that?* can perfectly well be answered by naming a human, but it never asks only for humans.) If *What is that?* were assigned the structure [what Ø [that is__]], it would be unclear why the 'Ø', in a supportive context, could not be understood as a predicate denoting people. The facts are that after *I met some people*, a respondent can continue *Which did you like?*, or *What person did you like?* but not *What did you like?*, as the proposal requires. But even considering only questions concerning non-humans, a difference can be felt. The difference between asking *What is that?* and *What berry is that?* is that the first asks what, from the totality of things, that is, while the second asks what berry, from all the berries, that is. Suppose *What is that?* is really *What Ø is that?*, where 'Ø' is understood as 'thing'. The problem with that is that *What thing is that?* is quite restricted in use, and, when it is allowed, does not mean what *What is that?* means. More tellingly, suppose someone says *I'm looking for berries.* You can respond *Which berries are you looking for?*, or *Which are you looking for?*, or *What berries are you looking for?*, but not *What are you looking for?* The reason the last is disallowed is that you have just been told what is being looked for: berries. While *Which are you looking for?* can, in this circumstance, be understood as *Which berries are you looking for, What are you looking for?* is not understood as, and apparently cannot be understood as, *What berries are you looking for?*

A reader has presented me with a possible counterexample to the last claim. Suppose I am browsing at the farmers' market in the berry section, and the grower asks *What are you looking for?* It seems right to say that the grower intends to be understood as asking what berries I am looking for, and that fact alone would appear to contradict what was just claimed. But it does not. And that is because, in the circumstance described, the mutually assumed portion of the universe of discourse from which the answer is to be drawn is restricted to berries. The grower assumes that I, inspecting what's on offer in the berry section, must be looking for berries. The question *What are you looking for?* is restricted, in this case, not because there is a silent syntactic restriction expressed in the sentence-type used, but because the use of a sentence-type in which there is no syntactic restriction is made in a circumstance in which that portion of the universe of discourse from which answers are to be drawn is restricted to berries. Not all tacit restrictions are syntactically expressed; some are purely circumstantial, as is the case here.

There is a way to see this. Suppose I am in the berry section, as before, and the grower asks any of the questions *Which berries are you looking for?*, or *What berries are you looking for?*, or *Which are you looking for?* And suppose, in each case, I am not in fact looking for berries, but apples. To none of these questions may I respond *Apples*. In each case, I must correct the grower's presupposition with something along the lines of *Actually, I'm looking for apples*. In contrast, if the grower has asked *What are you looking for?*, I may perfectly well respond *Apples*, to which the grower might respond *You're in the wrong section!* In conclusion, then, we have both 'what' and 'what N', but we have only one 'which', appearing always with a restriction that may or may not be spoken. Furthermore, tacit restrictions may either have syntactic support or not.

We here touch an issue that arises more famously in the analysis of incomplete definite descriptions. On Russell's (1905) account, a sentence such as *The book is unpublished* comes out false if there exists more than one book in the selected world. Among the responses to this problem is the idea that definite descriptions may contain unpronounced or elided material, material which serves to limit the definite description to picking out a unique object in that world. Call that the 'ellipsis' account. An alternative is the claim that, in general, the universe that the truth conditions of a sentence are responsible to varies over the course of a discourse, that the universe of discourse is often smaller than all of the selected world. Strawson (1950a) contains a version of this second proposal; he said that when the speaker "uses the expression 'the such-and-such' in a uniquely referring way, the presumption is that he thinks both that there is *some* individual of that species, and that the context of use will determine which one he has in mind" (1950a: 14). So a sentence such as *The book is unpublished* may rightly occur only when the current universe of discourse is, with respect to books, limited to a single one. Call that the 'contextual' account. Hanging over the choice between these approaches is the question what Russell's account of definite descriptions should be taken as applying to: sentence-types, uses of sentences, or usings of sentences.

Now it has repeatedly been argued that the ellipsis account is unworkable, one reason being that there seldom is a unique supplementation for the description.[7] A second reason to oppose the ellipsis account is that there is no *syntactic* reason to believe that definite descriptions generally contain unpronounced material of

---

[7] For discussion of this and related issues, see Barwise and Perry 1983, and Soames 1986.

the sort that would be required. So, for those who would defend the purity of syntax, some version of the contextual account would appear to be the last, best hope. Our current discussion of 'which' and 'what' is helpful here. We do, in this case, have syntactic reason to believe that 'which' contains unpronounced material, and, perhaps more importantly, we also have reason to believe that 'what' never does. So there is reason to believe that 'which' falls under the ellipsis account and that 'what' falls under the contextual account. While the use of 'what' teaches us that interlocutors can tacitly agree to limit the universe of discourse their utterances are responsible to, the use of 'which' teaches us there are sentence-types containing syntactically real but unpronounced restrictions on the universe of discourse. (It is a good question to what extent each account should be extended to quantifiers. I suspect that *Each did what he was told* falls under the ellipsis account and that *All is lost* falls under the contextual account, but I will not argue those points here.)

The specific behaviors of 'which' and 'what' indicate that the effects of the ellipsis account and the contextual account can be much the same: in both cases restrictions are provided that serve to limit the kind of thing from which the answer is to be chosen. Given the nature of the case, neither restriction could serve to limit reference to a single individual; individual reference is not in point. In particular, the elision in the 'which' example does not, and could not, have that character. So, while we do have an argument for a manner of ellipsis, it is not one that easily transfers to the problem of incomplete definite descriptions.

4.2.4 The inadequacy of D-linking in distinguishing 'which' from other *wh*-expressions

Because 'which' is different in manner from other *wh*-expressions, it also contrasts with them in syntactic distribution and in use. This will be argued at length. At least some of the syntactic facts have long been known. It was observed, for example, in Fiengo 1980, Kuno 1982, and Kayne 1984 that there is a contrast between *Which movie did which man see?* and *What did who see?* — the last usually being held to be ungrammatical. These facts were of interest within syntactic theory, since it was then thought important to determine under what conditions a syntactic constituent could, by movement, 'cross' another of the same type (Fiengo 1980, Rizzi 1990). It was theorized then that 'crossing' was not allowed; from that perspective, the 'which' example just cited is a counterexample to be explained.

One such explanation, due to Pesetsky (1987), began with the idea that 'which' is different from other *wh*-expressions in that its occurrence must be licensed by, or 'D-linked' to, an expression already appearing in prior discourse. He writes:

When a speaker asks a question like *Which book did you read?*, the range of felicitous answers is limited by a set of books both speaker and hearer have in mind. If the hearer is ignorant of the context assumed by the speaker, a *which*-question sounds odd . . . . No such requirement is imposed on *wh*-phrases like *who, what,* or *how many books.* (Pesetsky 1987: 108)

On that foundation, Pesetsky builds a theory aiming to account for the differing syntactic distributions of 'which' versus other *wh*-expressions. His idea is that 'which', being D-linked, is not a quantifier, is interpreted *in situ* and so avoids the crossing violations under which other *wh*-expressions fall. I will not speak to that analysis; my point will be that the facts have been mischaracterized. Nor will I take the point about discourse too seriously. Pesetsky concedes in a footnote that it is not in fact true that every occurrence of 'which N' must be licensed by the prior mention of things falling under 'N'. He points out that "if Mary is looking at a shelf of books, John might sneak up behind her and ask *Which book are you planning to steal?*, without any preceding utterances" Pesetsky (1987: 123). To account for this while preserving his proposal, he appeals to Lewis's (1979) theory of accommodation. In this, he follows Heim (1982), who had already made the same move when she faced an analogous difficulty in her account of the distribution of 'the'.

In contrast to quite specific and overly technical proposals that have been made in this area, I think there is a very general and quite humble conversational principle at work. It says, roughly, that you should not say something unless you think that the person you are talking to will know what you are talking about. Sometimes we know what someone else is talking about because it has been already mentioned; other times we know what someone is talking about because there is only one thing of its kind, or because it is staring us in the face, or biting us in the leg. Whether we know what someone else is talking about can often depend not on the content of previous discourse, but on how well we know each other. If I know you very well, I might know what you are talking about without any of the above clues, while, if a stranger said the same thing to me that you did, I might not. Prior discourse is by no means the only source from which we may be enlightened, and it is that enlightenment, on my view, that licenses the use of many other expressions as well.

So to ask a question using 'which', we should have in mind, and believe our addressee has in mind, which items we are talking about. But that is true of practically every word we utter. If I utter a sentence containing the word 'Maxwell' I should be careful that you will know which Maxwell I am talking about. If I utter the word 'bank', I should be careful not only that you know whether I am talking about sides of rivers or financial institutions; I should also be careful that you know which examples are in point. Returning to the *wh*-expressions, if the D-linking proposal were correct, it would follow that the licensing requirements of 'which' contrast with those of other *wh*-expressions such as 'who'. But that is not the case. All *wh*-expressions alike fall under the requirement that, to use them, one must be careful that one's interlocutor knows what is being talked about. Suppose, for example, I round on you and, out of the blue, demand: *Which student is smart?* We have a violation. Now suppose, on other occasions, I round on you and demand: *Who is smart?*, or *What student is smart?*, or *How many students are smart?* It seems plain that I have committed the same violation as before in each case. On the humble account, all of these violations arise from the simple fact that I had no reason to believe that you knew what group of students I wanted you to choose from. The point can be made more sharply: if there were, for example, no such constraint on 'who', it would always be perfectly acceptable to ask the question *Who is smart?* out of the blue. But that's not how things are at all.

The data that Pesetsky presents to support the view that occurrences of 'who', as well as 'what' and 'how many', are *not* D-linked are quite limited. He notes that if a speaker asks *How many angels fit on the head of a pin?*, "there is no presumption that either the speaker or the hearer has a particular set or quantity of angels in mind" (1987: 108). But that is not completely right: the set of angels that both speaker and hearer have in mind is the one composed of all of them. Now it may be the view of some people that this set has no members, and consequently, when that question is asked by a speaker of a hearer who is taken not to believe in angels, it is not asked so as to receive an answer; rather, the question is asked rhetorically, or to achieve some other, perhaps ironic, effect specific to the current discourse. Therefore, this example, when used by such speakers, certainly *is* a case where both the speaker and the hearer have a set of angels in mind, a set with no members. Besides, if the thesis is that D-linking is motivated by the requirement that the hearer have in mind some set of items *from which the answer is to be drawn*, the relevant set for any *how-many* question is the set of natural numbers, not the set of things being numbered. The natural numbers—as well as the sun, the atomic number of gold, the capital of Montana, and the special theory of relativity—are the kinds of things that are fair conversational game in many circumstances. For them, many speakers carry around varyingly active, but sufficiently active 'file cards', to use Heim's metaphor. The 'the' borne by these expressions needs no prior encouragement. Since the numbers are always fair game, *how-many* questions should always be in order, as far as their answer-set is concerned, a fact that has nothing to do with prior discourse, and everything to do with the fact that when we talk of numbers, we can assume that the person we are talking to will know what we are talking about.

Perhaps the most important cases offered in support of D-linking are *what-the-hell* questions, which Pesetsky calls "aggressively non-D-linked". He characterizes these in the following terms: "Roughly speaking, the whole point of uttering a question like *What the hell did you read that in?* is to express surprise in the answer. The appropriate answer is presumed not to figure in previous discourse" Pesetsky (1987: 111). This can't be right. If a speaker asks an open question, he presents himself as not knowing the answer to the question, and, if that is true, he will have no idea whether the answer has been given in previous discourse or anywhere else. (Some might think that *what-the-hell* questions are always rhetorical, but the current example can certainly be used non-rhetorically; I can perfectly well ask a friend *What the hell have you been up to lately?* in expectation of an answer.) So, if the answer has already been given, and if, furthermore, it has been given in such a way that it is clear that it *was* the answer, and if, lastly, the speaker knows these things, then he cannot ask the question as an open question at all, since he already knows the answer. On the other hand, if he is asking a question, he cannot "express surprise in the answer", since he does not know the answer.

The true explanation for the distribution of 'the hell', and other expressions of its ilk, such as 'in the name of God', or 'in the name of all that's holy', has nothing to do with D-linking. The reason that 'the hell' is allowed with 'what N' and not allowed with 'which N' is that 'the hell' is a Totalizing intensifier. This aspect of its distribution, in my terms, follows from the semantic distinction between 'which' and 'what', and not from any fact concerning their licensing, either by discourse or anything else.

To see this, take the question *What color did you paint your house?*, the logical structure of which is: [what Tx: color x [you painted your house x]]. A speaker who uses a sentence with that logical structure presents herself as ignorant of what color from the totality of colors you painted your house. Now take *What the hell color did you paint your house?* Since 'the hell' is a Totalizing intensifier, it serves to emphasize the totality in point is completely inclusive, lacking no potential member. Of course, if a totality loses a member, it is no longer a totality, 'the hell' serves to emphasize that the totality *is* a totality. So that is the force of saying *What the hell color did you paint your house?* This makes the question very useful when a speaker feels that you have painted your house a color not from the restricted range of normal colors, but from the absurd totality of colors, such as hot pink, or purple. In contrast, *Which color did you paint your house?* has the logical structure: [which Ix: color x [you painted your house x]]. A speaker who uses a sentence with that logical structure presents herself as ignorant which color is such that you painted your house that color. In contrast with the 'what' example, no totality is in point. But since 'the hell' is not an Individualizing intensifier, we cannot have *Which the hell color did you paint your house?*

That 'the hell' is a Totalizing intensifier is supported by other data that Pesetsky presents. Note that 'the hell' cannot appear with 'how many'—for example, *How many the hell angels can dance on the head of a pin?* or *How the hell many angels can dance on the head of a pin?* are no better than *Which the hell angels can dance on the head of a pin?* (*What the hell angels are you talking about?* is, of course, fine.) Pesetsky gives his *How many angels . . . ?* example as an illustration of a non-D-linked case. On his account, the restriction against 'the hell' appearing with 'how many' is unexpected: if his principle is to be that 'the hell' is disallowed in D-linked contexts, one would expect 'the hell' always to be allowed in non-D-linked ones. The analysis here offers a simple explanation. It is intuitively clear that *how-many* questions are Individualizing; they ask for a particular number, that number being the particular number of objects that fall under a predicate—in this case, the predicate 'angel that can dance on the head of a pin'. Like 'which', because it is Individualizing in manner, 'how many' resists 'the hell'.

To summarize, the contrast between 'each N' and 'every N' has served to distinguish 'which N' from 'what N'. Quantifiers and *wh*-expressions are directly comparable in terms of manner. Individualizing manner is marked in the case of 'which N', and the Individualizing manner of interpretation is forced in sentences that contain 'which N' as a matter of linguistic legislation. The same is true of the Totalizing manner of 'what N'. Also, some well-entrenched errors concerning the status of 'which N' have been cleared away—the use of 'which N', like the use of the rest of language, falls under the general rubric that one should not speak unless one feels that the addressee is in a position to understand what one is talking about. Finally, a last small fact about 'the hell' has been shown to follow from the semantic manner of 'which', not from discourse structure.

4.3 Incompleteness

4.3.1 Are *wh*-expressions incomplete, or do they lack something?

Wh-expressions are like quantifiers in that they can exhibit manner, but different from quantifiers in that they do not have force. Should this lack be represented as a syntactic incompleteness? In the overall conception of questions that I have advanced, questions arise from ignorance, ignorance is a lack, and we speak in such a way as to indicate our lack. In the case of open *wh*-questions, we choose a sentence-type that displays that lack through its incompleteness—incompleteness as compared with corresponding sentence-types used in answer. In open *yes-no* questions, what I have called 'the glue' is missing; the predicate denotes an (unsaturated) function, a function that may be saturated by the item denoted by the subject. But where is the incompleteness in an open *wh*-question? Is the incompleteness in the *wh*-expression itself? Are *wh*-expressions syntactically incomplete quantifiers, or are they syntactically complete? Formally speaking, should 'which', for example, be represented as '__I', where the gap indicates a site of incompleteness, the site where force would be indicated if 'which' were a quantifier, or as 'I' alone?

If 'which' is to be represented as '__I', a question such as *Which men left?* would be directed toward the cardinality of the men that left, as opposed to the men that left. The position represented as empty is the position in which the force of the expression would appear, if a quantifier were being represented. If this were the correct representation, then we would have, as perfectly responsive answers: *Forty-seven men left*, *Both men left*, and *Some men left*. But these answers, which provide quantificational force, are not perfectly responsive answers to the question that was asked; although, if we did not know which men left, we might respond in one of these ways. Completely responsive answers provide not cardinalities but men: *Those men left*, *Sam and Dave left*, and *The cowardly ones left*. This suggests that 'which men' should not be analyzed as '__ I', and that the incompleteness in *which*-questions is not to be found in the *wh*-expression itself. Assuming *which*-questions are representative, we face the broader prospect that the incompletenesses of *wh*-questions generally are not to be found in the *wh*-expressions they contain. The exception to this is the syntactically complex 'how many', which plainly is directed toward cardinality. If 'how many' is analyzed as '__ many', this would follow naturally.[8]

The obvious alternative is that the variable bound by the *wh*-expression is the site of incompleteness in a *wh*-question. This seems natural, since men, not quantities, are the objects the variable ranges over in a propositional function-name such as '[x left]'. What distinguishes the variables bound by *wh*-expressions from those bound by quantifiers is that they are bound by operators that lack quantificational force, a point that I will expand upon in the next chapter. For now, I will simply assume that a variable bound by a *wh*-expression is a site of incompleteness. Of course *wh*-expressions appear not only in sentence-types used to ask questions, but in relative clauses as well. The extension of these proposals to relative clauses is clear. In *the man who we talked to*, the site of incompleteness follows 'to', but no question is asked by uttering a relative clause because the site of incompleteness is 'filled' by the head of the relative clause, in this case, 'the man'.

4.3.2 The incompleteness of indefiniteness

I have provided only a partial speciation of the *wh*-expressions. 'When', 'where', and 'why' have been neglected in favor of those *wh*-expressions that cover either argument or predicate positions. But to do justice even to those that I have addressed, I must also consider the common circumstance in which indefinite NPs, not *wh*-expressions, are used to ask that either items or predicates be produced. In the case of open questions, displaying ignorance involves deploying incomplete linguistic forms. The contrasting behaviors of definite and indefinite NPs within questions allow us to learn something about incompleteness, and something else about ignorance.

The speaker of *Did Max see a movie?* presents himself as not knowing whether Max saw a movie. But if one presents oneself as not knowing whether Max saw a movie, one certainly presents oneself as not knowing what movie Max saw. Such is the logic of ignorance. But if one presents oneself as not knowing what movie Max saw, one may, given the logic of questioning, be taken as asking what movie

---

[8] 'How many' is perhaps also unique in that it always asks only for one item: a single number.

Max saw. And so, although the path is indirect, the speaker of *Did Max see a movie?* may be taken, and may have been intended to be taken, as asking what movie Max saw.

The speaker of *Did Max see the movie?*, on the other hand, presents himself as being able to specify the movie in ways independent of whether Max saw it, and as being in no way concerned that he can do so. The speaker may be able to name the movie, or describe the movie, or only know the movie as the one that was just mentioned in the current conversation—there are many possibilities here. But whatever the speaker's acquaintance with the movie, by using the definite article, he reveals his intention not to present himself as not knowing what movie is in question. It is the one that he knows by name, or the one that he can describe, or the one that was just mentioned. And since the speaker does not present himself as not knowing what movie is in question, the speaker of *Did Max see the movie?* will not be taken, and so will not intend to be taken, as asking what movie Max saw. It is this asymmetry between indefinite and definite NPs that would help to explain why, in many languages, the 'question-words', the analogues to the *wh*-expressions of English, are not morphologically distinguished from indefinite expressions.

Although the speaker of *Did Max see a movie?* may intend to be taken as asking what movie Max saw, he may also not intend to be so taken. He may intend to be taken as asking simply whether Max saw a movie. What determines which way the speaker will be taken? How does a speaker determine which way he will be taken? The speaker must calculate whether he will be understood as being interested not so much as to whether Max saw a movie but rather in what movie Max saw. And that depends upon a great many circumstantial factors. Perhaps the question is asked by a parent who is concerned, and knows that he will be taken as being concerned, with what movies his son Max watches. There is no general way to define the circumstances under which such an utterance will be understood in this way. But there is one rule: a sentence-type containing an indefinite description can be deployed in this way, and a sentence-type in which the indefinite description is replaced by a definite description cannot.

So sometimes a speaker of a question containing an indefinite description intends to be taken as being interested in having the item in question produced, and sometimes not. In all such cases, the speaker presents himself as ignorant of the item in question, but the ignorance is inferred, not expressed. If the speaker calculates that the inferred ignorance will be addressed by the respondent, the speaker may ask such a question so as to have the item produced. If not, not. But while the use of indefinite descriptions may, indirectly, give rise to inferences that reveal ignorance, they do not, at least in English, directly express ignorance. Indefinites, or the variables they bind, are not sites of incompleteness. In contrast, in *wh*-questions, the ignorance is expressed, not merely inferred. The expression of that ignorance is achieved through the presence of an incompleteness at the site of the *wh*-variable. Since the ignorance is expressed in the sentence-type, not merely inferred, the speaker should intend that the ignorance be addressed by the respondent—although we have seen cases where the incompleteness in the sentence-type is used with some other intent.

Among the indefinite expressions that may be used to angle indirectly for items or predicates, the so-called negative polarity items such as 'any' deserve special mention. If I ask *Do you have any problem with that?*, I may intend to be taken as asking you what problem you have with that. But quite apart from their use, negative polarity items pose the problem why they should be allowed not only in negative sentences but in sentence-types used to ask questions as well. Their distribution is not allowed indiscriminately in either kind of sentence, but they are prominent enough in both kinds that it is clear that there is something to be explained. Furthermore, negative polarity items may be found in sentence-types used to ask open questions, but not in sentence-types used to ask confirmation questions, a consideration that has direct impact on the speciation of questioning speech-acts defended here. There is, however, no hope of taking on the complex topic of polarity within the confines of a book about asking questions. An accompanying volume would be more appropriate. But if I may be allowed to speak broadly, there are a few things to say that bear on the presence of polarity items in questions and on my analysis of questions in particular.

If Ladusaw (1979) is right, polarity items such as 'any' are licensed only in downward-entailing positions. The notion 'downward-entailing position' is a simple one. To illustrate, suppose Max owns cats. It does not follow that Max owns gray cats. So the position after 'owns' is not downward entailing. Now suppose that Max doesn't own cats. It does follow from this that Max doesn't own gray cats, so the position following 'doesn't own' is downward entailing. In the former, positive case, the entailment doesn't migrate downward from superset to subset. But in the latter, negative case, the entailment does migrate down from superset to subset. There are some positive environments that contain downward-entailing positions; consider the generic interpretation of *Max loves cats*. If Max loves cats, then Max loves gray cats. The term 'cats' here denotes all cats; any gray cats there are are included among them. Consequently, the generic *Max loves any cats* is also allowed. So, correctly, if 'any' only is licensed in downward-entailing positions, the non-generic *Max owns any cats* will not be allowed, while *Max doesn't own any cats* and *Max loves any cats* will be fine.

The question now comes why negative-polarity items such as 'any' may appear in questions. The answer, broadly speaking, is that questions display ignorance, and that ignorance is downward entailing. Suppose I don't know whether Max own cats. Then I also do not know whether Max owns gray cats. The 'subject' of my ignorance is downward entailing, and therefore *Does Max own any cats?* is licensed. Suppose I do not know whether cat owners are happy. Then I also do not know whether the owners of gray cats are happy. So *Are the owners of any cats happy?* is licensed. Now suppose I don't know whether the woman who owns cats has left town. Does it follow that I also don't know whether the woman who owns gray cats has left town? Certainly not. I may know nothing about the color of her cats. So my ignorance of whether the woman who owns cats has left town does not automatically extend to ignorance of the color of her cats. The position following 'owns' in *The woman who owns cats has left town* is not downward entailing, ignorance-wise. It follows, correctly, that the presence of 'any' in the question *Has the woman who owns any cats left town?* is not licensed.

These examples involve the kind of ignorance expressed through the asking of *yes-no* questions. Let's now consider the ignorance displayed by using *wh-*questions. Suppose I don't know who would be willing to adopt cats. Then I also do not know who would be willing to adopt gray cats. It follows that I should be able to ask *Who would be willing to adopt any cats?* But suppose I don't know who teased the man who owned cats. It doesn't follow that I don't know who teased the man who owned gray cats—the man in question may have owned only orange cats. It follows that *Who teased the man that owned any cats?* is not licensed.

It is a complicated question what syntactic conditions there are on the distribution of downward-entailing positions. I will not go into that here. But I do wish to address how polarity items are licensed. In the assertive cases, we have pairs of statements, S' and S", where S" is the downward entailment of S'. By making a statement, one expresses a belief. By expressing a belief, one commits oneself to the beliefs that follow from it—even beliefs that one is unaware of. So in the negative cases, a speaker has 'downward commitments' to beliefs. This logic applies to the case of questions as well. By asking a question, one expresses an ignorance. By expressing an ignorance, one commits oneself to ignorances that follow from it, even ignorances one is unaware of. One is committed to the downward commitments of one's ignorance. As we have seen, downward commitments are enjoined in both positive and negative statements and in questions as well. But not all parts of the propositions these kinds of sentences express give rise to downward commitments. Downward commitment is enjoined by some positions but not others. Those positions by which it is enjoined, and only those, allow the presence of 'any' in the sentence-types used to express them. Ladusaw's account, of course, is semantic; (downward) entailments in his account are the entailments of sentences. I have recast his notion in terms of the (downward) entailments of commitments. I depart from Ladusaw in locating the licensing of 'any' in the commitments of speakers, not the entailments of sentences, but the generalization I exploit is Ladusaw's.

It should now be clear why 'any' is licensed in (some) open questions, but not in confirmation questions. Confirmation is not downward entailing. Those confirmation questions that are asked using complete sentence-types are asked by speakers who lack the confidence to use those sentence-types to make assertions. Suppose I want to confirm that you've had something to drink. It does not follow that I want to confirm that you've had a cola. So *You've had anything to drink?* is no better as a confirmation question than it would be as a statement. Of course, *You haven't had anything to drink?* may be asked as a confirmation question, the 'any' being licensed by the negative.

In some positions, in some sentence-types, indefinites, including negative polarity items, are used to reveal ignorance. One may use an indefinite so as to indicate that one cannot use the corresponding definite. The maxim of quantity holds sway here. But there is also a logic of ignorance, and it is grammatically marked. Polarity items track it.

4.4 The manners and structures of 'who' and 'what'

4.4.1 The syntax of 'who' and 'what'

'Who' can cover an argument position, but can it cover a predicate? Take *Who is that?* A possible answer is *Teddy Kennedy*, but that answer suggests that the position following 'is' (in [who [that is__]]) is an argument position, not a predicate position, and that we have an identity question, not a copular question. *A liberal* is another possible answer, but would it be completely responsive? This sounds like a case in which a predicate is being offered as an answer when an argument was being asked for, a reason to doubt that 'who' can cover predicates. In support of the proposal that 'who' only covers arguments, there is also the contrast between *Who considers Nixon what?* and *Who considers Nixon who?* The latter is quite bad, the second 'who' being forced into a position that only a predicate can occupy (there is no *I consider Cicero Tully*). I conclude that, when we are speaking strictly, *Who is that?* is understood as an identity question, 'that' and 'who' (or the variable it binds) being its arguments. When we are answering strictly, *Who is that?* must be answered by bringing forth a name, such as *Teddy Kennedy*, or a definite description, such as *The senior senator from Massachusetts*. Again, this point can be obscured, since often we cannot come up with the name or a definite description that will serve. Then we offer a predicate instead. The speaker who answers *A liberal* may be dismissive of the original question, lazy, evasive, or just unable to provide a definite description denoting Teddy Kennedy that will serve in the current setting. Without doubt, the response is natural, but given what the questioner asked, it is not good enough.

So 'who', or the position it moved from, covers the entire position of an argument, but may not, strictly speaking, cover the position of a predicate. In that respect, it differs from 'which' and 'what' as they appear in 'which N' and 'what N'. And 'what', or the position it moved from, when it appears without a syntactic restriction, may also cover the entire position of an argument, but it is not restricted to that role; it may cover the entire position of a predicate as well. How do 'who' and 'what' differ? The first asks for people and the second asks for things, in the natural sense of 'things', in which people are not things. They stand in the human/non-human contrast, which is to be expected if 'who' and 'what' are expressions that can cover entire arguments. 'Who' and 'what' can also show grammatical number, but only grudgingly. *Who are leaving?* and *What are falling down?* are passable, but not idiomatic; speakers who know that more than one person is leaving, or that more than one thing is falling down, nevertheless naturally say *Who's leaving?* and *What's falling down?* So 'who' and 'what', when appearing without any syntactic restriction, are morphologically marked for a human/non-human restriction.

4.4.2 The weak manner of interpretation of 'who' and 'what'

The syntactic speciation of *wh*-expressions is stated in terms of (i) whether the expression has a linguistically associated restriction, whether expressed or not, and (ii) whether the expression may cover argument positions, predicate positions, or both. In those terms, we have now uncovered the following distribution. 'What N' and 'which N' cover both predicate and argument positions. They contrast in manner. 'Who' and 'what' appear without syntactic restriction. 'Who' covers only argument positions, and 'what' covers both predicate and argument positions. I have argued that 'what N' and 'which N' are mannered and are distinguished by manner. So the question is forced whether those *wh*-expressions that do not have linguistically associated restrictions—'who' and linguistically unrestricted 'what'—are mannered.

The Individualizing manner of interpretation, and in many but not all cases, the Totalizing manner, share a trait: exhaustiveness. The evaluation of *Each man left* and, in many circumstances, the evaluation of *Every man left* require that the domain of men be exhaustively assessed; it must be determined whether every man in the domain left. Another quantifier that has exhaustive manner is 'most'. The truth of *Most men left* requires that the domain be exhaustively assessed; it must be determined whether the total number of leavers in the domain exceeds the total number of non-leavers in the domain. We often do not begin already knowing the cardinality of the chosen domain; that is determined, when it is determined, by manner of interpretation. Knowing that there are one hundred senators in the US Senate, *Most senators voted for the bill* might be evaluated non-exhaustively, but where the cardinality of the domain is not known, this option does not arise.

The quantifiers and *wh*-expressions that require exhaustiveness, such as 'each', I will call 'strong'. The quantifiers and *wh*-expressions that do not require exhaustiveness I will call 'weak'. Not all manners need be exhaustive. The truth of *Some man left* is assured once a positive case is found. To find that case, it might be necessary to exhaust the domain, but it is not required, to establish truth, that the domain be exhausted. So in that respect, 'some' differs from 'most' and 'each'. There are other quantifiers like 'some', including '47', 'between 3 and 8', 'several', and many others. Among the *wh*-expressions, it appears that 'who' and 'what' (as opposed to 'what N') are weak, as 'some' is. To answer a *who*-question, all one need do is produce an item, or, in the case of a *what*-question, either an item or a predicate.

These points about 'who' and 'what' can be argued empirically. Suppose you see Tom and Dick leaving a party, a party you yourself did not attend, and suppose they are animated and laughing. Imagine how you would respond to the question *Which men at the party had a good time?* Could you respond *Tom and Dick had a good time* even though you neither know who else was at the party nor whether they had a good time? I think not. You might say: *I don't know, but I do know that Tom and Dick did.* Now consider *What men at the party had a good time?* Again, you are up against it. You might say: *Tom and Dick did, and I don't know how many more.* But to the question *Who at the party had a good time?* I think you can flatly respond *Tom and Dick did.*

The differences among these answers derive from the respective manners of interpretations of 'which N', 'what N', and 'who'. In the case of *Which men at the party had a good time?* the questioner presents himself as ignorant of the number of confirming cases derived from an exhaustive Individualizing manner of interpretation. If the person to whom this question is addressed does not know the extent of the domain, she is not in a position to answer it. In the case of *What men at the party had a good time?* the questioner presents himself as ignorant of the number of confirming cases derived from an exhaustive Totalizing manner of interpretation. If the addressee does not know the extent of the Totality, because she does not know the extent of the domain itself, she again cannot answer the question as asked. But the person to whom *Who at the party had a good time?* is addressed may answer perfectly well by providing an instance of a person at the party that had a good time. Such a respondent need not know the extent of the domain.

Of course, in the example as given, if the respondent, when asked *Who at the party had a good time?* answers *Tom had a good time*, knowing that at least two men did, she violates the maxim of quantity. Such a speaker does not lie by saying *Tom had a good time*, but she does give rise to a false implicature. That stands in contrast with the speaker who says flatly *Tom and Dick had a good time* to either *Which men at the party had a good time?* or *What men at the party had a good time?* Such a speaker, in both cases, presents herself as being in a position to exhaust the domain of men at the party, something she cannot do. Here the speaker presents herself as knowing more than she really does. In the 'who' example, in contrast, the speaker presents herself as knowing less than she really does.

What was said for 'who' may be said for 'what'. Both are mannered, and weakly so. We will see that this makes them good choices if one wishes to ask that an instance of something be provided. In Austin's (1953) terminology, they are used when asking Exemplifying questions.

A final point about manner of interpretation. When classifying some manners as strong and others as weak, I have deliberately followed the terminology of Milsark (1974), who observed that in *there*-insertion sentences there is a restriction concerning what sort of noun phrases may appear after the verb 'be'.

Those NPs that are allowed he called weak, and those that are not allowed he called strong. Among the weak NPs are those headed by 'many', 'few', 'a', 'two', 'between five and eight', and 'several'— *There were some men in the garden, There were many men in the garden,* and so forth are allowed. However an NP headed by 'each', which is strong, is not allowed— *There was each man in the garden* is bad. Other strong NPs include those headed by 'all', 'the', and 'most'. It has been noted in Safir (1982) and Heim (1987) that *Who is there in the garden?* and *What is there in Austin?* are natural in comparison with *Which man is there in the garden?* or *Which thing is there in Austin?* Given my analysis that 'who' and 'what' are weak and 'which' is strong, these facts follow. The behavior of 'every' is instructive. I have noted that Totalizing 'every', when it appears in expressions such as 'every reason to believe', is not necessarily exhaustive. When someone says *I have every reason to believe you,* he does not say that he has added up all possible reasons to believe you and found none lacking; he is not claiming to have exhausted the reasons. Rather, he is saying that he can imagine no reason not to believe you. So we would expect such a non-exhaustive use of 'every' to be allowed after 'be' in *there*-insertion sentences, and it is: *There is every reason to believe that you will succeed* is fine, while the normal case of exhaustive 'every', as in *There was every man in the garden,* is not. Note that if quantifiers were distinguished only by force, it would be very difficult to account for this contrast. The two occurrences of Totalizing 'every' differ not in force, but in manner, specifically whether the manner is necessarily exhaustive. On the speech-act side of the problem, *there*-insertion sentences are used to Exemplify; the speech-act of Exemplification does not tolerate exhaustive manner such as one finds with 'each' and 'which'.

There is much more to say about manner of interpretation and *there*-insertion sentences. I am certainly not claiming to have given a final diagnosis for the strong/weak distinction. Suffice it to say that the weak and strong manners of 'who' and 'which' allow an explanation for their contrastive behaviors in *there*-insertion sentences. But the *wh*-expressions are also separated by syntactic differences, the topic of the next chapter.

4.5 Multiple questions

4.5.1 Multiple *which*-questions

In asking a question, one can deploy a sentence-type that contains more than one *wh*-expression: *Who saw who?* is one example. Multiple questions are to be distinguished from conjoined questions, such as *What did the president know, and when did he know it?* Here there are two questions, not one, and two answers are called for. A true multiple question is one question, and has one answer, or one list of answers. But there can be a problem in individuating multiple questions. Plainly the sentence-types *Which man saw which movie?* and *Which movie did which man see?* differ overtly, but are they used to ask the same question or different ones? If the same, then the overt difference in the scopes of the *wh*-expressions would not count semantically, nor in terms of use. If different, either meaning or use would be sensitive to that fact. As it happens, they differ semantically and also in use; they are different questions. The semantic distinction between them derives from the distinct scopes of the *wh*-expressions they contain. The scopal distinction entails a distinction in manner of interpretation.

As before, it will be useful to consider first an analysis of a pair of sentence-types involving 'each', in order to focus on manner of interpretation without at the same time bringing in the nature of *which*-questions.

The sentence *Each man saw each movie* is scopally ambiguous as shown below. In the first, 'man' has wide scope; in the second, 'movie' has wide scope.

(i) $\forall$Ix: man x [$\forall$Iy: movie y [x saw y]]

(ii) $\forall$Iy: movie y [$\forall$Ix: man x [x saw y]]

The first can be roughly paraphrased as each man is such that he saw each movie; and the second as each movie is such that each man saw it.

The compositional structure of (i), and, specifically, Individualizing manner, imposes the following procedure. Select an item from the universe of discourse. If that item is not a man, discard it, but if it is a man, select another item from the universe of discourse. If that item is not a movie, discard it, but if it is a movie, determine whether the man selected saw the movie selected. If he did see it, we have a confirming case, otherwise we have a disconfirming case. Retaining the man already selected, repeat the procedure. Select an item from the universe of discourse. If it is not a movie, discard it, but if it is a movie, determine whether the man selected saw that movie. If he did see it, we have a confirming case, otherwise we have a disconfirming case. Continue in this way until it is determined, for the man already selected, whether he saw each movie in the universe of discourse. When the movies are exhausted, a 'chapter' of the interpretation is complete: a set of pairings of a man with each movie he saw (the confirming cases) and a set of pairings of that man with each movie he did not see (the disconfirming cases). A new chapter is then opened by selecting another man from the universe of discourse, if there is any, and then determining, for each movie in the universe of discourse, whether that man saw it. And so on. Each chapter of the interpretation, once completed, will state for a man which movies he saw and which he did not see; there will be as many chapters in the interpretation as there are men in the universe of discourse. '$\forall$Ix: man x [$\forall$Iy: movie y [x saw y]]' will be counted as true if and only if there are no disconfirming cases in any chapter of the interpretation.

For (ii), the interpretation proceeds as follows. Select an item from the universe of discourse. If that item is not a movie, discard it, but if it is a movie, select another item from the universe of discourse. If that item is not a man, discard it, but if it is a man, determine whether the movie selected was seen by that man. If it was seen by him, we have a confirming case, otherwise we have a disconfirming case. Retaining the movie already selected, repeat the procedure. Select an item from the universe of discourse. If it is not a man, discard it, but if it is a man, determine whether the movie selected was seen by that man. If it was seen by him, we have a confirming case, otherwise we have a disconfirming case. Continue in this way until it is determined, for the movie already selected, whether it was seen by each man in the universe of discourse. When the movies are exhausted, a chapter of the interpretation is complete: a set of pairings of a movie with each man that saw it (the confirming cases) and a set of pairings of that movie with each man that did not see it (the disconfirming cases). A new chapter is then opened by selecting another movie from the universe of discourse, if there is any, and then determining, for each man in the universe of discourse, whether it was seen by that man. And so on. Each chapter of the interpretation, once completed, will state for a movie which men saw it and which did not see it; there will be as many chapters in the interpretation as there are movies in the universe of discourse. '∀Iy: movie y [∀Ix: man x [x saw y]]'will be counted as true if and only if there are no disconfirming cases in any chapter of the interpretation.[9]

Now consider the contrast between *Which man saw which movie?* and *Which movie did which man see?* Here the difference in the scopes of the *wh*-expressions is overtly marked; we have the logical representations:

(iii) Ix: man x [Iy: movie y [x saw y]]

(iv) Iy: movie y [Ix: man x [x saw y]]

A speaker who uses a sentence-type whose logical structure is (iii) presents himself as not knowing, for any individual man, which movies he saw, and a speaker who uses a sentence-type whose logical structure is (iv) presents himself as not knowing, for any individual movie, which man saw it. With (iii), the speaker angles for an answer organized by man, while in the case of (iv) the speaker angles for an answer organized by movie. The overt distinction between *Which man saw which movie?* and *Which movie did which man see?* allows the speaker to make overt how he wants the answer organized. By asking *Which man saw which movie?*, the speaker presents himself as not knowing how many man–movie pairs, organized by man, satisfy the exhaustive search required by Individualizing manner. That is what the questioner wishes to know.

Although a true and complete answer to *Which man saw which movie?* will also be a true and complete answer to *Which movie did which man see?*, answering truly and completely is not all that is involved in responding to a question. A true and complete answer to *Which man saw which movie?* will be the confirming instances of *Each man saw each movie*, when 'each man' has wide scope. A true and complete answer to *Which movie did which man see?* will be the confirming

---

[9] See Higginbotham and May 1981 and Higginbotham 1993 for related ideas.

instances of *Each man saw each movie*, when 'each movie' has wide scope. The two sets of confirming instances are distinct, one organized by man, one by movie. The choice between uttering *Which man saw which movie?* and *Which movie did which man see?* allows the speaker to present himself as having distinct ignorances concerning one and the same situation.[10] A speaker might care deeply which man saw which movie, but not care at all which movie which man saw. Given what the speaker cares about, he may present himself as ignorant in one or the other way. By presenting oneself as ignorant in a particular way, an answer of a particular structure is angled for.

Recall that while *wh*-expressions lack force, they are mannered. And recall that by uttering a sentence that is incomplete in a particular way, a speaker can indicate his particular ignorance, and thereby ask a question. By uttering *Which man left?*, a speaker indicates that he cannot give an exhaustive Individualizing classification of the men into the leavers and the non-leavers. The logical structure of *Which man left?* is 'Ix: man x [x left]'; the final variable constitutes the position of incompleteness. By using a sentence-type with that logical structure, the speaker indicates that he does not know which men are confirming cases of an exhaustive Individualizing of 'Ix: man x [x left]'. And of course the same holds with multiple questions. By using a sentence-type whose logical structure is 'Ix: man x [Iy: movie y [x saw y]]', a speaker indicates that he cannot exhaustively Individualize men by movies they saw. Again, *wh*-expressions, not being quantifiers, lack quantificational force. But some manners, such as Individualizing, require that each item in the universe of discourse be classified—a different matter entirely from requiring that a certain number of them must satisfy some propositional function.

4.5.2 Which *which*-question to ask?

A speaker, deciding whether to say *Which man saw which movie?* or *Which movie did which man see?*, chooses between them on the basis of the structure of the answer he or she is currently seeking. But in what ways would the structure of an answer matter? What is the difference between wanting to know which man saw which movie and wanting to know which movie which man saw? There are various possibilities. If one's goal were to classify the movies in question, to find out, for each movie, what sort of man saw it, one might want to know which movie which man saw. Conversely, if one's goal were to classify men, to find out, concerning each man, what sort of movies he saw, one would want to know which man saw which movie. Such distinctions are common. To want to know which breakfast cereals which kinds of people prefer is primarily curiosity about breakfast cereals. The question would be: Is this the kind of breakfast cereal that that sort of person enjoys? To want to know which kinds of people prefer which

---

[10] Can one achieve the same effect by choosing between active and passive forms? Do *Which man saw which movie?* and *Which movie was seen by which man?* ask for differently structured answers?

breakfast cereals is primarily curiosity about people. The question would be: Is this the kind of person that enjoys that kind of cereal?

Suppose that a speaker either does not care what structure the answer is presented in or—and this is the more interesting case—believes that there are no differences worth choosing among in the structures of the answers that might be given. There are various reasons why a speaker might hold the latter view. He might believe that the answer to his multiple question is a one-to-one pairing, with no overlap. That is, he might believe the answer to be a single pair, or many pairs; but in either case, he believes that no item appears in more than one pair. A speaker, believing that the answer to his question will be structured in this way, might well not care in which order the members of the pair or pairs is given. To take a concrete example of this, imagine the questioner knows that, in a particular horse-race, each jockey is riding one and only one horse and that each horse is being ridden by one and only one jockey, but does not know the horse–jockey pairing. Given the choice between asking *Which jockey is riding which horse* and asking *Which horse is which jockey riding?*, the intuition is that the speaker would choose the former. Note that, syntactically, the former is the 'simpler' of the two, involving no crossing of one *wh*-expression by another. Consequently, we might propose a principle that, where a speaker is indifferent as to which answer-structure he wishes to adduce, the syntactically simpler variant is chosen. It will become important to state this principle more clearly in the next chapter. But for now, in contrast, suppose that the questioner knows that, in the course of an afternoon, each jockey may have ridden more than one horse, and that each horse may have been ridden by more than one jockey. Then the choice between asking *Which jockey rode which horse?* and asking *Which horse did which jockey ride?* becomes relevant, the choice depending on how the questioner wants the answer to the question structured. The choice between them depends on the current interests of the speaker.

If these intuitions are granted, it should be already clear that the question as to whether one *wh*-expression may cross another cannot be settled in totally syntactic terms. Intuitions are even sharper when single-pair cases are considered, as occurs in a kind of chess problem involving 'retrograde analysis', devised by Smullyan (1979). In a retrograde chess problem, the task is to determine, from the position on the board, what happened on the previous move. The poser of the problem knows that the answer consists simply of a pairing of a white piece and a black piece. The problem is usually posed as *Which white piece captured which black piece?*, but not as *Which black piece did which white piece capture?* Only if the poser has some reason for having the answer structured black–white as opposed to white–black would the latter be chosen. If the poser asks *Which black piece did which white piece capture?* under the circumstances given, I think we must suppose that he has some particular reason for making that choice. Perhaps he likes black things to be given prominence. Or perhaps we would wonder whether the terms of the challenge allowed more than one pairing as the answer. But one thing which we must not say is that the question, uttered under those circumstances, is ungrammatical, defective as a matter of grammar. Rather we should say that the justification for the use of that sentence is hard to fathom; we should say that the basis for the choice of that sentence as against its alternative is, in the circumstance given, mysterious.

4.5.3 Multiple *who*-questions and multiple *what*-questions

Unlike the Individualizing 'which N' and the Totalizing 'what N', the manners of 'who' and 'what' are not necessarily exhaustive. Let's use the letter 'W' to symbolize the weak manner of interpretation. If, apart from questions of manner, 'who' is to be treated scopally as parallel to 'which', the question *Who saw who?* will be assigned the structure 'Wx: person x [Wy: person y [x saw y]]'.[11] The procedure determined by this structure is to find a pair composed of a seer and a person seen. And the question *Who did who see?* will be assigned the structure 'Wy: person y [Wx: person x [x saw y]]'—find a pair composed of a person seen and a seer. There is no semantic distinction between 'Wx: person x [Wy: person y [x saw y]]' and 'Wy: person y [Wx: person x [x saw y]]' other than the ordering of the pair. In the case of a single pair, this consideration can easily be immaterial. This is in contrast with the behavior of the strong Individualizing 'which N', where switching scope can easily have a semantic effect.

This has visible consequences. As already mentioned, it has long been known that while both *Which man saw which woman?* and the crossed *Which woman did which man see?* are available in English, there is no crossed *Who did who see?* corresponding to *Who saw who?* Now we have seen that while *Which man saw which woman?* and *Which woman did which man see?* ask different questions, there is no difference that can be registered by asking *Who did who see?* instead of *Who saw who?* It has generally been held that *Who did who see?* is ungrammatical—that is to say, ruled out by a syntactic restriction—but in light of this discussion, I think this has been a mistake. The correct analysis is that both *Who saw who?* and *Who did who see?* are syntactically well-formed, and both impose the same grammatical restriction on what would constitute an adequate answer. In both cases, that adequate answer is one (or more) pairings. Since there is no difference in adequate answer imposed by the two forms, speakers prefer the simpler, uncrossed *Who saw who?* to the crossed *Who did who see?* The absence of *Who did who see?* is due to practical considerations, not syntactic ones; the intuition of oddness that attaches to *Who did who see?* is not an intuition of ungrammaticality or syntactic ill-formedness, but an intuition of unavailingness. There is nothing gained by using the more complicated form; only useful variation in form is tolerated. Laying out a syntactic theoretical environment for this principle will be the task of the next chapter.

---

[11] In Chapter 5, I will argue that 'who' and 'which' should be given distinct scopal treatments.

To summarize my discussion of the speciation of *wh*-expressions, I have indicated that some *wh*-expressions are strongly mannered (exhaustive), and that some are weakly mannered (not necessarily exhaustive). And I have noted that while most *wh*-expressions may cover either argument positions or predicate positions, 'who', when speaking strictly, may only cover argument positions.[12] And lastly I have noted that the variables that *wh*-expressions bind are the sites of incompleteness in questions. These considerations are important when considering which questioning speech-act a speaker may perform when using a sentence-type containing one or another *wh*-expression in one or another position. Therefore, I will conclude the present discussion by introducing Austin's speciation of assertive speech-acts, which neatly complements the speciation of *wh*-expressions just presented.

4.6 On the speciation of the questioning speech-acts as reflected in the choice of *wh*-expressions

Austin (1953) distinguished between assertive speech-acts in which an item is given and a predicate produced, and assertive speech-acts in which a predicate is given and an item produced. He called this a difference in 'direction of fit', and proposed that there are two speech-acts of each kind. Calling and Describing are speech-acts in which the item is given and the predicate produced, while Exemplifying and Classing are speech-acts in which the predicate is given and the item produced. Each pair is differentiated by cross-cutting 'direction of fit' with another distinction called 'onus of match'. The resulting four assertive speech-acts are, I believe, echoed in the questioning speech-acts. Furthermore, once Austin's distinctions are recognized, the distributions of the various *wh*-expressions become more clear.

Let's begin with the correspondence between questioning speech-acts and, assertive, replying, speech-acts in terms of 'direction of fit'. If I wish to know what something is called, I may ask *What is that?*, and you may perform the Calling answer *That is a croze*. If, on the other hand, I want to be given an example of a croze, I may ask *What is a croze?*, and you, pointing at the cooper's tool, might perform the Exemplifying answer *That is a croze*. In the first case, you performed a Calling, producing a predicate that the given item falls under. In the second case, you performed an Exemplifying, producing an item that falls under the given predicate. Extending Austin's terminology, I will call *What is that?*, in this case, a Calling question, and I will call *What is a croze?*, in this case, an Exemplifying question. A perfectly responsive answer to a Calling question is a Calling assertion, and a perfectly responsive answer to an Exemplifying question is an Exemplifying assertion.

[12] This point will be revisited in Section 6.6.2.

Calling and Describing have the same direction of fit, as do Exemplifying and Classing. The speech-acts in each pair are distinguished by 'onus of match'. To appreciate this distinction, it is necessary to introduce Austin's proposal concerning predication. It is normal in the field of linguistic semantics to say that the relation between subject and predicate is the asymmetrical relation of set membership. Truth results if and only if the value of the subject belongs to the value of the predicate. Austin, in contrast, proposed that the relation between subject and predicate is symmetrical: that (not truth, for him, but) satisfactoriness results if and only if the value of the subject is of a type that matches the sense of the predicate. Of course, in the rough-and-tumble world of items and predicates, one cannot expect perfect matches. One might doubt whether some item or other is of a type that matches the sense of a predicate, or one might doubt whether the sense of a predicate is such that some item is of a type that matches it. In the first case, one's doubt falls on the item, in the second case, on the predicate. What Austin called the onus of match rests on the place where one's doubt might fall. The predicate or the item on which one's doubt does *not* fall is 'taken for granted'. As an example, consider a Classing question such as *Which birds are yellow?* In Classing, one has a predicate that is taken for granted and one worries, concerning each of the items to be Classified, whether it is of a type that matches the sense of the predicate. The onus of match is on the items. Here we make contact with the semantics I suggested for 'which', in particular, that 'which' is Individualizing and exhaustive in manner. To Class birds effectively as to whether they are yellow or not, one must have a firm notion *of* yellowness (the sense of the predicate is taken for granted) and one must exhaustively classify the produced birds *by* yellowness.

Different questioning speech-acts call for the use of different *wh*-expressions. 'Who' and 'what' are used for Exemplifying questions, while 'which N' is used for Classing questions, a point that Austin noticed in a footnote. The expressions 'how', 'how A', 'when', and 'where' are used to ask Describing questions. 'How' is the most general of these, and perhaps the most commonly used *wh*-expression in Describing questions. We use it when a friend says that he has just seen a movie and we ask *How was it?* (This 'how' is underappreciated; it is different from the commonly appreciated adverbial 'how' we find in a sentence such as *How did you do it?*) To ask Calling questions, one may use either 'what', or 'what N'.[13] Table 4.1 summarizes the system Austin suggested for assertions, adapted for questioning speech-acts, with characteristic questions included.

I have noted that the manners of interpretation of Exemplifying 'who' and 'what' differ from the manner of interpretation of Classing 'which N'. The former need not be exhaustive, but the latter must be. To Exemplify one need only produce an instance; to Class one must exhaust the domain.

In this chapter, a number of facts concerning the scopes of *wh*-expressions have been discussed, as well as the correlations between scope and the structures of

---

[13] We must wait until Section 6.4.1 to present Calling questions containing 'who'.

Table 4.1. Austin's quartet

	Onus of match	
	On predicate	On item
Direction of fit		
Item given, predicate produced	Calling:	Describing:
	What is that?	*How is it?*
	What tool is that?	*How tall is it?*
	Who is that?	*Where is it?*
		When is it?
		Why is that?
Predicate given, item produced	Exemplifying:	Classing:
	Who is brave?	*Which is yellow?*
	What is yellow?	*Which bird is yellow?*
	What bird is yellow?	

overt sentence-types. *Wh*-expression-types differ in these regards. They also differ pragmatically. In Chapter 6, I will return to Austin's quartet, further applying his analysis to the questioning speech-acts. But first, to express the relationship between scope and overt form, it is necessary to provide an accompanying account of the syntactic structure of the sentence-types I have been considering. That is the business of the next chapter.

5

Syntactic Structure

5.1 Syntactic notation and the representation of phrase-markers

Syntacticians study sentence-types, and sentence-types are abstract objects.[1] There are notations in which syntacticians write down their findings. What relationship is there between syntactic notation and the abstract objects they are studying? Often it is said that what syntacticians write down are 'representations' of the things that they are investigating. But the term 'representation' can be misleading. In one common way of speaking, a representation of an object bears a likeness to the object it represents, and we commonly think of representational likeness as relating two physical things, as in the case of portraiture. But there is no physical likeness between what a linguist writes down and an abstract sentence-type. If used in this context, the term 'representation' cannot connote portraiture.

Oddly, the verb 'represent' and its nominalization 'representation' differ in this respect. The verb 'represent' has one sense that seems appropriate to our case, as when we say *Let 'QB4' represent the fourth square in the Queen's Bishop file*. Here no physical likeness is implied. The noun 'representation', on the other hand, tends to suggest physical resemblance; it seems a little odd to say: *'QB4' is a representation of the fourth square in the Queen's Bishop file*. Nevertheless, I propose to retain the term and tolerate any oddness it might occasion. Furthermore, I will call syntactic sentence-types 'phrase-markers', not 'trees', since the term 'tree' suggests a particular method of representation of syntactic sentence-types, and tends to foster a confusion between syntactic sentence-types and representations of them.[2]

Some notations are better, in certain respects, than others. On the suggested usage, a phrase-marker representation is accurate if and only if each item in the representation corresponds to some property of the sentence-type, and

---

[1] See Katz 1981.

[2] I won't, however, be using the term 'phrase-marker' in the same sense that Chomsky (1955, 1975) uses it. There is, between that account and the one I offer here, a great terminological difference, and, perhaps, a great philosophical difference. For example, the objects of syntactic study in Chomsky (1955, 1975) are called 'utterances'.

no property of the sentence-type goes unrepresented by some item in the representation. Ideally, in representations of syntactic sentence-types, all and only the syntactic properties of the sentence-type would be represented. On this view, an analogue to phrase-marker representations would be the traditional molecular models composed of colored spheres and sticks. Like phrase-marker representations, they are representations of structure, and reflect scientific claims about that structure. But at the same time the physicists tell us that molecular models such as these do not look like that which they represent. Neither do linguistic representations look like what they represent. Both embody specific theoretical claims, accurate to the extent that they correspond to the structures of molecules or to the structures of sentence-types.[3]

It is necessary to distinguish the representations of phrase-markers from the notation in which the representations are written. Phrase-markers have certain properties. In a complete representation, each of those properties must be represented. The notation in which a complete representation is written must allow the representation of all of those properties. But no notation is ever unique in that respect. There are always distinct notations that allow the representation of the same properties, which are called 'notational variants'. One may use '*C4*' or '*QB4*' to represent the fourth square in the Queen's Bishop file; one may use trees or labeled bracketings to represent sentence-types. One task of syntactic theorizing is to produce a notation in which syntactic representations may be written. But there is no notation uniquely suited to the task.

As in the case of the term 'representation', the term 'notation' must be handled with care. There are differences between syntactic notation and other notations. Musical notational systems allow the representation of musical structure, but they also allow both the transcription of the structure of what has been heard, and the transcription of instructions to the musician. Syntactic notations serve neither of these functions. In particular, the syntactic constituency of a sentence-type is not something that we 'take down'. We could only 'take down' syntactic constituency if syntactic constituency were open to inspection. But it is not. So there is no syntactic notation parallel to phonetic notation. Again, our understanding of syntactic structure is only inferential.

There is not only a tendency to confuse representations with the things they represent but also a tendency to think that representations represent things that they do not. Specifically, there is a tendency, when reading syntactic

---

[3] There are many further issues. Suppose we wish to represent a complex object, indicating in the representation all of its parts, all of the properties of each part, and all of the relationships between those parts. And suppose the separation into objects, properties, and relations can at least in part be achieved empirically. We would wish, in our preferred theoretical talk, to refer to what we would take to be relations between parts. Should a term that refers to a relation be chosen (e.g. 'attraction'), or should a relational term be chosen ('attract')? Does it matter? There are many questions such as this that I cannot entertain here.

representations in one of the standard notations, to take the horizontal dimension as representing temporal priority. Tree structures and labeled bracketings both invite the idea that they notate representations of things that stand in time. But this cannot be right: phrase-marker representations are representations of sentence-types, which do not stand in time, not of utterances, which do. There is as little justification in reading phrase-marker representations as representations of things that stand in time as there would be in reading {2, 3} or <8, 6> as representations of things that stand in time. The things these notations represent are not temporal objects. I am, of course, specifically denying that phrase-marker representations represent utterances. Utterances *are* temporal; they have acoustic and articulatory structures, the first stated in terms of frequency against time, the second stated as a sequence of muscular gestures. Nothing could completely represent them that did not acknowledge their temporal nature. But utterances do not have syntactic structure, so no syntactic representation could correctly represent them.[4]

I will represent phrase-markers as sets of sets. Some parts of phrase-markers will be represented as ordered sets, and other parts will be represented as unordered sets. But no ordering indicated in the representation of a phrase-marker is temporal ordering. Sentence-tokens are ordered in time (or, in the case of written sentence-tokens, in space), but I am representing sentence-types, not sentence-tokens. Nevertheless, as I will argue directly, there *is* a kind of ordering that occurs in sentence-types that needs to be represented, a type of ordering that is neither temporal nor spatial. I will represent syntactic constituent-types that are ordered in this way as ordered sets. There are also syntactic constituent-types that are not ordered in this way, and these will be represented as unordered sets. By adopting set notation for syntactic ordering and its lack, I believe I can avoid the temporal confusions that have arisen from other notations. But since sentence-tokens are ordered in time, it will be necessary to state the relationship between the (atemporal) ordering (or lack of ordering) of linguistic expression-types and the temporal ordering of their tokens. I will take that up in due course.

In the fragment of syntactic theory that I present, much will be left unexamined. I assume, for example, that we are given a set of syntactic categories, but will not argue what the categories should be. It would be best, I think, if we could limit the theory to only two—a function category and an argument category—and much that I will have to say would go through if only this binary categorial distinction were allowed. The motivation for positing a syntactic category can only be given in syntactic terms; the tendency to 'syntacticize' all sorts of linguistic phenomena whose treatments more correctly lie in pragmatics, semantics, and even phonetics should be resisted.

---

[4] As regards Chomsky (1955, 1975), the question would be whether he meant, by calling the objects of inquiry 'utterances', to be referring to things that stand in time.

5.2 Ordering in syntactic representation

Each element in a phrase-marker stands in a 'privileged' relation to no more than one other element. This privileged relationship is represented as co-membership in a binary set, and may be asymmetric or symmetric.[5] An asymmetric privileged relationship is represented by an ordered set containing two members; a symmetric privileged relationship is represented by an unordered set containing two members.

A phrase-marker is represented as a set of sets. Some of the sets are ordered and some are not. I will say that the ordered set $<\alpha, \beta>$ has a first member and a second member, while the unordered set $\{\gamma, \delta\}$ has no first or second member. The terms 'first' and 'second' will apply only to members of ordered sets. To give examples of both types, the relation between a function and its argument is an asymmetric relation, and so is represented as ordered, while the relationship between members of an adjunction cluster is symmetric, and so is represented as unordered. This means there are no first or second members in adjunction clusters, a point that will become central to the discussion of multiple *wh*-questions below.

In the semantic tradition that originated with Frege (1892), it has been customary to distinguish three things: linguistic expressions, what they mean, and what they refer to. Also since Frege, it has been customary to consider the function/argument distinction as central. There are function-names, function-senses, and functions, and there are argument-names, argument-senses, and arguments.[6] I follow this tradition in assuming that the only asymmetric privileged relationship is that between function and argument. The relationship between a function and an argument will be represented as $<F, a>$, where 'F' is a function-name, and 'a' is an argument-name. This relation is asymmetric; all ordered sets represent the privileged asymmetrical relationship between a function and its argument in a phrase-marker. It should be understood that 'a' need not always be the name of an item: 'a' may represent the scope of the quantifier 'F'. In that case, 'F' would represent a second-level concept and 'a' would represent not an object, but a first-level concept. If 'F' represents the universal quantifier, and everything falls under the first-level concept 'a', the result is truth. Ordering indicates asymmetry in this case, just as it does in the case of a verb and its object.

---

[5] The assumption that structural relations are fundamentally binary has deep roots, even within the study of natural language. See Yngve 1960 and Kayne 1984. I assume binary branching for convenience only. Ternary branching could easily be accommodated here, as it could in other systems.

[6] Furth's (1967) introduction to Frege 1893 lays this out clearly.

5.2.1 'Horizontal' ordering, 'vertical' ordering, and the containing node

In traditional representations, there is both left-right, or 'horizontal' ordering, and 'vertical' ordering, which is usually called 'containment'. In the representations $<\alpha, \beta>$ and $\{\gamma, \delta\}$, what is the containing node? Of what categories are they? In traditional tree-structure notation, all nodes are labeled; in traditional bracketing notation, all brackets are labeled, overtly expressing the identity of the containing node. Sometimes the representation of containment is redundant; in the representation of phrasal structure, for example, it is redundant to represent both the head and the containing phrasal node.[7] Since there is no reason to believe that there is anything in phrase-markers that this redundancy represents, the distinct representation of containment must, at least in this case, be eliminated. Set theoretic notation does this; in a notation that uses ordered and unordered sets, there is no need to distinguish two directions of ordering, and no need to represent containing nodes. For an ordered set, the first member of the set is the containing node, while for an unordered set, the containing node is the conjunction of the elements of the sets. In $<\alpha, \beta>$, α is the containing node, while in $\{\gamma, \delta\}$, 'γ and δ' is the containing node. In $\{\beta, \{\gamma, \delta\}\}$, the containing node is 'β and γ and δ'. In $<<\alpha, \beta>, \gamma>$, the containing node is $<\alpha, \beta>$, which is of category α. Recalling that unordered sets do not have 'first' or 'second' members, these two proposals may be united under the following generalization:

> The containing node of a set is the conjunction of all of its elements, minus its second member.

This proposal is incomplete; I will refine it further. Here the point is only that, given the suggested notation, there is no need to represent containing nodes separately: their identities are transparent. Set notation simultaneously indicates both the identities of the members of a set, and the identity of the containing node, without redundancy.

In most traditional theories of syntactic structure, phrasal structure is taken as basic, while adjunction structures arise through the application of an adjunction operation. In the account I advocate, phrasal structure and adjunction structure are on a par. Concerning the identities of containing nodes, it would be desirable that, if both γ and δ can dominate α and β (whether α and β are horizontally ordered with respect to each other or not), then $\gamma = \delta$. In other words, it would be desirable that containing nodes be determinable as a function of the contained nodes, both in the phrasal and adjunction cases. The present suggestion concerning the identity of containing nodes achieves this.

---

[7] This has long been recognized. See Chomsky 1970 and Chomsky 1994.

But in empirical research pursued using a more standard notational framework, there is the risk that this ideal cannot be met. Suppose it is allowed, in such a framework, both that N may adjoin to V, yielding a constituent of category V, and that V may adjoin to N, yielding a constituent of category N. If the containing node is to be a function from the contained nodes (solely) to the containing one, the ideal must be dropped, at least for structures 'created' by adjunction. Furthermore, the proposal that containment is a function from contained nodes to containing ones runs afoul of the desideratum that the well-formedness conditions on phrase-markers be neutral as between phrasal-structure representations and adjunction-structure representations. In the notation suggested here, whether N 'adjoins' to V or V 'adjoins' to N, we have the unordered notation {V, N} and 'V and N' would be the containing node. The prediction is that the structure that results when V adjoins to N and the structure that results when N adjoins to V are of the same category: 'V and N'. If this is correct, phrase-markers are simpler than previous representations of them have been claiming.[8]

I have emphasized that the ordered (or unordered) constituents in phrase-marker representations indicate only syntactic asymmetry (or symmetry), and are not to be thought of in temporal terms. But there is a relationship between the ordering in sentence-types and temporal or spatial ordering in tokens of these types, which can be expressed as pronunciation rules. One such rule is that all ordered expression-types in a language are pronounced in the same direction. A language may be such that asymmetrically related pairs of expression-types, represented as $<F, a>$, are pronounced 'F, a', or it may be such that they are pronounced 'a, F'. It is well known that in some languages, such as English, the head temporally precedes its argument, whereas in other languages, such as Japanese, the head temporally follows its argument. These rules have exceptions, and there are many complexities that I am ignoring, but there do appear to be generalizations of this sort applying in individual languages.[9] Crucially, I express these generalizations as pronunciation rules, not rules of syntax.

This view has implications for parametric theories of language acquisition. It might be thought that if, in English, constituent-types of the form $<F, a>$ are pronounced 'F, a', and if, in Japanese, constituent-types of the form $<F, a>$ are pronounced 'a, F', then English speakers have nothing to learn concerning ordering, while Japanese speakers have to learn that the ordering of pronunciation

---

[8] I assume, merely for purposes of illustration, that there is a syntactic distinction between V and N. That is usually assumed, but it might be questioned. Plainly, empirical questions arise here. One empirical question, which this proposal would force into the open, is what the categories of syntax actually are. Categorial status is conferred by syntactic argumentation, of which this issue is a part. It is not conferred by naming constituents for their use. That is appropriate when naming kitchen utensils, say, but not here. That said, can it be maintained in general that the result of adjoining α to β and the result of adjoining β to α yield the same category? What categorial theory would that assumption give rise to?

[9] See Greenberg 1963.

is the reverse of the ordering of the expression-type. But that way of viewing this matter would be confused. The notation $<F, a>$ has no temporal interpretation; it serves only to indicate an asymmetrical relationship between a function and its argument. The correct way to state the matter is the following. There are two empirical possibilities. Either (i) Speakers of both English and Japanese must learn the temporal direction in which constituents of the form $<F, a>$ are pronounced, or (ii) One set of speakers must learn that temporal ordering and the other need not. Suppose the first is true. Then, as far as learning is concerned, the asymmetry of function and argument is not partial as to direction of pronunciation. All speakers know the asymmetry, but must learn the direction of pronunciation, which varies from language to language. If the second is true, then one temporal ordering of asymmetry is unmarked. That ordering would be the 'first guess' on the part of the learner. Then the question would be why that should be so; why, in particular, the chosen ordering has priority of place in learning. Of course these matters have been studied empirically, but I am not yet certain that we know which of the possibilities mentioned is correct. Similarly, it is not right to say that English has the traditional phrase-structure rule VP → V NP, while Japanese has the phrase-structure rule VP → NP V. Phrase-structure, whether given by phrase-structure rule, or by the operation of merge in current minimalism, is assigned to atemporal sentence-types, not their tokens.

Turning to the pronunciation of *unordered* constituents in *particular* languages, this account would predict two options: (i) If and where there is no learning, the temporal ordering of unordered constituents would be arbitrary; and (ii) If and where there are rules for the pronunciation of unordered constituents, those rules must be learned. One fairly clear and relatively simple example that might be of the former sort involves the distribution of adverbs in English. It is traditional to say that adverbs adjoin, and that they may adjoin to sentences and to verb phrases. If there are unordered structures such as {IP, Adverb} and {VP, Adverb}, the learner's first guess would be that the temporal ordering of adverbs with respect to the nodes they are adjoined to is free: that in tokens of these constituents an adverb may precede or follow the constituent it is adjoined to. *Amazingly, John left*, and *John left, amazingly* would now be tokens of the same syntactic type, as would *John suddenly left* and *John left suddenly*. The positioning of adverbs is a tricky business, however; here I can only gesture toward what I believe to be a promising direction to account for their behavior if the first option is correct.[10]

If and where the latter option is correct, rules—possibly language-particular rules—must be stated that specify the temporal ordering of tokens of unordered sentence-types. There are suggestions in the literature along these lines. For example, it has been suggested in various domains that there are certain syntactic

---

[10] See Jackendoff 1972.

output conditions that filter out illicit orderings. Perlmutter (1971) advances a modern theory of clitics in the spirit of traditional Romance language grammars, which state generalizations of clitic-ordering in terms of person, grammatical case, and so on. If multiple clitics are syntactically represented as adjunction clusters, then this might be a case in which unordered constituents are temporally ordered by a filter stating the order in which the syntactically unordered clusters of clitics are to be pronounced. A similar sort of filter might be appealed to in the cases of multiple overt *wh*-movement in languages such as Hungarian, Polish, and Bulgarian. Syntactic filters stated in terms of crossing and nesting have been suggested in these cases, but semantic considerations might also be in play. It would be crucial, of course, to distinguish *wh*-expressions comparable to 'who' and *wh*-expressions comparable to 'which', so that matters of scope can be controlled for. Liptak (2001) and Bošković (1999) have made suggestions along these lines.

There are other approaches to the 'linearization' problem, one of which is due to Kayne (1994), who holds that, despite appearances to the contrary, universal grammar imposes a subject-head-complement order on phrases in all languages. Among the tasks that must be faced to sustain this view is the task of stating the relationship between the grammatical structures of sentences and time. To this end, Kayne proposes to associate the string of terminals in a phrase-marker with a string of time slots in a particular way: associated with each time slot will be not simply the corresponding terminal, but the "substring produced up to that time" (1994: 37). The first terminal will appear in all substrings, but the final terminal will appear only in the last substring, yielding an asymmetry which, details aside, allows the conclusion that the interpretation of the set of terminals $<x, y>$, where x asymmetrically c-commands y, is that x precedes y. Kayne extends this proposal to all phrase-markers in a derivation.

In my view, Kayne's proposal is not adequate in certain respects. First, in deriving the consequence that asymmetric c-command should be interpreted as temporal precedence, temporal precedence is used to formulate the relationship between terminals and time slots. Secondly, if all phrase-markers are time-slotted, the implication would seem to be that movement rules move constituents in time, presumably from later times to earlier ones, a startling prospect. And thirdly, I can't help but feel that the mechanism of substrings that Kayne selects could be replaced by a mechanically no less plausible alternative to yield the opposite result. These points would have to be improved upon if the relation between structure and time could truly be said to be derived. More generally, Kayne's proposal does not make clear what the relationship is between time slots and time. If the time slots are slots *in* time, and time is the dimension we are familiar with, then the odd consequences just mentioned would seem to follow. But if the time slots are not slots in time, we are left wondering what the relation is between 'time-slot time' and time. There is no type-token talk in the sections of Kayne (1994) just discussed, so I think it is probably right to say that there is little relation between Kayne's goal and my own. I wish to state the temporal ordering of spoken sentence-tokens on the basis of the structures of the sentence-types they are tokens of. Kayne, in contrast, apparently seeks to place sentence-structures, and their derivations, in time. This may mean that Kayne and I also disagree concerning the subject matter of linguistics, but on this topic Kayne is not explicit.

But to return to the topic of horizontal and vertical ordering, I believe, in sum, that the best system of notation for syntactic constituency is one in which phrase-marker representations are notated as sets of sets, which may be ordered or unordered. Ordering represents asymmetry in phrase-markers, which is always the function-argument relation. Lack of ordering represents symmetry in phrase-markers, which is always the relation among the member of clusters. There are pronunciation rules stating the temporal ordering for ordered and unordered sets, but these rules are not syntactic. There may be universal aspects to these rules, such as the generalization that, in all languages, a choice is made as to the direction in which $<F, a>$ is to be pronounced. But the choice of direction, and other matters such as the filters I referred to, might be determined language by language.

5.2.2 The definitions of containment and dominance

In this section, I will define several relations between elements in phrase-marker representations. Let's start with two generalizations concerning immediate containment:

    i) Given $\{e_1, e_2\}$—or, equivalently, given 'e_1 and e_2'—e_1 and e_2 *immediately contain* each other.

    ii) Given $<e_1, e_2>$—or equivalently, given e_1—e_1 *immediately contains* e_2, and e_2 does not *immediately contain* e_1.[11]

In $\{a, \beta\}$, a immediately contains β and β immediately contains a. In $<a, \beta>$, a immediately contains β, but β does not immediately contain a. In a structure such as $\{\{\{a, \beta\}, \gamma\}, \delta\}$, a and β immediately contain each other; $\{a, \beta\}$ and γ immediately contain each other; and $\{\{a, \beta\}, \gamma\}$ and δ immediately contain each other. Furthermore, since $\{a, \beta\}$ is of category 'a and β', both a and β immediately contain γ, and γ immediately contains both a and β. The members of an unordered set are both the members of that set and the categories of that set. So, since $\{\{\{a, \beta\}, \gamma\}, \delta\} =$ 'a and β and γ and δ', all of a and β and γ and δ immediately contain each other.

In what environments may a constituent that is of a conjoined category appear? In $\{a, \beta\}$, a and β immediately contain each other, and $\{a, \beta\}$ is of the category 'a and β'. Let the principle be that a constituent that is of a conjoined category

---

[11] 'Equivalently', since $<e_1, e_2>$ is an instance of the category e_1.

meets a subcategorization requirement if one of the conjoined categories does. To illustrate, suppose $\{\alpha, \beta\}$ occurs in the structure $<\gamma, \{\alpha, \beta\}>$, and γ is subcategorized only to allow arguments of category α. Then this is allowed. If instead γ is subcategorized to allow arguments of category β, $<\gamma, \{\alpha, \beta\}>$ will also be allowed. Finally, if in $<\gamma, \{\alpha, \beta\}>$, γ imposes no subcategorization requirement, then $<\gamma, \{\alpha, \beta\}>$ is allowed. However, if γ is subcategorized only to allow arguments of category δ, $\delta \neq \alpha$ and $\delta \neq \beta$, then $<\gamma, \{\alpha, \beta\}>$ is not allowed.[12]

Let me now define the more general notion 'containment'. First, immediate containment is a kind of containment:

If e_1 immediately contains e_2, then e_1 contains e_2.

The general definition of containment will be:

e_1 *contains* e_n iff they appear in a series of the form '. . . e_1, e_2, e_3, . . . , e_{n-1}, e_n, . . .' where e_i immediately contains e_{i+1}.

To see how this works, consider the structure $<\alpha, \{\beta, \gamma\}>$. $\{\beta, \gamma\}$ is of the category 'β and γ'. So $<\alpha, \{\beta, \gamma\}> = <\alpha, '\beta$ and $\gamma'>$. α immediately contains 'β and γ'. 'β and γ' immediately contains β and 'β and γ' immediately contains γ. So we have the series 'α, 'β and γ', β' and the series 'α, 'β and γ', γ', in which each member immediately contains the next. So α contains β and α contains γ. The structure $<\alpha, <\beta, \gamma>>$ yields the same result. $<\beta, \gamma>$ is of the category β. So $<\alpha, <\beta, \gamma>> = <\alpha, \beta>$. α immediately contains β. And β immediately contains γ. So α contains β and α contains γ. On the other hand, in $<<\beta, \gamma>, \alpha>$, β contains α, but γ does not contain α.

Now let's turn to dominance. On this account, dominance is ordered containment: one element dominates another if it is ordered before it and contains it. Like containment, the ordered-before relation may be immediate or not: e_1 is immediately ordered before e_2 when e_1 and e_2 appear in the structure $<e_1, e_2>$. Generally speaking:

e_1 is *ordered before* e_n iff they appear in a series of the form '. . . e_1, e_2, e_3, . . . , e_{n-1}, e_n, . . .' where e_i is immediately ordered before e_{i+1}.

We may now combine the definitions of containment and ordered-before:

e_1 *contains and is ordered before* e_n iff they appear in a series of the form '. . . e_1, e_2, e_3, . . . , e_{n-1}, e_n, . . .' where e_i immediately contains and is immediately ordered before e_{i+1}.

And this, as a matter of terminology, is equivalent to:

e_1 *dominates* e_n iff they appear in a series of the form '. . . e_1, e_2, e_3, . . . , e_{n-1}, e_n, . . .' where e_i immediately dominates e_{i+1}.

---

[12] The force of these considerations depends on how many categories there are, and on how syntactically varied the members of clusters may be. If there are only two categories, and if clusters are syntactically homogeneous, never containing constituents of different categories, then this stipulation is trivial.

It should be clear that, in the theory of structure being presented here, dominance replaces c-command. In one standard definition, A c-commands B iff every node that dominates A dominates B.[13] But the relation 'dominate' used in that standard definition is not the relation I have just defined. As the term is traditionally used, α does not dominate β in $<\alpha, \beta>$. As I have defined the term, it does. The interpretation of ordered set representations, in which $<\alpha, \beta>$ is read as saying both that α is ordered before and contains β, gives a formal definition of scope. Thus it replaces c-command. There are, however, some interesting differences in the application of c-command and dominance, as I have defined it. Consider $\{\{\alpha, \beta\}, \delta\}$. $\{\alpha, \beta\}$ is of category 'α and β', and $\{\{\alpha, \beta\}, \delta\}$ is of the category 'α and β and δ'. Suppose that $\{\{\alpha, \beta\}, \delta\}$ appears in the larger structure $<\{\{\alpha, \beta\}, \delta\}, \gamma>$. Then all of α, β, and δ dominate γ; all of them are ordered before γ, and all of them contain γ. Since what is dominated by a constituent is that constituent's scope, γ is in the scope of all of α, β, and δ. The same will be true no matter what the complexity of the adjunction cluster that replaces $\{\{\alpha, \beta\}, \delta\}$; all of the elements of any unordered set of unordered sets dominate all of the elements that set dominates. (The prediction this makes concerning scope is fulfilled in the analysis of multiple *who*-questions below.)

Now that containment and dominance are defined, I wish to return to the generalization concerning the identity of containing nodes, proposed earlier to be:

> The containing node of a set is the conjunction of all of its elements, minus its second member.

Now a more inclusive definition is possible:

> The containing node of a set is the conjunction of all of its elements, minus any element dominated by an element of the set.

Let's work through a few examples. In the case of $\{\alpha, \beta\}$, neither α nor β dominates the other, so the containing node is 'α and β'. In the case of $<\gamma, \delta>$, γ dominates δ, but not conversely, so δ is subtracted and the containing node is γ. In $\{\alpha, <\beta, \gamma>\}$, γ is dominated, but neither α nor β is, so the containing node is 'α and β'. In $\{\alpha, \{\beta, <\gamma, \delta>\}\}$, '$\alpha$ and β and γ' is the containing node. In $\{\alpha, <\beta, \{\gamma, \delta\}>\}$, '$\alpha$ and β' is the containing node. Finally, in $\{<\alpha, \beta>, <\gamma, \delta>\}$, '$\alpha$ and γ' is the containing node. In general, the first member of an ordered set removes, in effect, all the elements it dominates from membership in the containing node of the set it is a member of.

In sum, phrase-markers are represented as sets of sets; sets may be ordered or unordered. Ordering represents asymmetry in phrase-markers, and lack of ordering represents symmetry. The containing category of a set is not represented but determined by rule, for both ordered and unordered sets. The ordering of representations is not to be confused with temporal ordering. There are two important relationships between elements: containment and dominance, which

---

[13] There are many variants, beginning with Reinhart 1976, 1983.

is defined in terms of containment. With these defined, we can approach a definition of movement.

5.3 Movement (splitting), and the lack thereof

One might think that an ideal language would be one in which there was no movement at all. In such a language, each utterance would be a pronounced logical structure. But there are many ways to be ideal, and we should, I think, treat with suspicion any preconceptions concerning what the ideal state of natural language might look like. At the end of the day, language is what it is. If we ever find out what language is really like, we might be very surprised. It is, rather, our *theory* of language that we want to be the best that it can be. That said, a consideration of the nature of movement suggests that movement might be more a benefit than a blot on language. Movement allows the circumstance in which the 'powers' of an expression may be divided among more than one syntactic position. Language might, 'ideally' for all we know, allow only one power to be expressed in any position. If that were true, then the blot on language would be the case in which an *unmoved* expression expressed more than one power.

Movement, simply put, is the rearrangement of elements in phrase-markers. In movement, no elements may be added, and none taken away. In Chomsky 1955, 1975, the first formal conception of movement in the framework I am following, movement was defined as a complex operation, consisting of copy and deletion. On this conception, copying μ is just the insertion of another occurrence of the same syntactic expression that μ belongs to. To move μ, there is first the insertion of an element under identity with μ, and then the deletion of the original occurrence of μ, again under identity with the inserted occurrence of μ.[14] 'Movement' denotes the circumstance in which copying is followed by deletion. Before movement, there is an occurrence of a syntactic expression at one position; after movement, there is a distinct occurrence of that expression at another position. Taking distinct occurrences of the same expression as syntactic equals, no syntactic element has been added, and none taken away.

There has always been a problem with the 'copying' part of this operation, as defined. It seems to ignore the fact that, completely generally, the moved element and its trace—what remains in the position moved from—exhibit different syntactic powers. If copying were really part of movement, one would not expect that it regularly results in two syntactic occurrences with distinct syntactic powers. On the contrary, one would expect two syntactic occurrences with the same syntactic powers, one pronounced, the other not.[15] Consequently, I have come

---

[14] In Fiengo 1974, the obligatoriness of deletion after copy followed from principles governing the obligatoriness of deletion generally.

[15] See Heycock 1995 for a good presentation of the issues here.

to prefer a different conception, according to which syntactic expressions have certain powers, and 'movement' is the *splitting* of those powers between distinct positions. Although I think the movement metaphor is now misleading, I will sometimes continue to use the term, for its familiarity and convenience. The important question is what powers syntactic expressions have, and the reasons for their being split.

5.3.1 The powers of positions, the powers of expressions, and incompleteness

The picture of syntax I am developing is as follows. Syntactic positions differ as regards what powers may be expressed in them; linguistic expressions differ as regards what powers they may express. Generally, if an expression is to appear in a phrase-marker, no power of it may remain unexpressed. Some expressions, for example, have the power to serve as adjuncts. To serve as an adjunct, an expression must appear in an adjunct position. Other expressions have the power to serve as arguments. To serve as an argument, an expression must appear in an argument position. Some syntactic positions are referring positions. Some syntactic expressions are referring expressions. For a referring expression to refer, it must appear in a referring position. Both argument positions and adjunct positions are referring positions. Some positions are obligatory and some are optional. In very many well-formed sentence-types, argument positions are obligatory, in the sense that there are no well-formed sentence-types, otherwise identical to them, but lacking those argument positions. In very many well-formed sentence-types, adjunct positions are optional, in the sense that there are other well-formed sentence-types, otherwise identical to them, but lacking those adjunct positions. Generally, argument positions are obligatory and adjunct positions are optional, although there is some slipping on either side.

When an expression is split, its powers are expressed in different positions. This occurs either (i) when the phrase-marker in which the expression appears contains no position at which all its powers may be expressed, or (ii) when the expression contains powers both of which may not be expressed in one position. Let's examine these two sorts of splitting in turn.

NP-splitting is of the former sort. NPs have the power to refer and the power to stand as arguments, which is not a problem when they appear in a referring, argument position, as direct object position of an active verb has been alleged to be. However, some argument positions are not referring positions, such as NP positions following passive participles. Since all the powers of an expression must be expressed, this might be thought to be a problem. But an NP may split in such a way that one of the positions in which it appears follows a passive participle, expressing its argumenthood, and the other position in which it appears allows its power to refer to be expressed. For example, the NP in *John was arrested__* is split in this way; the first NP-position is the referring position and the second

NP-position, the object trace following 'arrested', is the argument position. A single expression-type is split, appearing in two positions.

Wh-splitting is of the latter sort. *Wh*-expressions have complementary powers, the power to bind and the power to be bound. Since no expression may bind itself, *wh*-expressions must be split if both powers are to be expressed. The variable position is the dominated position, and may be an argument position or an adjunct position, depending on the *wh*-expression. The dominating position is the position of the variable-binder. If the *wh*-expression is not split, the power to bind and the power to be bound may cancel each other out, leaving behind only whatever other powers the expression may have.

The analysis of *wh*-questions begun in the previous chapter concluded that all *wh*-expressions move covertly in sentence-types used to ask open questions, and that no *wh*-expressions move, either overtly or covertly, in *wh*-confirmation questions. Since only the splitting of a *wh*-expression allows its logical binding powers to be expressed, that splitting must appear, at least covertly, at the logical level if those powers are to be expressed. Therefore, in confirmation questions, where no splitting occurs, *wh*-expressions do not express their logical binding powers. Thus in *wh*-confirmation questions such as *John saw who?*, a *wh*-expression with complementary powers, the power to bind and the power to be bound, is not split, and so these powers cancel each other out. What remains are the non-complementary powers: the so-called phi features. 'Who', when unsplit, expresses just the human element, and 'what' the nonhuman element. The uttered confirmation question *John saw who?* is incomplete, asking that the addressee complete the utterance *John saw (person)*.

I suggested that it might be the case that no syntactic position is such that it allows more than one power to be expressed in it. That would entail that there is no such thing as a referring, argument position, as I assumed in the case of direct objects above, and would also entail that all multi-powered constituents must be split. Perhaps, if that were true, only expletives would not have to be split. Expletives have neither the power to refer nor the power to serve as arguments, so perhaps only they might appear unsplit.[16] Such considerations are well beyond my topic here, but the operative principle would be:

> An expression may appear in a phrase-marker only if none of its powers remains unexpressed.

The expression *who* has the power to bind, the power to be bound, and the 'human element'. If the first two cancel each other out, and the human element remains; then, if the human element is expressed, none remain unexpressed. On the other hand, the NP that appears unsplit in the phrase-marker *Was arrested John* cannot express its power to refer, the ungrammaticality resulting from the fact that that power remains unexpressed.

---

[16] Here I have in mind the 'it' that occurs in such sentences as *It's raining*.

As mentioned, split expressions appear in dominating and dominated positions. A phrase-marker is not well-formed if it contains a split expression none of whose parts dominates the others. The following rule governs the appearance of a syntactic expression in a phrase-marker:

If an expression is split, one part of it dominates the others.

Splitting, however, is optional. Many of the arguments put forth earlier concerning *wh*-movement carry over to the new conception of *wh*-splitting. There is no bit of structure that triggers *wh*-splitting. While open *wh*-questions display *wh*-splitting, confirmation *wh*-questions do not. So the ideal theory would be that *wh*-splitting is optional. Again, it would be wrong to say that some sentence-types contain the morpheme 'Open Q', a morpheme that triggers splitting, while other sentence-types contain the morpheme 'Confirmation Q', which fails to trigger splitting. Structures should not be tagged for use. Sufficient for all purposes is to allow both split and unsplit forms, and to state the rules for using them, rules that must be stated in any event.

Wh-splitting is a relation between phrase-marker representations. In my view, it is optional. Derivations are sequences of phrase-marker representations, each tangent pair related by a rule.[17] The claim that a rule is optional is the claim that a derivation that contains a phrase-marker representation meeting the structural description of a rule is well-formed whether it is followed by a phrase-marker representation in which the structural change has been effected or not. The claim that a rule is obligatory is the claim that a phrase-marker representation meeting the structural description of the rule is well-formed only if it is followed by a phrase-marker representation in which the structural change specified by that rule is effected. (If rules are ordered, there are further complexities, which I will ignore.) Most generally, all sequences are allowed unless there is some prohibition against them. That being true, optionality is the null hypothesis. The claim that rules are obligatory must be expressed as a stipulation against certain sequences.[18]

I have suggested that splitting can result from the requirement that no power of an expression remains unexpressed. Is the splitting obligatory in that case? It is not. If there is a general principle that no power of an expression may remain unexpressed, that principle alone serves to rule out phrase-markers containing expressions one or more of whose powers remain unexpressed. It would be superfluous first to state the general well-formedness principle and then to state

---

[17] I assume that a derivation is a sequence of phrase-markers, each one of which meets the conditions laid down here, and perhaps others besides. The question whether phrase-markers are built top-down, or bottom-up, as assumed in current minimalism, is ignored here.

[18] I am assuming neither that the derivation of a phrase-marker is bottom-up, as in minimalism, nor top-down, as in the prior tradition. There are well-formedness conditions on phrase-markers, and well-formedness conditions on sets of phrase-markers. These conditions constitute the syntactic theory of sentence-types. There is no need to view the application of these conditions in a stepwise fashion, and it would be incoherent to view it in temporal terms.

that splitting is obligatory. These points apply to any rendering of syntax, including minimalism (Chomsky 1995). In minimalism, despite what might be thought, movement is optional; in some cases, when it does not apply, strong, uninterpretable features remain, features that would have been deleted had movement occurred. In the Standard Theory (Chomsky 1965), obligatoriness was a stipulated (global) property of a derivation. But these distinctions only involve the execution of obligatoriness; and obligatoriness is not, recall, the null hypothesis.

This optionality extends, of course, to what has been called 'vacuous' movement, the issue being whether *Who left?* contains an application of *wh*-movement or not.[19] On the theory offered here, there are two sentence-types, in one of which *wh*-movement applies and in the other of which it does not. The first is used to ask an open question, while the second is used to ask a confirmation question.

5.4 Ideal representation for variables, quantifiers, and *wh*-expressions

Wh-expressions and quantifier expressions differ semantically. With respect to a given universe of discourse, a quantifier states the quantity of items that must satisfy the open sentence in its scope, to yield truth. Quantifiers aim only to state the quantity of items. They are not directed to the identities of the items in question, as is the case with *wh*-expressions. The question *Which answer is false?* is directed toward the identity of the false answer. The statement *Each answer is false* is directed toward the quantity of the false answers.

There is an important difference, as well, between quantifier variables and *wh*-variables. Quantifier variables do not refer, and it is not required that they should. *Wh*-variables do not refer, but it is required that they should. Statements made using sentence-types containing quantifier variables are *true* if the right quantity of items satisfy a propositional function. Questions asked using sentence-types containing *wh*-variables are *truly answered* if the right items are produced. Note that neither kind of variable refers, and recall that both argument positions and adjunct positions are referring positions. Yet quantifier variables, which may appear in either position, do not refer. Rather, their presence in those positions results in a lowering of the referential requirement. With the lowering of the referential requirement, truth then depends on quantity of items, not on reference to items. *Wh*-variables also do not refer, but their presence does not reflect a lowering of the referential requirement, but rather a referential incompleteness. Answers must identify items; quantities will not suffice.

---

[19] See Chomsky 1986*a*.

This last point is central to my doctrine concerning questions, which began with the idea that questions spring from ignorance, that ignorance is a lack, and that, to express the lack one has, one utters a sentence-type containing a corresponding incompleteness. *Wh*-variables indicate a site of referential incompleteness. Syntactically, however, sentences that contain *wh*-variables are in fact complete.[20] They are syntactically complete by virtue of the fact that the *wh*-variables they contain are bound. But they are referentially incomplete, in contrast with sentences containing quantifiers. This is what makes them useful for the asking of questions.

Syntactic representations must indicate all aspects of the structures of sentence-types, and nothing must be represented that a sentence-type lacks.[21] In this connection, consider a logical structure that contains two quantifiers, Qx, and Qy, Qx binding x, and Qy binding y. Apart from the relative order of the variables, which has no bearing on the point to be raised here, there are two possible logical structures in the traditional notation meeting these conditions: $[Qx\,[Qy\,[\ldots x \ldots y \ldots]]]$ and $[Qy\,[Qx\,[\ldots x \ldots y \ldots]]]$. Suppose further that these are truth-conditionally equivalent; that the two quantifiers may commute without changing truth conditions (as in the English sentence *Someone loves someone*). Given this, does either logical structure meet the representational standard that I have imposed?

Plainly, if the two traditional structures are truth-conditionally equivalent, both may not be allowed. The principle is that there can be no superfluity in representation; these representations violate that by making opposite claims about the relative scopes of quantifiers where there is in fact no contrast to be represented. Now quite independently it might be held, for syntactic reasons alone, perhaps having to do with the application of movement, that one or the other structure is disallowed. But whichever structure syntax plumps for, the selected structure will itself represent something superfluous; there is no fact of relative scope that *either* logical representation represents. So not only is it the case that both should not be allowed; it is also the case that neither should be allowed. In a case like this, the unordered representation that I have proposed does a much better job. Instead of the two logical representations above that make opposing claims, there is the one representation $<\{Qx, Qy\},$ $<\ldots x \ldots y \ldots >>$, which correctly indicates that there is no relative scopal ordering of the two quantifiers, and also indicates, at the same time, that both variables are within their scopes.[22]

---

[20] These contrast with the case, discussed in Section 3.1.2, where a speaker literally fails to complete a sentence-type, namely, *You just talked to . . . ?*, said with a rolling motion of the hand. Such sentences *are* incomplete syntactically, as well as referentially.

[21] Here, at least, I follow the spirit of minimalism.

[22] This contrasts with the account of commutability given in May 1985 and Chomsky 1986*a* under very different structural assumptions.

5.4.1 The logical representation of *wh*-expressions and the overt marking of relative scope

On the basis of differences of interpretation between 'each' and 'every', I argued above that natural language quantification varies not only with respect to the force of the quantifiers it contains but also with respect to their manner of interpretation. 'Each' and 'every' differ as regards manner but not as regards force. Furthermore, 'which' and 'what' parallel 'each' and 'every' in that 'which' is Individualizing in manner and 'what' is Totalizing in manner. These facts have scopal consequences. Since 'which' is Individualizing, the distinction between asking *Which man saw which movie?* and asking *Which movie did which man see?* depends on a scopal contrast in their logical representations. But now we may ask what the connection is between the identities of the *wh*-expressions and the expression of scope. How can principles of syntax be sensitive to the fact that, generally, crossing one occurrence of 'who' by another is unavailing, while crossing one occurrence of 'which' by another generally is not? The answer is that syntax proper cannot know these things, but we can say that relative scope may be represented only if it is availing. The upshot of this is that distinct relative scopes of two quantifiers may be represented only if the reverse relative scope is distinct either in manner of interpretation (the intensional notion) or in truth conditions (the extensional notion). That conforms with what I have argued.

A process quite analogous to *wh*-movement is allowed in all languages; in Indo-European, the process is overtly marked, while in many non-Indo-European languages the process is entirely covert. In some languages, such as Bulgarian and Serbo-Croatian (Boščović 1999), and Hungarian (Liptak 2001), more than one *wh*-expression may be fronted overtly, but this does not occur in English. English allows *Who gave what to whom?*, but not *Who what whom gave to?* The conclusion has been reached that the distinction between languages that allow multiple overt *wh*-movement and those that do not is syntactic. For those languages like English in which only one *wh*-expression fronts overtly, there is reason to believe that they do all front covertly; the idea is that all *wh*-expressions front in all languages, but languages vary as regards how many are fronted overtly. There are many arguments to that conclusion, some independent and some theory-internal. I will rehearse here only one independent argument. It has been understood since Postal 1971 that the question *Who does his mother love?* cannot be awarded a logical structure which, in the traditional account, would be [who x [x's mother loves x]], since this question does not ask for people whose mothers love them. Assuming *wh*-movement, the generalization appears to be that an operator cannot bind a variable that it crosses, even one that does not c-command the original position of the operator. (Because the variable does not c-command the initial site of the *wh*-expression in this example, the crossing is called 'weak', in contrast to 'strong' cross-over in a sentence such as *Who did he think was wise?*, where the prospective variable pronoun does c-command the original site of the *wh*-expression.) But now consider *What did his mother give to whom?* Here we cannot understand the question as [what y [whom x [x's mother gave y to x]]] — that is, the question does not ask for pairs *x, y* such that *x*'s mother gave *y* to *x*. If 'whom' is analyzed as moving covertly, we simply have another instance of weak cross-over, but if it is not analyzed in this way, it is left a mystery why the sentence should not be understood in the indicated way. A parallel argument explains the fact that *His mother loves everyone* cannot be taken to mean [every x [x's mother loves x]], assuming a rule of quantifier raising (May 1985). The conclusion is that *wh*-expressions, as well as quantifiers, move covertly.

Consequently, the sentences *Which man saw which movie?* and *Which movie did which man see?* will be given the logical representations <Ix: man x, <Iy: movie y, <x, <saw, y>>>> and <Iy: movie y, <Ix: man x, <x, <saw, y>>>>, respectively. By what principle are the pronunciations correlated with their logical representations? It seems clear that the contrast is overtly marked in these cases. If a speaker wants his answer structured by men, the speaker should ask *Which man saw which movie?*, while if a speaker wants his answer structured by movies, the speaker should ask *Which movie did which man see?* The contrast is scopal. For a language such as English, the generalization in this case is:

> Given a sentence containing two or more *wh*-expressions, a *wh*-expression is split in overt syntactic structure if and only if it has wider scope than the other *wh*-expressions in logical structure.

This generalization does not exhaust the topic; it is silent concerning the relative scopes of non-fronted occurrences, such as the scopal relationship between 'which book' and 'which woman' in *Which man gave which book to which woman?* In addition, the principle leaves out cases in which two *wh*-expressions fail to stand in relative scope to each other. While in a sentence containing more than one expression of the form 'which N', there is a scopal relation between them, this is not so in the case of multiple *who*-questions, the topic of the next section, where the above generalization will have to be further refined.

5.5 The explanation for restrictions on crossing

I have argued that the oddness of sentence-types such as *What did who see?* is not to be explained as a syntactic violation, and that our intuitions concerning this type of sentence have been misinterpreted. We correctly consider such sentences odd, but that oddness is due to the recognition that the choice of such a sentence is, in a particular way, unavailing. It is clear that there can be no simple principle prohibiting one *wh*-expression from crossing another, since *Which movie did which man see?* is perfectly fine. Furthermore, for triple multiple questions, English allows not only *Who saw what where?*, but also *What did who see where?* and *Where did who see what?*, all of which are fine, a point due to Kayne (1984). The problem these data pose would seem to be why any crossing is prohibited at all. Why, specifically, is *What did who see?* unavailing? And why are *What did who see where?* and *Where did who see what?* not unavailing?

If, as I have suggested, *Who saw what?* and *What did who see?* are assigned the same logical structure, $<\{Wx: \text{person } x, Ty: \text{thing } y\}, <x, <\text{saw}, y>>>$, why is *Who saw what?* the preferred pronunciation?[23] Suppose that, other things being equal, crossing is not preferred. And suppose that other things are equal if the crossing leads to overt forms with the same logical structure. The overarching principle would be the following.

> In *wh*-questions, overt syntactic structures and covert logical structures are in one-to-one correspondence.[24]

According to the principle, there would not be cases in which one logical structure is derivationally related to two (or more) overt structures. Nor would there be cases in which one overt structure is derivationally related to two (or more) logical structures. When the former situation threatens, the syntactically more complex overt possibilities—the crossing cases—are pared away. It is important to add that the principle could not be extended to quantification, since there are sentences that are quantificationally ambiguous, which is to say, there are sentences with more than one covert form. Since, in English, *wh*-movement is overt and quantifier raising is covert, it is natural to think that the apparent limitation of this principle to *wh*-questions reflects the fact that speakers may choose among sentences containing distinct overtly moved *wh*-expressions for the very reason that they are overtly distinct. Given the choice of a potentially ambiguous sentence containing more than one quantifier, however, the speaker must take care that the intended scope is understood, there being no overt syntactic disambiguation.

The set-theoretic notation that I have adopted again shows its power in these examples. Where there are only two *wh*-expressions that do not interact scopally, such as in *Who saw what?* and *What did who see?*, there is only one unordered set in logical structure that contains them. Consequently, only one overt form is allowed; If the more complex form is pared away, only the simpler *Who saw what?* survives. However, when there are more than two *wh*-expressions in a sentence, set theory allows more distinguishable possibilities. Given three elements, and only unordered relations between them, there are three ways to

---

[23] Between the weak 'who' and the Totalizing 'what' we do not find a scopal interaction that would force a semantic choice sensitive to the structure of the answer sought. However, as mentioned in Section 4.5.2, that does not mean that a choice might not be made.

[24] Whether this principle can withstand the factual challenges that might be brought by the relative scopes of unfronted *wh*-expressions is not clear. The facts themselves are not clear.

combine them: $\{\{\alpha, \beta\}, \gamma\}$, $\{\alpha, \{\beta, \gamma\}\}$, and $\{\{\alpha, \gamma\}, \beta\}$. In the cases at hand, we may use these distinct structures to accommodate *Who put what where?*, *What did who put where?*, and *Where did who put what?*, whose logical structures will be, respectively:[25]

$<\{Wx: \text{person } x, \{Ty: \text{thing } y, Wz: \text{place } z\}\}, < x, <<\text{put}, y>, z>>>$,

$<\{Ty: \text{thing } y, \{Wx: \text{person } x, Wz: \text{place } z\}\}, < x, <<\text{put}, y>, z>>>$, and

$<\{Wz: \text{place } z, \{Wx: \text{person } x, Ty: \text{thing } y\}\}, < x, <<\text{put}, y>, z>>>$.

From this, it follows that crossing will be tolerated whenever there are more than two *wh*-expressions in a sentence. In such cases, there are, corresponding to each of the overt structures, distinct covert structures—which is not the case when there are only two *wh*-expressions. On a set-theoretic understanding of structure, the puzzles concerning the crossing of *wh*-expressions dissolve.

But there is a last point. I have argued that the preference of *Who saw what?* to *What did who see?* derives from their both having the logical structure: $<\{Wx: \text{person } x, Ty: \text{thing } y\}, <x, <\text{saw}, y>>$.[26] The uncrossed form is unmarked. But markedness only applies between competing forms; the sentence-types *Who saw what?* and *What did who see?* compete precisely because they have the same logical structure. And *Which man saw which movie?* and *Which movie did which man see?* do not compete, and are both allowed, precisely because they have different logical structures. I have suggested that the embracing principle is that there is a one-to-one correspondence between overt and covert structure, at least in the domain of multiple questions in English. One might give a derivational cast to the operative principle: the idea would be that *wh*-movement may not apply if the sentence that would be produced by doing so has the same logical structure as the sentence that would be produced by not doing so. But I believe that this would be an unfortunate way to view the matter. The application of *wh*-movement ought not to depend on the logical structure of the sentence. Rules such as *wh*-movement should be local, not global. Besides, there is a better alternative.

I have suggested as a bit of methodology that, ideally, there should be no notational distinctions in our representations of language where there are no differences to distinguish. Here we see a principle of that tenor applying within the object we are studying. It says that, at least in a certain domain, there may be no distinctions in pronunciation where there are no logical

---

[25] I assume here, without argument, that the manner of 'where' is weak.

[26] But it is equally true, notationally speaking, that they are both of the form $<\{Ty: \text{thing } y, Wx: \text{person } x\}, <x, <\text{saw}, y>>$. These two logical structures represent the same phrase-marker. Is this a defect of the notation I have chosen? In one sense it is. The ideal representation of an unordered set would be one in which there is no distinction between the positions of the inscriptions representing the members, since, when positional distinctness of two inscriptions exists, there will always be another representation in which the two are reversed in position. On the other hand, the positions of the inscriptions cannot coincide. So, while unsurpassed, our notation, if it is to be written down on a page, must stray from the ideal in this respect.

differences to be distinguished. Language, at least here, itself appears to embody a certain parsimoniousness of expression comparable to the methodological parsimony I have called ideal. Methodologically, the point is that a notational distinction should indicate a difference in expression-types being represented. Grammatically, within a certain domain, the point is that a distinction of pronunciation should indicate a distinction of logic.

5.6 Scopal differences and structural differences

Let us pursue the account of scope by further considering the logical structures for triple multiple questions, repeated here.

$$<\{Wx: \text{person } x, \{Ty: \text{thing } y, Wz: \text{place } z\}\}, < x, <<\text{put}, y>, z>>>,$$

$$<\{Ty: \text{thing } y, \{Wx: \text{person } x, Wz: \text{place } z\}\}, < x, <<\text{put}, y>, z>>>, \text{ and}$$

$$<\{Wz: \text{place } z, \{Wx: \text{person } x, Ty: \text{thing } y\}\}, < x, <<\text{put}, y>, z>>>.$$

In these three structures, each *wh*-expression dominates its trace, and each dominates the same nodes as the other two. Scopally, they are the same, yet each is dedicated to one and only one covert form. How do these forms differ, and how are they related to their overt forms?

Differences in scope are differences in dominance relations. Let the list of all ordered pairs of nodes in a phrase-marker that are such that the first node dominates the second be called the 'dominance set' of that structure. As dominance constitutes the structural expression of scope, two structures are scopally equivalent if and only if they are expressions of the same dominance sets. But given the coarse-grained definition of dominance assumed here, two phrase-markers that are scopally equivalent may nevertheless show structural differences. The above examples show that there may be significant differences in structure without there being any differences in scope. Difference in scope entails difference in structure, but the reverse is not true.

While the overt contrasts between *Who put what where?*, *What did who put where?*, and *Where did who put what?* are reflected in logical structure, assuming their representation as unordered sets, those structural contrasts are too fine to be reflected as differences in scope. Recall that in the case of the scope-bearing element 'which N', I was able to state the generalization:

> Given a sentence containing two or more *wh*-expressions, a *wh*-expression is split in overt syntactic structure if and only if it has wider scope than the other *wh*-expressions in logical structure.

But now we must cut finer. Let's say that in both $\{\alpha, \{\beta, \gamma\}\}$ and $<\alpha, <\beta, \gamma>>$, α is structurally 'prominent'. Formally defined:

> α is *prominent* with respect to β in set Σ if and only if α and β are members of Σ, α is an element of Σ, and β is not an element of Σ.

For example, in $\{\alpha, \beta\}$ and $<\alpha, \beta>$, neither α nor β is prominent with respect to the other, since both α and β are elements of their sets. In $\{\alpha, \{\beta, \gamma\}\}$ and $<\alpha, <\beta, \gamma>>$, however, $\{\beta, \gamma\}$ and $<\beta, \gamma>$, while they are members, are not elements; α is both an element and a member in both cases; so in both cases α is prominent. Note that an element with wider scope than another element will be prominent with respect to it, but that not all prominent elements will have wide scope. Given this, the previous generalization can now be replaced with the following principle:

> A *wh*-expression is promoted in overt structure if and only if it is structurally prominent in logical structure.

To illustrate, the sentence-type *What did who put where?*, in which 'what' is promoted overtly, can only be tied to the logical structure $<\{$Ty: thing y, $\{$Wx: person x, Wz: place z$\}\}$, $<x, <<$put, y$>$, z$>>>$, where its logical spelling-out is prominent, and the spellings-out of the other two *wh*-expressions are not. Taking this one step further, if quadruple multiple *wh*-questions are considered, it will be necessary to define *maximal* prominence, since these will have the covert structure $<\{\alpha, \{\beta, \{\gamma, \delta\}\}\}, \ldots >$, where both α and β are prominent.

Prominence is a syntactic relation, but it plays a role in the choices speakers face when they are deciding what to say. A speaker may ask a question in such a way as to indicate the structure of the answer he seeks. In order to do so, he chooses among sentence-types in the logical structures of which different *wh*-expressions are structurally prominent. If he intends to be taken as asking a question whose answer is in terms of a particular range of items, he should choose a sentence-type whose logical structure contains a structurally prominent expression binding a variable ranging over those items. Sometimes, as in the case of 'which N', the decisions will have scopal consequences; at other times, as in the case of multiple *who*-questions, the decision will have structural but not scopal consequences.

5.6.1 Dominance and prominence

Let's pause to consider the implications of a theory such as the one offered here, in which differences of structure cut finer than differences in scope.

Dominance syntactically expresses scope. Structures that are defined by the same dominance sets are semantically equivalent scopally, but need not be structurally equivalent. To accompany the notion of dominance set, let the list of all ordered pairs of nodes in a phrase-marker representation that are such that the first node is prominent with respect to the second be called the 'prominence set' of that representation. Representations that express the same prominence sets are structurally equivalent in every way; equivalence of syntactic structure may be defined in terms of equivalence of prominence sets.

I have observed that dominance replaces c-command in the notation advanced here, by which I meant that dominance expresses scope, which is what c-command has been said to do. But that is a functional way of viewing the matter. If the question is: What syntactic relation has the function of expressing scope?, the answer is c-command in standard accounts, and dominance in this one. But if the question is the purely formal one: What syntactic relation in the system I advocate is structurally most similar to c-command?, the answer is prominence, not dominance. In that formal sense, then, I believe syntacticians have been mistaken to think that c-command expresses scope. Again, the logical representation of multiple *who*-questions is telling.

There are also implications for speech-act theory. Speech-act theory concerns itself with the question how a speaker decides what to say. In deciding which sentence-type to utter a token of, we have seen that a speaker must sometimes go beyond dominance-equivalence to prominence-equivalence. Pragmatic choice imposes a finer-grained syntactic requirement than semantic choice. It has long been appreciated that pragmatics cuts finer than semantics, that semantics is a blunt-edged tool in comparison with pragmatics. But it has not often been appreciated, I think, that pragmatics and semantics might depend on different degrees of syntactic coarseness.

Certainly, in deciding what to say, a speaker must consider the linguistically determined meanings of sentence-types. And certainly the speaker must also consider the pragmatic implications of what is said. But these truisms may be implemented in different ways. To take a classic example from Grice (1975), suppose that a speaker wishes to assert that A and B. There are two candidate sentence-types to choose from. If the speaker believes that A occurred before B, and believes that his addressee believes that the maxim of manner is in force in the current circumstance, then he should use the sentence-type *A and B*, not *B and A*. The distinct sentence-types are semantically, but not pragmatically, equivalent. It is likely that this is typical of this kind of pragmatic choice, that the speaker chooses between distinct sentence-types with the same meaning.

But speakers do more than this. When deciding whether to say *A and B* or *B and A*, they are choosing among overt forms that are logically equivalent. That was Grice's point. But I have now gone a bit further, arguing that in some cases, speakers choose among overt forms that have the same logical dominance-structure, but distinct logical prominence-structures. If the term logic cuts no finer than dominance-structure, then speakers choose among logically equivalent but syntactically distinct structures.

To return to Grice's case, if a speaker wishes to say something with the logical structure [A & B], the choice depends on a belief concerning the order of events. A speaker chooses to say *A and B* instead of *B and A* because if he were to say *B and A*, he would be taken to believe that the event denoted by 'B' occurred first. So the choice depends on the speaker's desire not to misrepresent his beliefs. The reason behind the choice in Grice's example is different in kind from the reason behind the choice in the questioning case. The decision in the questioning case depends on how a speaker wants his answer structured. If the speaker intends to be taken as asking for an answer structured in terms of places, not people, the speaker should utter *Where did who see what?*, not *Who saw what where?* If the speaker nevertheless utters *Who saw what where?*, he will not have asked for an answer structured in the way that he intended the answer to be structured. He will be taken to have asked for something, and indeed will have asked for something, that he did not intend to ask for. So the choice depends on which answer the questioner intends to ask for.

There are both differences and points of comparison between a speaker's desire not to misrepresent his beliefs and a speaker's desire not to ask for information he does not want. Grice's maxims, by and large, state circumstances a speaker should avoid so as not to misrepresent his beliefs. The questioning case suggests that there are also circumstances a speaker should avoid so as not to misrepresent his goals. The maxim governing the conjunction case is the maxim of manner, one provision of which is that the speaker should be orderly. The maxim governing the questioning case is in some ways similar. Speakers are sensitive to a rule that states that the overtly promoted *wh*-expression is prominent in logical structure. This rule expresses a purely syntactic relationship between different syntactic levels of representation. Relying on that rule, the speaker may choose the sentence-type that correctly indicates his goal. The maxim might be stated as:

Be clear as to your goals.

The principle of sentence choice for asking a *wh*-question will then be:

If one wants one's answer structured in terms of a particular class of items, choose a sentence-type in which the *wh*-expression binding a variable ranging over that class of entities is prominent.

5.7 The indication of saturation

A syntactically well-formed phrase-marker representation may contain an argument position or an adjunct position that is referentially incomplete. A phrase-marker representation may also lack the glue. A sentence-type such as *Who did Jack see?* shows incompleteness in both ways. I have suggested that when phrase-markers contain expressions in particular positions, the predicate is saturated; and when phrase-markers lack expressions in those positions, the predicated is unsaturated. Let's call the corresponding positions in phrase-marker representations 'completion positions'. Without exception, phrase-marker representations whose completion positions are unfilled represent phrase-markers containing unsaturated predicates. And generally, phrase-marker representations whose completion positions are filled represent phrase-markers containing saturated predicates. The expectation is that all sentence-types used to ask open questions, including those that show *wh*-splitting, should show inversion: an uninverted sentence-type signifies that the predicate is saturated, and that cannot be the case if either (part of) the subject or (part of) the predicate is incomplete.

There is, however, one class of sentence-types used to ask *wh*-questions which appear to be exceptions to this last generalization: in English, we have *Who left?*, in which the completion position would appear to be filled.[27] Why is this allowed? In English, Tense fills completion position. Phrase-marker representations containing Tense in completion position represent phrase-markers whose predicates are saturated.[28] I assume that Tense position is the first position in a predicate; complete sentence-types will be represented as $<a$, $<$Tense, $\beta>>$, and incomplete sentence-types will be represented as $<$Tense, $<a$, $<t$, $\beta>>>$. In the first case, a represents a subject, and $<$Tense, $\beta>$ represents a saturated sentential predicate, while in the second case $<t$, $\beta>$ represents an unsaturated predicate, where 't' is the trace of Tense. This suffices to describe inversion in open *yes-no* questions. In the case of *wh*-questions, we have the generalization that if either the subject or the predicate *properly* contains a *wh*-trace, the completion position must be unfilled. Thus we have *Who were you looking at?*, where the predicate properly contains a *wh*-trace, but not *Who you were looking at?* And where the subject properly contains a *wh*-trace, we have *Who was a picture of lying on the table?*, but not *Who a picture of was lying on the table?* There is, however, an important asymmetry between subjects and predicates. (The trace of) a *wh*-expression may completely cover subject position, but no trace of a *wh*-expression may completely cover predicate position. We have *Who left?*, but neither *What did John?* or *What John?* (angling either for the predicate minus Tense or the whole predicate) nor the multiple open question *Who said John what?* (said as a confirmation question, this last sentence is, of course, fine). Thus traces of *wh*-expressions in predicates will always be properly contained in those predicates, while traces of *wh*-expressions in subjects may fill those positions. When this last occurs, we have subjects that are *wh*-traces and no inversion: Tense remains in completion position in *Who left?*, and that is unexpected.

One way to face the difficulty, and the one I prefer, is to say that inversion indicates lack of saturation only in the circumstance in which neither subject position nor predicate position constitutes a site of incompleteness. In English,

---

[27] I am talking here of the sentence-type *Who left?* which is used to ask an open question and in which *wh*-movement applies, discussed at the end of Section 5.3.

[28] Note that the analysis of inversion is different from the analysis of *wh*-splitting, according to which the moved element and its trace contain complementary powers. That analysis is appropriate for *wh*-splitting, since, in essence, *wh*-splitting expresses a linguistic universal: splitting a *wh*-expression into an operator and a variable yields a logical 'construction'. This is probably not the case with the inversion of Tense; certainly not every language that has Tense displays inversion overtly, as English does. I have chosen to use the term 'predicate' to denote a constituent that has Tense on its edge. Whether completion positions must be on the edge of predicates is left open, though various languages clearly speak to the issue.

only the first occurs, and when it does, it is otherwise plain that the predicate cannot be saturated, since the subject is incomplete. Alternatively, it might be proposed that the exception is removed at the level at which it really counts, logical structure. There is a difficult choice here between use and grammar; more will have to be learned to make it in an informed way. In either case, by asking a *wh*-question, the speaker asks that an item be produced such that, if it is taken as the value of the variable, a yet-to-be-saturated predicate becomes saturated.

5.7.1 The completeness of indirect questions and the absence of inversion

I have argued that *wh*-splitting results in a site of referential incompleteness at the position of the variable. I have now also argued that inversion occurs in *wh*-questions because the presence of Tense in the completion position would incorrectly indicate that the predicate was saturated. This second principle explains why we do not see inversion in relative clauses, which are referentially complete, as mentioned in Section 4.3.1. Things are quite different in indirect questions such as *John asked who you were looking at*, however. Note that, generally speaking, when one utters a sentence that contains an indirect question one does not thereby ask a question. Also, there is no inversion in indirect questions. But are they referentially complete or incomplete?

It should be said at the outset that the term 'indirect question', as it applies to this construction, is partly misleading. It seems reasonable to say that, in the example just cited, 'who you were looking at' does refer to what the question *Who were you looking at?* expresses. To be sure, John need not have used those particular words; there are many ways to ask who someone is looking at. For *John asked who you were looking at* to be true, it is required only that what would be expressed by *Who were you looking at?* be close to what John in fact expressed. How close depends on circumstance. There are hard questions here, but it seems clear that the indirect question 'who you were looking at' refers more or less to what John's question expressed.

What I have said about 'ask' can be said for some other verbs that take similar complements, such as 'wonder', 'be curious', and 'worry about'. But the indirect question construction occurs after another class of verbs, which includes 'know', 'forget', and 'remember'. In these cases, it cannot be said that the indirect question refers to what some question expresses. In *John knew who you were looking at*, the indirect question refers not to the question, but to the proposition expressed by what would count as a correct *answer* to the question *Who were you looking at?*[29] The term 'indirect question' does justice to only one side of an ambiguous construction.

---

[29] I realize how rough this is.

On either side of this ambiguity, however, it can be argued that indirect questions are referentially complete expressions. If John asked who you were looking at, then there is something that John asked. If John knew who you were looking at, then there is something that John knew, and so forth. But there is a further fact to be noted. The reference that we find in indirect questions is indeed indirect. So in this respect, indirect questions are well-named. *John knew who Cicero was* may be true while *John knew who Tully was* is false. So, if we are to follow Frege here, if there is any referential incompleteness in indirect questions, that incompleteness is incompleteness of *indirect* reference.

Although indirect questions display *wh*-splitting, I have now observed that they are referentially complete. In that respect, they contrast with *wh*-questions, which are referentially incomplete. The indirect question 'who you were looking at' names what is expressed by a question. What is expressed by the question *Who were you looking at?* includes an incompleteness and the proviso that the incompleteness be filled by one or more people. The corresponding parts of 'who you were looking at' refer to those two things. It is therefore not surprising that *wh*-splitting must occur in indirect questions; there are two things in what *wh*-questions express that must be referred to, and the expressions referring to what *wh*-questions express must make provision for that fact.

As for inversion, things are a little less clear. It should be noted that the tense morpheme that actually appears in an indirect question is not independent; its identity depends on the tense morpheme that appears in the matrix sentence. A sequence-of-tense rule determines whether the tense is present or past. In *John asked who you were looking at*, the verb 'were' must be past tense because the verb 'asked' is in the past tense, whether John asked a past-tense question or not. It is therefore possible to say that there is no (independent) Tense in indirect questions, and that the completeness position (indirectly) denotes the absence of saturation. No inversion is needed, since, unlike the case of *wh*-questions, we need reference to only one thing, in this case, the absence of saturation. But this is speculative; there is certainly a great deal about indirect reference and indirect questions that we do not know.

5.7.2 The absence of inversion and *wh*-splitting in confirmation questions

Recall that in confirmation questions such as *You saw who?*, there is neither inversion nor *wh*-splitting, even covertly. I have argued that confirmation questions are, in comparison with assertions, incomplete in the performing of them. While open questions are referentially incomplete, what is missing in the repeat question *You saw who?* is not the person seen, but an expression referring to the person seen. When the *wh*-expression is not split, the complementary power to bind and power to be bound cancel each other out, leaving behind only the phi features—in this case, the human element. The confirmation question

You saw who? asks that the addressee complete the sentence *You saw (person)*. If an expression such as 'Max' replaces 'who', there is completion. The expression 'Max' would be the correct answer to the repeat question *You saw who?*, if the addressee had said *I saw Max*. In contrast, Max is the correct answer to *Who did you see?* if the addressee saw Max. The absence of *wh*-splitting in confirmation questions indicates that it is not values of expressions that are missing, but expressions themselves. Similarly, the absence of inversion in confirmation *yes-no* questions indicates that the predicate is saturated; what is lacking are beliefs of sufficient strength to license assertion. From this it follows that confirmation questions cannot be pair-list questions. While the open question *What did you give to whom?* asks for a list of pairs of gifts and people, the confirmation question *You gave what to whom?* cannot do that. If asked as a multiple repeat question, the correct answer would be *I gave money to the NRA* if the addressee had previously said *I gave money to the NRA*. If the addressee had previously said *I gave money, food, and lodging to Tom, Dick, and Harry*, then the answer to *You gave what to whom?* will be *I gave money, food, and lodging to Tom, Dick, and Harry*, but that is not a pair-list answer since the two (conjoined) expressions that were originally said are merely repeated.

There is a difference between not knowing whether a particular item falls under a particular predicate and not having beliefs strong enough to license the assertion that a particular item falls under a particular predicate. In the first instance, one takes up item and predicate and wonders whether the first falls under the second. In the second instance, one takes up a complete sentence and wonders whether it is 'true enough' to assert. In the first case, one is concerned about items and properties, things-in-the-world. In the second case, one is concerned about bits of language that might be used to assert something concerning things-in-the-world. The first concern gives rise to open questions; the second concern gives rise to confirmation questions.

5.8 Summary

The fragment of syntax that I have sketched contains phrase-marker representations composed of both ordered and unordered sets. It is neutral as between phrasal structure and adjunction structure. Phrase-marker representations represent phrase-markers, which are themselves atemporal. Syntax also contains splitting rules, which are optional in their application. There is no feature-driven movement; there is no 'Q' morpheme that serves to trigger movement. Dominance and prominence are relations between elements in phrase-marker representations. The first represents scope, the second is finer-grained.

It has been my goal to distinguish grammatical structure from use, and within grammatical structure, to distinguish syntax from semantics. One of the findings is that syntactically related structures have distinct uses. *Which man saw which movie?* and *Which movie did which man see?* are syntactically related by optionality of application, but they are distinct in use. Similarly, *Is Max here?* and *Max is here?* are syntactically related by optionality of application, but distinct in use. In this latter case, however, we also have a formal difference, involving the lack or presence of saturation.

It has also been my goal to distinguish representations from the things they represent. We found that this bit of methodology is echoed in grammar itself: at least in one domain, overt distinctness of pronunciation is allowed only if there is distinctness in what would be expressed. Otherwise, the syntactically marked structure is pared away. There are principles that allow speakers to choose which sentence-type to utter, depending on the structure of the answer they wish to receive. These decisions are sensitive to the detailed syntactic structures of sentence-types; to a certain extent, sentence-types overtly indicate structural properties that would make them suitable for the performance of certain tasks.

6

On the Questioning Speech-acts
and the Kinds of Ignorance they Address

6.1 What the questioner is asking for

In this book, I have isolated some aspects of the syntactic structure of English that a speaker commands, some speech-acts that sentence-types may be deployed to perform, and some of the rules that a speaker must be sensitive to when deciding which structure to put to a particular use. On the side of form, there is the fact that speakers know a great many bits of linguistic legislation, some of it involving the meanings of words, some of it involving the structures of sentence-types, and some of it involving the interpretations of sentence-types. Prominent among these, for a questioner, are: the formal distinction between deformed and undeformed sentence-types and the kinds of incompleteness that deformity results in; the distinction between sentence-types that contain *wh*-expressions and those that do not; and the distinctions of manner among *wh*-expressions, such as the Totalizing manner of 'what' and the Individualizing manner of 'which'. Languages vary in these regards: many do not have this last distinction overtly marked, if at all, and neither do inversion and splitting always appear overtly, if at all. On the side of use, there is the broad distinction between asking an open question and asking a confirmation question, and a great many variations of each on either side of the divide. Many of these were exemplified in Chapter 3, and I will be cutting the uses of open questions, at least in one important respect, even finer in this chapter. Also on the side of use, there are certain rules that speakers follow when deciding which sentence-type to utter a token of. Our ignorances are varied; certain usings of incomplete sentence-types, and certain incompletenesses in the usings of sentence-types, lend themselves to addressing them. Further, at least in the case of multiple *wh*-questions, choices among overt structures depend in part on whether those structures are syntactic variants of logically the same sentence-type. In sum, the sentence-types formally allowed are, in virtue of the fact that they have the structures that they do, appropriate tools for performing certain tasks but not others, and there are rules of use making reference to this kind of consideration.

In this chapter, I will again be leaning heavily on Austin's (1953) analysis of speech-acts—his 'quartet'.[1] I will take up some very short, if not very simple, sentence-types so as to illustrate the interplay between the various factors that go into the asking of a question. With the formal analysis now in place, I wish here to position this analysis within a broader speech-act theory. In speech-act terms, some apparently simple cases, such as *Who is the thief?*, will turn out to be quite complex, as will *Who is stealing what?*, *Who is who?*, and *Which is which?* These last cases will allow me to consider the nature of identity statements and their corresponding identity questions. Over and above these matters, there is the fact that by asking a question, a speaker may ask either for a thing-in-the-world, such as an item or a property, or a piece of language, such as a name or a predicate. This fact, noticed by Austin, has enormous implications for the analysis both of questions and of questioning.

6.2 Asking for things-in-the-world and asking for bits of language

Austin is well known for pointing out, in *How to do Things with Words* (1962) and in other places, that there are a great many different speech-acts; part of his complaint against the logical positivists is that, once this fact is understood, truth, as far as the analysis of natural language is concerned, is not as central as it is cracked up to be. He argues that a great many speech-acts are not in the business of being true or false, and that, if they are not in that business, it seems wrong to call them nonsense because they are not in principle provable. The speech-acts could justly say in their own defense that they were not in the least trying to be provable.

Austin is less well known for pointing out, in 'How to Talk—some simple ways' (1953), that the one speech-act that arguably is in the business of being provable—the assertion—is, if examined closely, not one speech-act, but four. So in addition to arguing that truth and provability are not criterial to the speech-act, he also argues that truth is too coarse-grained a notion to distinguish among the speech-acts in which it does figure. He arrives at this second conclusion by concocting an artificial, minimal language that contains only sentences of the form 'I is-a T', where 'I' may be replaced by individual-referring expressions and 'T' by predicates, and imagining the use of such sentences in an austerely minimal speech-situation. He finds that even in such reduced circumstances, four distinct assertive speech-acts can be discerned. We are left to infer that any language that properly contains Austin's minimal language, used in any speech-situation that properly contains his austere speech-situation, will perforce give rise to the

---

[1] Austin's quartet is pervasive. To see its application in the analysis of a quite different phenomenon—the behavior of the Japanese particle '-wa'— see Fiengo and McClure 2002.

distinctions he uncovered. We are also left to infer that the differences in assertive speech-acts that he uncovered in English arise neither because of the structural complexities of English nor because of the complexities of the settings in which it is used. They arise with the possibility of predication, as he understands it.[2] Given the nature of his brief, Austin looks only at the very simplest sentence-types; I will be examining some more complicated cases here.

In Section 4.6, I suggested that, corresponding to Austin's quartet of assertive speech-acts, there are four questioning speech-acts, and I organized the *wh*-expressions of English with respect to the four questioning speech-acts they may be standardly used to perform. I now wish to examine the relationship between the questioning speech-acts and the assertive speech-acts further. Austin's quartet of assertive speech-acts, reproduced in Table 6.1, results from the cross-cutting of 'direction of fit' with 'onus of match'—in a Calling, for example, the item is given and the predicate produced, with the onus of match on the predicate.

Table 6.1. Austin's quartet

	Onus of match	
	On sense of predicate	On type of item
Direction of fit		
Item given, predicate produced	Calling	Describing
Predicate given, item produced	Exemplifying	Classing

In questioning, a speaker asks that something be produced. In answering, the respondent produces something. If the answer is responsive to the question, the thing produced is the thing asked for. So it makes sense that, if the assertive speech-acts are individuated, in part, with respect to the kinds of things that are produced, and if the questioning speech-acts are individuated, in part, with respect to the kinds of things that are to be produced, and if, lastly, there really are responsive answers to questions, as seems clear, the speciation of the questioning speech-acts will, in part, complement the speciation of the assertive speech-acts. It is reasonable to expect that the two dimensions, direction of fit and onus of match, that distinguish Austin's assertive four speech-acts, are echoed in the questioning speech-acts—one can, for example, ask a Calling question, a question specifically designed to elicit a Calling in response.

Often, responses are assertions. An assertion is true if the item referred to by the subject is of a type that matches the sense of the predicate. The matching of type to sense, or sense to type, is Austin's glue. Like most other conceptions of predication, it is asymmetrical, designed in such a way that it allows him to distinguish the four ways in which it might arise. A question, on the other hand,

[2] In his system, the distinct assertive speech-acts are defined in terms of the matching of type of item and sense of predicate. Without matching, they cannot arise.

asks that something be produced which is such that, if it is added to the mix, a matching between type of item and sense of predicate is achieved. There is no matching in the question. Rather, different kinds of things may be given, and different things asked for, to yield match.[3]

When asserting, we take one thing as given and produce the other. The speaker either takes an item as given and produces a predicate to fit to it, or takes a predicate as given, and produces an item to fit to that predicate. At least that is how it works in the simplest cases. In correspondingly simple questions, there is also one thing given and one thing to be produced. When questioning, we may lack either an item or a bit of language, a predicate perhaps. If we have an item, we may ask that a predicate be produced, or, if we have predicate, we may ask that an item be produced. Responsive answers take the form of assertions, in which the predicate or the item is produced. Of course, when we ask our interlocutors to produce items, we know they do not carry those items around with them, as Jonathan Swift imagined, ready to place them on the table should they be asked for; rather we expect that those items will be produced by name or by description, or by one of a number of other linguistic or non-linguistic devices. Sometimes, what we primarily want produced are the relevant items; the verbiage is just the means by which the items are produced. But at other times, the verbiage is exactly what is in question.[4]

We can, of course, talk about bits of language. When we do, we treat them as we would any other things-in-the-world. When we say that 'mouse' is ambiguous, we say something about an item that happens to be a bit of language. We can ask that items that happen to be bits of language be produced, and we can take them as given. We can ask that a predicate be produced, or we can ask that the property that it refers to be produced. We can ask that a name be produced, or the item that it refers to. And we can take any of these as given. But Austin noticed a distinction between using a name or a description to refer to an item, and using a name or a description to Call the item *by* its name or description. If you ask me to identify a bird—if you ask, for example, *What bird is that?*—and I respond *That is a nuthatch*, the term 'nuthatch' is used to call the bird a nuthatch, and in such an act of Calling, the identity of the expression used is precisely what is important. But, in the sentence *That is a nuthatch* the expression 'nuthatch' is not mentioned. The traditional use/mention distinction does not comfortably accommodate the Calling use of expressions, although that use is very common.[5]

---

[3] Austin (1953) barely mentions questions. Here I am assuming that he would agree with me as against Frege that *yes-no* questions are glueless, not expressing complete thoughts.

[4] Here we make contact with the distinction between referential and attributive use, introduced in Donnellan 1966 and discussed in Kripke 1979. If, in the referential use, the words are incidental, merely a means to an end, the question would be whether the referential use is only appropriate when the item is given. And if, in the attributive use, the words are not incidental, the question would be whether the attributive use is only appropriate when the item is produced. There is fertile ground here.

[5] Specifically, the traditional use/mention distinction underrates the complexity of use.

The example just given is perhaps the simplest and most overt kind of Calling, and Calling is only used here to exemplify the complexities of the quartet. We will see that many more complex kinds of sentence-types may also be used to perform the questioning speech-acts.

To what extent is the choice between asking for a thing-in-the-world and asking for a bit of language reflected in the structures of the sentence-types that are used in each case? May a sentence-type that in one circumstance is used to ask for a thing-in-the-world be used in another circumstance to ask for a name or description that refers to it? I will offer at least the beginnings of an investigation of this largely unexplored area.

6.3 Asking for properties and asking for predicates; the distinction between Calling questions and Describing questions

Suppose I want to find out what something is called. Although I might say *What is that called?*, I might also say *What is that?* In this last case, several things might be meant, and care would have to be taken that, when I say *What is that?*, I will be understood to be asking what it is called. Whichever way the question is asked, what is desired to be produced is a bit of language. This point is easy to miss, due to an assumption, commonly made, concerning the semantic structures of sentence-types. It is commonly held that, in the case of sentence-types that are used to express singular propositions, the subject refers to an item and the predicate to a property. There are various doctrines as to what an item is, what a property is, and how one cashes in the idea that an item *has* a property, but accounts generally agree that if the item has the property, the sentence, or a statement making use of it, counts as true. But this picture can lead to the conclusion that, when a *wh*-expression 'covers' the position of a predicate, as it does in *What is that?* (which, recall, is of the form '[what [that is___]]'), a property is always being asked for, not a predicate. That is not correct, as the current example shows: when a question such as *What is that?* is used to ask someone what he calls a thing, as it quite often is, a predicate is being asked for, not a property.

Let's look at some cases. An adult French speaker learning English might hold up a screwdriver and ask *What is this?* Now in a perfectly straightforward sense, most adults know what screwdrivers are, and screwdrivers are common in France. What French speakers learning English might well not know is what screwdrivers are called in English, and to alleviate that ignorance, one of them might well hold up a screwdriver and say *What is this?* The point can be made within a single language as well. Suppose that you hold up an odd-looking tool from my collection and say *What is this?* And suppose that you intend to be taken as asking me what I call that thing, and suppose further that I correctly divine your intentions and respond: *That is a croze*. The first thing to see is that, as the question is intended and as I have taken it, mine is a perfectly adequate response. On hearing the answer, you might not know what the tool is used for or what sort of person uses the tool—if, for example, you were unfamiliar with the predicate 'croze'—but that is not what you were asking for. You wanted to know what I call the thing, and I have told you. I did my job completely, and performed what Austin termed a Calling speech-act.

Now suppose that your curiosity goes further, and you go on to ask *What is a croze?* ([what [a croze is__]]). (Or suppose, exasperated, you say again *What is that?*) Here it is unlikely that you are asking what I *call* a croze. I just told you that. I call a croze a croze. Rather, you now wish to know what the thing that you now know I call a croze *is*. And taking you that way, I might answer: *A croze is a cooper's tool*. Now here my goal is not primarily to produce a predicate, but rather to produce a property. I produce a property *by* uttering a predicate, and there are related properties that I could have produced by saying other things: I could have said *A croze cuts the groove for the head of a barrel*. Both responses are appropriate because, when you ask *What is a croze?*, you do not know what property the term '(is a) croze' refers to, and want to find out. You want now to get past the verbiage and find out what the thing *is*. In my answer, I perform what Austin termed a Describing speech-act.[6]

So Calling and Describing are distinct assertive speech-acts that one may be performing when answering Calling and Describing questions. The speaker who asks *What is that?* may be angling either for a predicate or the property that it denotes; one sentence-type serves for both purposes. The distinction between Calling and Describing is perhaps easiest to see when we want to find out someone's name. If you ask me of the strange pet I own *Who is that?* and I respond *That's Teddy*, you cannot ask me to further unpack the name I have provided you with. That names, like predicates, are unpackable is something that Frege believed, and Mill did not. In common discourse, we treat them as not unpackable, and perhaps, from a certain point of view, this is an argument for Mill. In any event, in the case at hand, you ask for the name, I give it to you, and that is that. You may want to know more about Teddy, however, and, if you do, you may ask the Describing question *What's Teddy?* ([what [Teddy is__]]).

One last case. Suppose we are gazing at a flower in normal lighting conditions, both of us having normal vision, and I say to you *What color is it?* ([what color [it is__]]). You might respond *It is vermilion*. Plainly, I have again asked a Calling question, and you, answering appropriately, have performed a Calling. I have

---

[6] Here we touch the complicated question what speech-act defining is, and how defining relates to Austin's quartet. If I say *If something is a croze, it is used to cut the groove for the head of a barrel*, I describe crozes. If I say *The word 'croze' refers to tools that cut the groove for the head of a barrel*, I define 'croze'. Both respond to the question *What is a croze?* Or is it that we may ask both *What is a croze?* and *What is a 'croze'?* There are not distinct pronunciation-types for these last two.

asked you to produce a bit of language. I could not, without misleading, ask you to produce the color itself (by whatever means), since I *have* that, being able to see it clearly. What I do not have, and what you correctly take me not to have, is the name of the color. Notice that if instead you reply *It is a bright showy red*, you have failed me. I can *see* it is a bright showy red; what I want to know is the name of the color. I don't need you to Describe, I need you to Call. On the other hand, suppose we are discussing a flower that grows in Argentina that I have never seen. In this case, I might ask *What color is it?* to ask for the property, not a bit of language, a property that may be provided by name ('vermilion'), or by description ('a bright showy red').

It has been my doctrine that ignorance is a lack, and that, when questioning, one displays incompleteness either in the sentence-type chosen or in the performing of the speech-act in which the sentence-type is used. Open questions may be asked using sentence-types that display ignorance of predicates, and open questions may be asked by using sentence-types that display ignorance of properties. Let's now briefly revisit confirmation questions. Confirmation questions reveal incompleteness in their performance, and, at least sometimes, the completion requires the utterance of a predicate. A natural question arises. How are open questions that ask for predicates different from confirmation questions that do? To address this, we may compare Calling questions to those confirmation questions in which the predicate is covered by a *wh*-expression. Consider the open Calling question *What is that?* and the similar confirmation repeat question *That is what?* Both, it would appear, may be asked to elicit the Calling of a bird. Both may be answered by producing a predicate, such as 'a nuthatch'. Yet there are differences. If the confirmation question is a repeat question, the difference is obvious. In the open Calling case, the speaker asks by what predicate the item is called. In the confirmation repeat case, such as would occur when I have said *That is (mumble)*, and you ask *That is what?*, you are asking what predicate I have just called the item; you are asking that the previous utterance be completed. Though their answers may be the same, these are, of course, quite different questions.

Interrogation scenarios provide a closer contrast. Suppose that the district attorney has me on the stand, and, pointing to a tool from my collection, says *That is what?* Here I have not previously said *That is a croze*, as in the case of the repeat question. And, just as in the case of the open Calling question *What is that?*, my interrogator wants me to produce a predicate, a predicate by which the item is called. How do these two cases differ? Only in terms of how the questioner presents herself. By asking *What is that?*, the speaker presents herself as not knowing what predicate applies to that. By asking *That is what?*, the speaker presents herself as unable to complete her utterance.[7] Again, the answers are the same, but, also again, the questions are different.

---

[7] In leading questions, this presentation is often pretense; as is often said, a good lawyer never asks a question she does not know the answer to.

To return to the main argument, there is good reason to believe that open Calling questions ask for pieces of language to be produced. It is wrong to think that it is always a property that one is angling for, not a predicate; to think this is to assume that we always ask Describing questions, and never Calling questions. In the next section, we will see that when a speaker asks for a bit of language, the *wh*-expression deployed does not always cover 'predicate position'. In Austin's minimal language, and in the croze and vermilion examples, this was true, but when more complicated sentence-types are taken on board, it becomes clear that the phenomenon is more extensive.

6.4 Calling, Exemplifying, and Classing questions

6.4.1 The distinction between Calling questions and Exemplifying questions

When using a sentence-type of the form '[who [. . .___. . .]]', where the gap appears in any argument position, does a speaker angle for an item or for a bit of language? It turns out that a speaker may do either.

When one asks a question there is something that one does not have, but also, there are other things that one does have. Sometimes, one has an item and wants the addressee to say what he calls it; that is a good time to ask a Calling question. At other times, one has an item and wants the addressee to produce a property of it; that is a good time to ask a Describing question. Conversely, a speaker may have a predicate and want the addressee to provide an item that falls under it. In that event, the speaker might ask an Exemplifying question. At still other times, the speaker may have a predicate, and want items classified with respect to it; that is the time for a Classing question. Given the division between language and the world it is used to talk about, one often is in the position of having something from one side of the divide and then asking that something from the other side be produced. When 'who' is used, we have people on one side of the divide, and their names or descriptions on the other. A *who*-question may thus be used to elicit either a Calling or an Exemplifying response.

Suppose a speaker observes a boy before him. Assume that the boy is alone, well-lit, and that there is no trickery in the observation itself, no difficulty in singling the boy out. The speaker might say *Who is that?* The structure would be [who [that is___]], and it would be answered by something like *That is Oliver*, the bit of language 'Oliver' being produced. But the answer cannot be *That is him* (pointing at the boy). Take a another case. Assume the boy, still clearly lit as before, is again observed in the act of stealing a cow. The speaker, curious as to the identity of the thief, may ask the question *Who is stealing my cow?*, using a sentence-type whose structure is [who [___ is stealing my cow]], a structure in which the predicate is given. To this question, the answer might be *Oliver is stealing your cow.* Or the answer might be *Fagin's apprentice is stealing your cow.* But again, the answer *He is stealing your cow,* said while pointing at the boy, will not do. Why should that be? Clearly, in the cases considered, pointing out the boy provides the questioner with nothing that he does not already have. He has the boy; what he wants produced is a bit of language with which to refer to him. And the questioner wants that bit of language not so as to be able to pick the boy out (since the questioner can already do that), but rather so that he will have either the boy's name, or his description, something that he might use for other purposes. So, in the asking of *Who is stealing my cow?,* although the sentence-type is one in which a predicate ('stealing my cow') is given, the speaker is not using it to demand an item. The thief (Oliver, if the respondent is correct) is given, and the identifying expression ('Oliver', or 'Fagin's apprentice') is to be produced by the addressee. In the event, which sort of expression is produced depends on a variety of factors, but a demonstrative expression will not do. Demonstratives point to items, but that is not what the questioner is angling for. The questioner, rather, given an item, the boy, is angling for a bit of language to refer to him with. The questioner is asking a Calling question, demanding a Calling response.

A *who*-question may, in other circumstances, be used to demand an Exemplifying response. Suppose, suddenly noticing the absence of his cow, the speaker asks *Who stole my cow?* Then the answer might be *Oliver stole your cow,* or *Fagin's apprentice stole your cow,* or *He stole your cow,* this last said while pointing to the boy. Oliver might be well-known to the questioner, yet not be known to be the item *in* question. In producing Oliver, by whichever means, the respondent is performing an Exemplifying. Here the respondent knows that the questioner does not have the item, the thief, and helpfully produces him. In the previous case, I set the circumstances up in such a way that the item in question was in front of and plain to the questioner, and put the question in the present progressive, thereby setting the stage for the asking of a Calling question as against an Exemplifying question, in which the past tense was used to suggest the circumstance in which the item was not present. But such scenarios are not necessary to the asking of a Calling question. All that is necessary to the sincere asking of a Calling question, at least all that is of relevance here, is that the questioner not believe that he has the bit of language in question, and all that is necessary to the sincere asking of an Exemplifying question is that the questioner not believe that he has the item in question.

This brings us back to Austin's minimal language. Within the confines of that language, it is possible to see that either a thing-in-the-world or a bit of language may be produced. I have suggested that the questioning speech-acts mirror this: that distinct questioning speech-acts can angle either for things-in-the-world or bits of language, asking that one or the other be produced. But the division is not one simply marked by questions angling for subjects and ones angling for predicates, a conclusion that might be drawn if attention were restricted to Austin's minimal language. Rather, a question, in the expression of which a *wh*-expression binds an argument position, may angle either for a thing-in-the-world or a bit of language. And a question, in the expression of which a *wh*-expression binds a predicate position, may angle either for a property or a predicate.[8]

It is instructive that a demonstrative pronoun may be used to produce an item but not to produce a bit of language. In fact, a mere pointing, performed in silence, may be used to produce an item. This makes demonstratives useful for testing which questioning speech-act has been performed. To the questions asked, the respondent might have produced Oliver merely by pointing at him, or even at a picture of him. Might the respondent have pointed at a written occurrence of the word 'Oliver' and thereby have answered that Oliver stole the cow? The speaker might have been able to pull that off. The speaker would have required his addressee to reason that he has pointed to a written occurrence of the word 'Oliver' because he intends to be taken as meaning that a person whose name is 'Oliver' did it. Fine, but Oliver's name is not the same thing as that written occurrence of the word 'Oliver', and the speaker would have to be confident that my addressee could make the leap. The reference is indirect or 'deferred', via a spoken or written occurrence of the name, in the way that we refer to people by demonstrating their pictures.[9] Can an expression-type be directly referred to demonstratively? The problem is that names do not exist in space and time, and the use of demonstrative expressions is hazardous when pursued outside the normal dimensions. There certainly are cases in which the expression 'that name' refers to a name previously mentioned, but in each such case it could be argued that the occurrence of 'that name' is anaphoric.[10] So we arrive at the question whether there are any non-anaphoric occurrences of 'that name' that refer to some name or other. There are of course non-anaphoric demonstratives. If I begin a conversation by saying *That necklace is lovely*, I consider it safe to assume that we both know what necklace I (demonstratively) refer to. Lasnik (1976) noted that, during Watergate, among those following the events, the (demonstrative) pronoun in an utterance of *He resigned!* would naturally be taken to refer to Nixon. Could I, in those circumstances, have begun a conversation by saying *That name will live in infamy!*, intending 'that name' to refer demonstratively to 'Nixon'? This seems a stretch; in the normal course of events, bits of language like names are never as salient as necklaces, presidents, and the rest of the furniture. So it is by no means surprising that Calling questions can only with difficulty be answered demonstratively. Calling answers produce expression-types, and those things are hard to demonstrate.

---

[8] Here my use of the term 'predicate' departs from that of Chapter 5. There, the term embraces Tense and the remainder; here it does not embrace Tense. No issue of substance arises; the terminology might be squared in various ways.

[9] See Kaplan 1989.

[10] Begging the question in what sense an anaphoric expression refers—to settle that, one needs a theory of anaphora generally, a wider concern. For related discussion, see Fiengo and May 1994, and references there.

Let me sum this up. We have seen that a speaker should not ask an Exemplifying question if he knows the item in question to *be* the item in question. The speaker might ask *Who stole my cow?*, and his friend might answer *I did*, Exemplifying himself; but then the item in question, although known to the questioner, is not known to *be* the item in question. If the questioner has the item in question, and knows that he does, he has no business asking for it. (Or, at least, no *straightforward* business asking for it, since, for example, various kinds of irony and jocularity may be achieved by asking for something one already has. If one has just been given a huge slice of pie, one may ask *May I have some pie?* Such moves may be made, but here we are pursuing less exotic game.) In asking either that a thing-in-the-world or a bit of language be produced, and more generally in asking that *anything* be produced, a speaker implies that he has not got that thing. So the asker of an Exemplifying question implies that he does not have the item in question. The principle at work is: It is misleading to ask for something if you think you already have it. If a speaker considers himself to have that item, it would be misleading to ask an Exemplifying question; it would be misleading to ask that the item be produced. Equally, if an item stands before a speaker, and the speaker does not know what it is called, it is in no way misleading to ask what that item is called.

6.4.2 Classing questions

To round out Austin's quartet, let's take up *which*-questions. As noted earlier, in Classing questions, 'which' is the *wh*-expression of choice. Can 'which', like 'who', be used to ask both for things-in-the-world and for bits of language? It appears that 'which' may only be used to ask for things-in-the-world. Unlike the Calling question *Who is stealing my cow?*, asked when I see the boy clearly, I may not, in the same circumstance, ask *Which boy is stealing my cow?*, angling for the name of the boy. That may be said only if it is unclear which boy, from a number of boys, is doing the stealing, but not, I think, if a particular boy is plainly doing the stealing, and I am angling not for the boy, since I have him already, but for the name of the boy. Of course, bits of language can themselves be the things-in-the-world being talked about. The verb 'call' itself provides an example. This verb, as it occurs in the sentence *They called him Miles*, takes as its first complement an expression denoting an item and as its second complement an expression denoting a name. Notice then, that one may ask the Classing question *Which did you call him? Miles or Mr. Davis?* (or one might ask the Exemplifying question *What did you call him?*). Here the addressee is asked to produce a thing-in-the-world, which happens to be a name, selected from the options given.

Which-questions are Classing questions, and, like Exemplifying questions, angle for things-in-the-world, not bits of language. But the superficial form of the sentence-type used does not always reveal which speech-act is being performed. In particular, it does not always indicate whether the questioner lacks a thing-in-the-world or a bit of language. *Who*-questions, as we have seen, may be either Calling questions or Exemplifying questions. Speakers sort this out in context; very frequently it is obvious whether the questioner lacks a bit of language, or a thing-in-the-world. And in part it is obvious what the questioner lacks because, in a large variety of cases, it is obvious what the questioner does *not* lack. But this raises an interesting question, to which I now turn: How ignorant can a questioner be when asking a question?

6.5 Multiple questions

6.5.1 How ignorant can a questioner be?

To ask a question a speaker must know quite a few things. First, she must know the grammar of the language she is using, which includes the laws of sentence-hood for the language. The questioner must also know how to use the language. That know-how contains the general rules followed when choosing which sentence-type to use and knowledge of how to wield a sentence-type once it has been chosen. Beyond these two, the use of language, in normal speech-situations, brings with it a variety of factual commitments. Speakers have beliefs, for example, concerning the relationship between the bits of language deployed and the items-in-the-world that they intend to talk about.[11] One may know a term and not know what it refers to, and one may be acquainted with an item and not know what it is called. Exemplifying questions and Calling questions address these ignorances. But if one has no acquaintance with some thing-in-the-world, *and* has no bit of language, no name or predicate to use to refer to it, then one has no attachment to the item at all. In this case, one does not know enough to know that one is ignorant. One does not know that one does not know about such items, so one has no means or motivation to ask questions concerning them. Apparently, one must know something if one is to know further that one is in ignorance.

There are a few sentences that seem to express near total ignorance. If one asks *What is anything?* as a completely general Describing question, one might attempt to present oneself as totally ignorant concerning all items, as not knowing what properties anything has. But I am not certain that anyone can seriously, consistently, and unmisleadingly ask this question, in these words, to that end.[12] It seems that, to ask this question, one must know some properties that a great many items do have—one must know, for example, concerning a great many things, that they are things whose (other) properties one does not know.

---

[11] The 'Assignments' of Fiengo and May (2006) encode this sort of information.
[12] I allow that one can express this ignorance using other words.

Otherwise, when one asks the question, one does not know what one is talking about. To take a particular case, you might know that skillets are things that you do not know any properties of, apart from the property of being things that you do not know any (other) properties of. Now generalize. *What is anything?* is on the same level as *What is a skillet?*, more general but no deeper. And if the general question is seriously asked, the speaker should know of every thing that it is a thing that the speaker does not know any properties of, the sole exception being the property of being something that the speaker does not know any (other) properties of. And no speaker could possibly know so much as to be in a position to ask such a question.[13]

The things that a speaker may lack include bits of language and things-in-the-world. On the side of language there are names and predicates. On the side of the world, there are items and properties. In questions containing a single *wh*-expression, one of these things is being demanded. Multiple *wh*-questions allow that more than one of these may be demanded at once, and so these seem like a promising area in which to discover how ignorant a speaker may be when asking a question. What multiple combinations may we ask for? And when we ask for combinations of things, what must we know? Consider, for example, the question *Who saw who?* In principle, each *wh*-expression might ask either for items or bits of language. Plainly, pairs of people may be asked for, but is this the only possibility? By examining multiple questions like this, it becomes possible to assess how much one must know to be in a position to ask them. Multiple questions such as *What is what?* are particularly interesting in this regard. One might be asking for pairs consisting of items and properties, but nevertheless be acquainted with both the items and the properties. In this case, the speaker lacks neither items nor properties; it would only be the pairing of item and property that the speaker would be angling for. Thus the speaker of a multiple question may often be less ignorant—not more—than a speaker who asks a single question.

6.5.2 On the speech-acts that may be performed when asking multiple questions

As was the case with single questions, the speech-acts that may be performed when asking multiple questions constitute a large, unexplored territory. That being so, I will consider here only the simplest cases, and hope that at least some of what is uncovered will carry over to more complex examples. I will continue to neglect 'when', 'where', and 'why', and I will limit consideration to multiple questions containing two and only two *wh*-expressions. Recall that sentence-types used to ask open, single questions are grammatically incomplete, and may be answered

---

[13] And of course there is the point that once one property is granted, a flood of properties follow it.

either by producing things-in-the-world or bits of language. We saw that one circumstance under which a speaker might intend to ask for a name, not the item that bears it, occurs when he believes he already has the item, believes that the addressee believes that he has the item, and thus is in a position to assume that the addressee can conclude that a name or description is all that he could be being asked for. So while it is correct to say that *wh*-questions are grammatically incomplete, it does not follow that, when asking a *wh*-question, the speaker is always angling for a thing-in-the-world. Under some circumstances, even when using the word 'who', the speaker may be angling for a bit of language.

Sometimes, the things-in-the-world that (double) multiple questions ask for are pairs of things-in-the-world; at other times, they ask for pairings of bits of language. We will see that *Who saw who?* may ask for pairs of people or pairs of names. A question such as *What is what?* may ask for pairs of items and their properties. Two important questions arise: can all of the questioning speech-acts be performed by the asking of a single multiple question? And can more than one questioning speech-act be performed by asking a single multiple question?

6.5.3 Is there a quartet of multiple questions?

Multiple questions can be found in all corners of Austin's quartet. Multiple Exemplifying questions and multiple Classing questions ask, in different ways, for pairings of items—and these two kinds are the most straightforward and easily asked. Of course, one needs to know certain things to be in a position to ask for pairings of items. One might know a relation, and seek pairs of items to satisfy it. Or one might have two kinds of item, and seek the pairings between them. These kinds of situations are relatively common. In contrast, speakers need to know much more to ask a multiple Calling or Describing question. The circumstances appropriate for multiple Calling questions, which ask for pairings of bits of language, or multiple Describing questions, which ask for pairings of properties, are more limited. It is required, in each of these cases, that the questioner bring a considerable amount of knowledge to an unusual situation. Let's look more closely at all of these types, starting with the more common ones.

A simple Exemplifying question such as *Who left?* demands that one or more instances of leavers be produced. Each instance is a person. Similarly, the multiple Exemplifying question *Who saw what?* demands one or more instances of pairs be produced, each pair consisting of a seer and a thing seen: for example, *Max saw the perpetrator, and Maxine saw the get-away car.* Boscovic (1999) and others have claimed that the list of pairs being demanded should have more than one member—that a speaker cannot use a multiple question intending to be taken as asking for an answer in the form of a single pair. That is just a mistake. Suppose the manager of a supermarket has reason to believe that an employee has stolen one item from his store, having received an anonymous note to this effect. It seems plain that, in that circumstance, the manager can ask *Who stole what?*, intending to be taken as asking for the single pair consisting of the thief and the thing stolen. This is a multiple Exemplifying question, intended in this case to be taken as demanding a single pair of items. Retrograde analysis chess problems, discussed earlier, provide another example. Recall that these involve determining, on the basis of studying a position on the board and assuming the normal rules of chess, what the previous move must have been. Given a chess position, a particular puzzle might be posed by asking the multiple Exemplifying question *What captured what?*, the speaker clearly intending to be taken as asking for an answer in the form of a single pair. To ask a multiple question intending to be taken as asking for one and only one pair, the speaker need only be in a position to know that the answer, whatever it might be, takes the form of one and only one pair.

As with the case of multiple Exemplifying questions, a considerable amount of knowledge must be brought to the asking of multiple Classing questions. When a speaker asks *Which man saw which movie?* he must already have both the men and the movies—at least well enough to ask about them—what he lacks is an exhaustive pairing between them, and the Individualizing manner of 'which' guarantees that the pairing be exhaustive on both sides. Furthermore, as argued at length earlier, the speaker may indicate, through the overt form of the sentence, how the pairing is to be given. In this case, the pairing is to be given by man, not by movie. And, as in the case of Exemplifying questions, the speaker might ask this question knowing that only one man saw a movie and that only one movie was seen, or the speaker might expect many pairs in answer.

Multiple Calling and Describing questions occur in more limited circumstances. In performing a simple Calling question, one presents oneself as not knowing what name or predicate applies to a given item. In performing a multiple Calling question, one presents oneself as not knowing what pairs of names or predicates apply to given pairs of items. This last part expresses a condition on the asking of a multiple Calling question that did not arise in the case of multiple Exemplifying or multiple Classing questions. Specifically, to ask a multiple Calling question, the questioner must already have knowledge of the pairing of items. Take first a case in which a single pair of items is given. Suppose we are watching a sumo match, and one wrestler is lifting the other. I might ask *Who is lifting whom?*, and you might respond by performing a multiple Calling, giving me the name of each wrestler. As was true in the case of the stolen cow, I have the items in question; it is their names I am asking for. Now take a case in which more than one pair of items is given. Suppose that several sumo matches are in progress, and that, as luck would have it, one wrestler is lifting the other in each match. Can I, not knowing the names of any of the wrestlers, ask *Who is lifting whom?*, intending to be taken as asking for pairs of names to apply to the pairs of wrestlers? This might be done, but the answer cannot simply be a set of pairs of names. For the answer, to be a multiple Calling, must specify *which* pairs of names apply to which wrestlers. If that is not done, no wrestler has been called anything. And the task would be harder still if I had asked *Who is wrestling with whom?*, since the predicate does not suffice to order each pair. So the task imposed on the addressee is greater than merely to provide a set of pairs of names.

Constructing a circumstance under which one might ask a multiple Describing question might at first seem impossible. A multiple Describing question demands not pairs of bits of language but pairs of properties. The questioner asks that pairs of properties be produced that apply to given items, or to given pairs of items. As in the case of multiple Calling questions, the task requires that the questioner be in a fairly unusual circumstance, the circumstance of having the belief that there are some properties that are paired in a particular way. Furthermore, for understandable reasons of syntax, the sentence-types used to perform this task—those containing two 'property'-positions filled with *wh*-expressions—are awkward. For example, the multiple Describing question *What were the men really, who you thought were what?* might be asked if I wished to know how you had systematically misjudged the men. Here the answer is a list of pairs of properties, the first being a property a man really had and the second being a property that you thought he had: for example, *The one who was a liar, I thought was as honest as Abe; the one who was a philanderer, I thought was loyal to his wife; and the one who was manipulative, I thought was naive.* Given a set of people already known, the answer produces pairs of properties, both of which apply to the same person.[14] In general, the sentence-types that would be used to ask multiple Describing questions are ungainly, and it is furthermore hard to imagine the unusual circumstance in which one would need the answer to such questions. Nevertheless, their meanings and uses are plain. That said, certainly most multiple questions angle for pairs of items; most multiple questions are either multiple Exemplifying or multiple Classing questions.

6.5.4 Are there mixings of the questioning speech-acts?

We have seen that (multiple) *who*-questions and (multiple) *what*-questions may be Exemplifying questions or Calling questions, questions whose answers are pairs of items (multiple Exemplifyings), or questions whose answers are pairs of bits of language (multiple Callings). For reasons already discussed, Exemplifying questions and Calling questions are generally asked in different circumstances, but it is not precluded that circumstances might exist in which both might be asked at once. So we are led to ask whether there are circumstances in which one may elicit, for example, both a Calling and an Exemplifying by the asking of a single multiple question. Of course, one may perform distinct questioning

---

[14] A difficult exercise: could an example be found angling for an answer in which pairs of properties apply to different people?

speech-acts in successive utterances. But may one perform distinct questioning speech-acts in a single utterance, each perhaps tied to a particular occurrence of a *wh*-expression? I will conclude, concerning a few simple sentence-types, that while they may be used to elicit a multiple performance of a single assertive speech-act, these same sentence-types cannot be used to elicit any combination of distinct assertive speech-acts. While there are multiple Calling questions and multiple Exemplifying questions, there are no questions asking for both a Calling and an Exemplifying. I am not in a position to demonstrate that such a thing is impossible, but the limitations I will observe are suggestive.

Let's first construct a multiple Exemplifying example. Suppose I tell you that I have just bought a box of dweeber's tools. I open the box, you see some odd-looking objects, and you ask the multiple Exemplifying question *What does what?*, demanding pairs, each consisting of a tool and its purpose. Nothing hard about that. To answer, I must produce pairings of tools with their purposes. That may be accomplished by successively demonstrating a tool and stating its purpose: for example, *That one (pointing) fluffs the dib, and that one (pointing) separates the dab.* The answer takes the form of a succession of examples, each example composed of a produced tool and a produced purpose.

But in that same circumstance could you instead ask a Calling–Exemplifying question using the sentence-type *What does what?*, demanding pairs consisting of the *name* of the tool and its purpose? That is, can you ask *What does what?* in order to demand both a Calling and an Exemplifying speech-act for each tool in the box? I believe this is not possible. To answer such a Calling–Exemplifying question, I would have to call each tool by its name, as well as instance its purpose. No set of pairs will alone suffice as the form of this answer. For by producing pairs of names and purposes, one does not thereby join either the names or purposes to their items. No Calling is performed if a name is not attached to a tool. The pairs alone cannot inform the questioner what each tool is called and what that tool does. One way to overcome that, in the confines of one utterance, would be to demonstrate the tool while naming it and then give its purpose: *Dwibbers (said while pointing at one tool) fluff the dib, while dwoobers (said while pointing at another tool) separate the dab.* Here, the Calling is performed by saying the name of an item while demonstrating it, and the Exemplifying is performed in the normal way. So it is true that we can perform these two acts together, and perhaps there is a way to ask that we perform them together. But the intuition seems firm that the multiple question *What does what?* does not ask, and cannot be taken to ask, that we do all of this. And that is the point at issue. Here we see a contrast with the case of the multiple sumo matches. There the addressee not only had to provide pairs of names but attach the names to the appropriate wrestlers. The answer went beyond the mere providing of names. But the answer was uniform; only one speech-act, though multiple, was angled for by the question. In the case imagined here, more than one speech-act is angled for, and it is that which puts it in the pale. I conclude that there are no Calling–Exemplifying questions in the sense I am interested in, and it can be seen in the same way that the same considerations rule out the possibility of Calling–Classing questions.

What about other combinations? Are there cases of Exemplifying–Classing multiple questions? Recall the distinction between the multiple Exemplifying question *What man saw what movie?* and the multiple Classing question *Which man saw which movie?* An Exemplifying–Classing combination might be asked by saying *What man saw which movie?* or *Which man saw what movie?* How are these questions used? Do they differ from the previous two, and how do they differ from each other? Intuitions on these mixed 'which'–'what' cases can be somewhat murky. I believe that both questions may angle either for just a single example, or for an exhaustive list of men and movies seen. If that is right, then these putative mixed cases are really badly put versions of either multiple Exemplifying questions or multiple Classing questions. They are, in any event, puzzling sentence-types; it is difficult to know how exactly to interpret them. But if multiple questions cannot demand mixed speech-acts, the possibility of loosely saying either *What man saw which movie?* or *Which man saw what movie?* as a multiple Exemplifying question or a multiple Classing question follows, since there would be no danger of their being understood as demanding a mixed response. Context would have to be relied on to sort out which of the two possibilities the questioner intended. As for whether the questions differ, I believe that *What man saw which movie?* leans toward Exemplifying and that *Which man saw what movie?* leans toward Classing. Perhaps, in the absence of other evidence, the first *wh*-expression 'wins', but I cannot be certain.

Finally, we should consider whether there are combinations involving Describing. The multiple question *What is what?* can be said so as to demand that pairs of items and their descriptions be produced. But there is another possibility. It appears that the verb 'be' is sometimes followed by a predicate denoting a property and at other times by an argument referring to an item. In this latter case, an identity is expressed. So, before we can determine the speech-acts that may be performed when using sentence-types like *What is what?*, we must ask whether the sentence-type used to ask the multiple Describing question *What is what?* is the same sentence-type as that which is used to ask a multiple identity question. In what follows, I will assume that they are not the same sentence-type, but this is not the place to tackle the issues involved. Again, I will limit myself to a small bit of exploration.

6.6 Identity questions, manner, and Austin's quartet

The idea that 'be' is, in some of its occurrences, the copula, in other of its occurrences the identity sign, and in still other of its occurrences an existential predicate was perhaps first put forward by Plato in 'The Sophist' (Ackrill 1957). Frege (1892) also held this view, while others have suggested that the putative ambiguity of 'be' is either partially or totally eliminable. Quine (1960), for example, suggests that some occurrences of 'be' that might be thought to be copular, such as the occurrence of 'be' in *Agnes is a lamb*, are not really so: he proposes that 'be', when it appears before indefinite NPs, is really the identity sign. I do not follow Quine here and will assume that English contains both the identity sign and the copula, pronounced alike, the first occurring in sentences such as *Cicero is Tully* or *Two and two is four*, the second occurring not only before adjectives, but before indefinite NPs as well.[15]

There are multiple questions that seek answers in the form of identity statements. Let's consider answers of the form 'A = A' first. It is hard to imagine a speaker not knowing what items are self-identical, or not knowing which instantiations of 'A = A' are true. It is easier to imagine a speaker presenting himself as not knowing these things. If a speaker wishes to present himself in this way, one way to do so is to say *What is itself?* Statements either of the form 'A is A' or of the form 'A is itself' count as replies, both of which have '[X is X]' as their logical structures.[16] Binding Theory (Chomsky 1981) generally requires that if two expressions of the same type flank a verb, the second should be the reflexive, but when we 'speak arithmetic', as we do when we say *Four equals four*, we speak a language in which pronounced form can be relied on to determine reference uniquely, and Binding Theory does not figure. The identity statement *John is John*, when of the form 'A = A', and other non-arithmetic identities, are built on this model.[17]

However, intuition suggests that if one is angling for answers of the form 'A is A', it will not do to ask either *Who is who?* or *Which is which?* It appears that the variables flanking 'is' in the logical structures of these sentences cannot easily be occurrences of the same variable-type. Consequently, the logical structures of these sentence-types have '[X is Y]' as parts, and thus questions using them must angle either for answers of the form 'A = B' (or for answers of the form 'A is a B', if the difference is acknowledged). As for the various lacks that the questioner might have, he might lack the relevant things-in-the-world, and have bits of language, or the reverse might be true. In other circumstances, he might have all of the relevant things-in-the-world and all of the relevant bits of language, but not know how they pair up. This is difficult terrain; I will start with *Which is which?*, and then consider *Who is who?*, but much will remain unexplored.

---

[15] See Fiengo and May 1994.

[16] In languages generally, the reflexive pronoun serves to indicate expression-identity. The choice whether to say 'A is A' or 'A is itself' is, in this particular case, not subject to hard-and-fast grammatical rule, but if the verb were anything other than 'is', the reflexive would be strongly preferred. See Fiengo and May 1994.

[17] See Fiengo and May 2006.

6.6.1 Which is which?

As a first example, suppose I can tell alligators and crocodiles apart. I know they are different animals, and that the shape of the snout is a distinguishing species-property. Seeing a mix of the two, I can accurately sort them into two species. And assume that I know the names that apply to them and can tell *them* apart; one name has three syllables and the other has four. But suppose that I cannot classify the animals by name, in the sense that I am unable to match the right species-name with the right animal. Faced with two specimens, one of each type, I might not be sure whether the one with the narrow snout is the alligator or the crocodile. In these circumstances, I can address my lack by asking *Which is which?*, hoping to get the right name associated with the right animal. I have both the items and the names; what I lack are their pairings. To answer my question, you might say *That (pointing to an alligator) is an alligator, and that (pointing to a crocodile) is a crocodile*. Each of these is a Calling; after producing a specimen, you call it by name. More precisely, in each case, you produce a specimen, and, taking it as given, produce a predicate whose sense matches the type of the specimen. By doing these things, you answer my question as I intended it to be taken.

There is a very different kind of circumstance in which I might ask *Which is which?* Suppose that I *cannot* tell two species apart, and want, by asking the question, to become able to do so. There might, for example, be two species of bird whose members are indistinguishable to me, grackles and starlings, say. Nevertheless, I might know the species-names 'grackle' and 'starling'; suppose that I do. When I see a bird from one of these species, I cannot tell which species it belongs to. You, on the other hand, might be able to identify them instantly, but I do not know how you can tell. I might try to get you to straighten me out by asking *Which is which?* Now here what I lack are properties distinguishing the two species of bird. Unlike the alligator and crocodile case, if you just demonstrate each— *That (pointing) is a starling and that (pointing) is a grackle*— you will not answer my question, because the birds will still look indistinguishable to me. Nor will you relieve my lack if you say *That bird (pointing) is speckled, and that bird (pointing) is not*. By saying just that, you have provided me with a distinguishing property, but you have not told me the name of the bird that has it. What you need to say here is something more like *Starlings are speckled, and grackles are not*. If you say that, you produce pairs composed of items (species, let us say) and (distinguishing) properties. Both the items and the properties are produced by name, and it is crucial that neither be produced by demonstration. Here we have a multiple question answered by Describings.

But in the two cases just given, what kind of question was asked? In the former case, *Which is which?* elicited multiple Callings; in the second, multiple Describings. I have, however, followed Austin (1953) in claiming that *which*-questions are Classing questions, and I have, up to this point, been assuming that the speech-act of the question elicits the corresponding assertive speech-act in response. But there is no contradiction. By asking *Which is which?* a speaker asks either that species (or their members) be classified by what they are called or classified by what properties they have. To answer either occurrence of the question, the addressee performs a Classing, in one case constituted by a set of Callings and in the other case constituted by a set of Describings. At the end, there must be no item uncalled (or undescribed), and no name or property unapplied. Classings are always exhaustive.

It is much more difficult to ask the Classing *Which is which?* angling for an exhaustive Exemplifying or Classing. The reason for this has to do with the overt ordering of the *wh*-expressions that the sentence-type contains. The question *Which is which?* asks that items be classified either by the properties they have or by the bits of language that apply to them. To do that, one first produces items and then classifies them in the relevant way. Thus the form of the question itself imposes a particular direction of fit on the answer. Since in both Calling and Describing, the items are given and the predicates, or properties, produced, the question *Which is which?* is naturally taken as asking for the material for Callings or Describings, as we have seen. But to ask for the material for Exemplifying or for Classing, the direction of fit must proceed in the opposite direction. The most accurate, though inelegant, way to do that is to ask *Which might which be?* The 'which' that covers the position of the predicate is overtly fronted, signaling that it has wider scope than the 'which' left behind. To answer this accurately, one should produce a property by name and then, taking it as given, produce items of a type that match its sense. To do that is to perform either an Exemplifying, or a Classing, depending on where the onus of match falls.[18]

6.6.2 Who is who?

What kind of question may *Who is who?* be used to ask? And what kind of sentence-type is it? If, speaking strictly, 'who' may not replace predicates, as I suggested above, the occurrence of 'is' in *Who is who?* must expresses identity. I am not completely sure that 'who' might not cover predicates in some circumstances, but I believe that it does not in the examples I address here. Now, as was mentioned, when a speaker asks *Who is who?*, he does not ask that answers be produced of the form 'A = A'. If *Who is who?* did ask this, it could be completely answered by saying *Everyone*. But that answer, which is a fine answer to the question *Who is him- or herself?*, is not an answer to *Who is who?*,

---

[18] It is much more difficult to see the relationship between scope, manner, and direction of fit in sentences such as *Which saw which?* and *Who saw who?* I do not attempt here to lay down how these relationships play out generally; it is enough that they do interact in copular and equative sentences.

which apparently asks for answers of the form 'A = B'. But what speech-act is performed by asking *Who is who?*

We here touch Frege's puzzle. He asked how 'A = B' can be informative when true, and he gave his answer. But Frege's puzzle may be cast in question form. Put that way, the puzzle is: How could one not know who is who? One answer to the puzzle is that a person who does not know who is who does not know certain facts, facts expressed by certain uses of certain identity statements. Not any use of any identity statement will express what such a person does not know. Probably, the identity statement should be a Calling.[19] The speech-act diagnosis for the informativeness of 'A = B' (or at least one such diagnosis) is that, when sentence-types of the form 'A = B' are used informatively, they are used to perform Callings. By asserting 'A = B' truthfully, the speaker calls A B, (and, by asserting 'B = A' truthfully, the speaker calls B A). A person might not know that A is called B (or B A). But let's return to the main thread. How may *Who is who?* be used?

Suppose, regarding a baseball team on the field, I ask *Who is who?* By asking that question, I may demand that you provide me with the names of each of the players. If the players are standing at their positions, you might respond *The first baseman is Moose Skowron; the second baseman is Bobby Richardson,* and so on. I already have the items and the positions they play, what I lack are their names. In your answer, you have paired the items (by position) with their names, but you also could have done so demonstratively: *That guy (pointing) is Moose Skowron, that guy (pointing) is Bobby Richardson,* and so on. Or suppose we are at a masked ball, each guest costumed as a character from *Alice's Adventures in Wonderland,* and costumed so well that I ask you *Who is who?* You might point to the one dressed up as the Mad Hatter and say *He is Melvin,* or without pointing, say *The Mad Hatter is Melvin.* When you point to the man, or refer to him as 'the Mad Hatter' (which costume I recognize as such), and say that he is Melvin (which I did not know), you have relieved my lack; you have paired an item (by demonstration or by description via the costume) with its name. In each case, you have performed Callings; by saying *The first baseman is Moose Skowron,* you called the first baseman Moose Skowron.[20]

As a second example, suppose I am introduced to Standish Brewster Chipplethwaite, VI. Curious as to his background, I later consult the book called

---

[19] I say 'probably' because I cannot exhaust the circumstances under which identity statements might be said. And there is the case of arithmetical statements, which seem unlikely to be Callings: *Cicero is Tully* and *Tully is Cicero* are used to perform distinct Callings, but $2 + 2 = 4$, as a statement of arithmetic, is not 'used to perform' anything distinct from $4 = 2 + 2$. It seems likely that the equations of arithmetic don't fall within Austin's quartet.

[20] But did you refer to Moose Skowron by saying 'Moose Skowron'? Here it gets hard. Plainly, if the sentence is equative, you do not equate Skowron with his name. But if not equative, then perhaps copular, which would force 'who' to cover a predicate. As previously mentioned, the use/mention distinction seems too crude if the complexities of use are taken seriously, and the calling of someone by name is taken into the mix. Or are the formal distinctions too crude?

Who's Who. I have a man, and I have a name, and I know that the name is his. What I lack is a description of him. The book is organized by name; next to each name, a description is provided. "The only son of Standish Brewster Chipplethwaite, V", the *Who's Who* might inform me. The book displays names next to (definite) descriptions of the people that bear them. By reading *Who's Who*, I learn a description of the man I met. The book pairs items (by name) with their descriptions, and is thus answering one use of the question *Who is who?*

As a third example, suppose I am presented with the names of the Greek gods and the names of the Roman gods and I want to know the correspondence between the names. I may ask *Who is who?* and you may begin your answer by saying *Aphrodite is Venus.* I must know a great deal to ask this question. I bring to the question the knowledge that the gods each have two names, that the pantheon was named differently in Greek and Latin, and I have all the names before me; what I lack is the correspondence between them.

In all of these cases, *Who is who?* is a multiple Calling question. It asks for pairs of expressions such that the first applies to the same person that the second does. We may have descriptions and seek names (the masked ball case or the baseball case), or have items and their names and seek definite descriptions (the *Who's Who* case).[21] We may even have lists of names, assume that there are items that members of each list refer to, yet not know which names refer to the same item (the pantheon case). Sequences of Callings of the form 'A = B' address these lacks.

As a final example, suppose that you come to my course to give a guest lecture. Not knowing the students, and wanting me to tell you their names, you can ask, when you see them, *Who are they?*, or *What are their names?* But if I have not previously told you the names of my students, you cannot ask *Who is who?* to get their names. Suppose, however, that we have previously discussed all my students by name, and you want to attach the students to those names. Then you may ask *Who is who?*, and I can respond *This is Gertrude (the Gertrude I told you about), and this is Max (the Max I told you about)* . . . , going around the room. This again underlines the point that a questioner must know a great deal to be in a position to ask a multiple question.[22] Only if a speaker has names (or descriptions) already may a speaker ask *Who is who?* to attach further names (or descriptions) to those same items. The pantheon case shows that we may ask *Who is who?* even if we cannot attach any name to any item, so long as we have the names. So, with some hesitation, I conclude that *Who is who?* is a multiple Calling question, asking always for Calling responses. Some very hard issues are playing themselves out on some very tricky examples.

---

[21] Again we hit the question whether 'who' may cover predicate positions. If this is allowed, then asking *Who is who?* comes to asking *Who is what?*, and a multiple Describing may be performed.

[22] Which makes multiple questions useful when one wants to present oneself as knowing far more than one does. Upon meeting my students, having never heard of any of them, you may choose to ask *Who is who?* in the ingratiating circumstance in which you (falsely) present yourself as knowing all about them.

In summary, in these last sections, and in this chapter, we have considered only a few of the vast array of multiple questions that exist, but some of the issues that will arise in the further exploration of this domain are already clear. We have not yet seen a questioning composed of more than one of the speech-acts in Austin's quartet; perhaps other more complicated examples will also yield to a unified analysis. Then there is the fact that 'who', and other *wh*-expressions, may ask either for things-in-the-world or for bits of language. The question becomes how general this bivalence is. At the end, we have been able to face Frege's puzzle in its questioning guise, and to consider the contribution of Calling to the informativeness of true identity statements. But there is a great deal of syntactic and semantic research that remains to be done in this rich area.

6.7 What is a question?

Wittgenstein was right when he said that, "if you do not keep the range of uses of language in view, you might be inclined to ask 'What is a question?'" (1958: 24). Even if you do try to keep the range of uses of language in view, you might be inclined to ask that question. I have tried to avoid some of the pitfalls. There is no one questioning speech-act, just as there is no one assertive speech-act. Austin saw that one and the same sentence-type may be used to perform four distinct assertive speech-acts. I have echoed him by saying that, corresponding to each assertive speech-act, there is a questioning speech-act. And within each corner of the quartet there are further divisions, which shade off in various directions.

I have approached questions from the point of view of ignorance; the relationship between questioning and answering is more central than either pole. It is not that there is a definition of questioning, and a definition of asserting, and some relation between them. Rather, questioning and asserting can only be appreciated mutually. Incompleteness is characteristic of questioning, but incompleteness comes in many guises and in many degrees. There is a prominent distinction between incompleteness in the form of the sentence-type and the presentation of incompleteness in the performing of a speech-act. This is the divide between open questions and confirmation questions. But taxonomy is, in this case, ultimately futile. The complexities of what we do, once we attend to them, should remind us that our behavior is shaded and complex. When we speak, we do many things at once, to many degrees. We may discern prominent distinctions in this terrain, but we should not seek to tidy it up too much. Our behavior is what it is.

While declarative sentences have received a substantial amount of scrutiny, asserting has received far less. Similarly, while sentence-types used to ask questions have been the subject of analysis, particularly semantic analysis, the terrain of asking questions remains largely unexplored. My goal has been to give a first sketch of our questioning behavior, trying to give due consideration both to matters of use and matters of grammar. Perhaps there are domains within language that may be studied without consideration of use, but I suspect those domains are much smaller than is generally recognized—certainly the domain of questions is not one of them. I have also pursued a methodological goal. I have tried to show through example that it is all right to consider matters of grammar and matters of use together, so long as one does not confuse them. To the syntacticians, I would say that we all should acknowledge that the sentence-types syntacticians study are used, and that syntacticizing use is an error. To the students of pragmatics, I would say that we all should acknowledge that the sentence-types we use have form, and that pragmatizing structure is an error. Syntax, no matter how baroque, cannot render pragmatics superfluous, and pragmatics, no matter how clever, cannot render syntax superfluous. Both types and tokens must be in view. But what to say to the semanticists? Perhaps only that, if the entire language is its domain, truth, and conditions on it, are not the central semantic notions. There is no central semantic notion.

Bibliography

Ackrill, J. L. (1957) 'Plato and the Copula: Sophist 251–259', *Journal of Hellenic Studies* 77 (Part I), reprinted in A. O. Rorty (general ed.) *Modern Studies in Philosophy*; G. Vlastos (ed.), *Plato: A Collection of Critical Essays I: Metaphysics and Epistemology*, Garden City, NY: Anchor Books, Doubleday and Company, Inc., 1971.

Aristotle (1973) *On Interpretation*, Loeb Classical Library, Volume 1, William Heinemann Ltd. Cambridge, MA: Harvard University Press.

Austin, J. L. (1950) 'Truth', *Proceedings of the Aristotelian Society*, Supplementary Volume xxiv. (Also collected in Austin 1961.)

—— (1953) 'How to Talk–some simple ways', *Proceedings of the Aristotelian Society, 1952–3*. (Also collected in Austin 1961.)

—— (1961) *Philosophical Papers*, 3rd edn., J. O. Urmson and G. J. Warnock (eds.), Oxford: Clarendon Paperbacks, Oxford University Press.

—— (1962) *How to do things with words*, Cambridge, MA: Harvard University Press.

Barwise, J. and Perry, J. (1983) *Situations and Attitudes*, Cambridge, MA: MIT Press.

Beaney, M. (1997) *The Frege Reader*, Oxford: Basil Blackwell.

Belnap, N. and Steel, T. (1976) *The Logic of Questions and Answers*, New Haven and London: Yale University Press.

Boščović, Ž. (1999) 'On multiple feature checking: multiple *wh*-fronting and multiple head movement', in S. Epstein and N. Hornstein (eds.), *Working Minimalism*, Cambridge, MA: MIT Press, 159–87.

Brown, P. and Levinson, S. C. (1978, 1987) *Politeness: Some universals in language usage*, Studies in Interactional Sociolinguistics 4, Cambridge: Cambridge University Press.

Chomsky, N. (1955, 1975) *The Logical Structure of Linguistic Theory*, New York: Plenum Press.

—— (1965) *Aspects of the Theory of Syntax*, Cambridge, MA: MIT Press.

—— (1970) 'Remarks on nominalization', in R. Jacobs and P. Rosenbaum (eds.), *Readings in English Transformational Grammar*, Waltham, MA: Ginn.

—— (1980) *Rules and Representations*, New York: Columbia University Press.

—— (1981) *Lectures on Government and Binding*, Dordrecht: Foris.

—— (1986a) *Barriers*, Cambridge: MIT Press.

—— (1986b) *Knowledge of Language*, New York: Praeger.

—— (1994) 'Bare phrase structure', Cambridge, MA: MITWPL.

—— (1995) *The Minimalist Program*, Cambridge, MA: MIT Press.

—— and Halle, M. (1968) *The Sound Pattern of English*, New York: Harper and Row.

Curme, G. (1935) *The Grammar of the English Language*, reprinted 1977, Essex, CT: Verbatim.

Darwin, C. (1899) *The Origin of Species*, 6th edn., New York: D. Appleton and Company.

den Dikken, M. and Giannakidou, A. (2002) 'From *hell* to polarity: "aggressively non-D-linked" *wh*-phrases as polarity items', *Linguistic Inquiry* 33.1: 31–61.

Donnellan, K. S. (1966) 'Reference and definite descriptions', *Philosophical Review* 75: 281–304.

Eimas, P., Siqueland, E., Jusczyk, P., and Vigorito, J. (1971) 'Speech perception in infants', *Science* 171: 303–6.

Fiengo, R. (1974) *Syntactic Conditions on Surface Structure*, Doctoral dissertation, MIT.

_____ (1980) *Surface Structure*, Cambridge, MA: Harvard University Press.

_____ (2003) 'Talking, topics, types, and tokens', in W. McClure (ed.), *Japanese/Korean Linguistics* 12, Stanford: CSLI Publications, 325–39.

_____ and McClure, W. (2002) 'On how to use *-wa*', *Journal of East Asian Linguistics* 11.1: 5–41.

_____ and May, R. (1994) *Indices and Identity*, Cambridge, MA: MIT Press.

_____ _____ (2006) *De Lingua Belief*, Bradford Books, Cambridge, MA: MIT Press.

Fowler, H. W. (1926) *A Dictionary of Modern English Usage*, Oxford: Clarendon Press.

Frege, G. (1879) *Begriffsschrift, eine der arithmetischen nachgebildete Formelsprache des reinen Denkens*, Halle a. S.: Louis Nebert. Trans. by S. Bauer-Mengelberg: *Concept Script, a formal language of pure thought modelled upon that of arithmetic*, in J. Van Heijenoort (ed.), 1967, *From Frege to Gödel: A Source Book in Mathematical Logic, 1879–1931*, Harvard University Press

_____ (1882) Letter to A. Marty, in *Philosophical and Mathematical Correspondence*, trans. by H. Kaal, ed. by B. McGuinness, 1980, Chicago: University of Chicago Press.

_____ (1891) 'Function and concept', in *Philosophical Writings of Gottlob Frege*, trans. by P. Geach and M. Black, 1966, Oxford: Basil Blackwell.

_____ (1892) 'On sense and reference', in *Philosophical Writings of Gottlob Frege*, trans. by P. Geach and M. Black, 1966, Oxford: Basil Blackwell.

_____ (1893) *The Basic Laws of Arithmetic*, trans. and ed. by M. Furth, 1967, Berkeley and Los Angeles: University of California Press.

_____ (1918*a*) 'Negation', in *Philosophical Writings of Gottlob Frege*, trans. by P. Geach and M. Black, 1966, Oxford: Basil Blackwell

_____ (1918*b*) 'Thought', in M. Beaney (ed.), *The Frege Reader*, 1997, Oxford: Basil Blackwell.

Furth, M. (1967) 'Introduction' to Frege 1893, *The Basic Laws of Arithmetic*, Berkeley and Los Angeles: University of California Press.

Geach, P. (1962) *Reference and Generality*, Ithaca, NY: Cornell University Press.

Greenberg, J. (1963) 'Some universals of grammar with particular reference to the order of meaningful elements', in *Universals of Language*, Cambridge: MIT Press, 73–113.

Grice, P. (1975) 'Logic and conversation', in P. Cole and J. L. Morgan (eds.), *Syntax and Semantics 3: Speech Acts*, New York: Academic Press, 41–58.

Hamblin, C. L. (1976) 'Questions in Montague English', in B. Partee (ed.), *Montague Grammar*, New York: Academic Press.

Hare, R. (1949) 'Imperative sentences', *Mind* 58: 21–39.

Heim, I. (1982) *The Semantics of Definite and Indefinite Noun Phrases*, Doctoral dissertation, University of Massachusetts, Amherst.

_____ (1987) 'Where does the definiteness restriction apply? Evidence from the definiteness of variables', in E. Reuland and A. ter Meulen (eds.), *The Representation of (In)definites*, Cambridge, MA: MIT Press, 21–42.

Heycock, C. (1995) 'Asymmetries in reconstruction', *Linguistic Inquiry* 26: 547–70.

Higginbotham, J. (1993) 'Interrogatives', in K. Hale and S. J. Keyser (eds.), *The View from Building 20*, Cambridge, MA: MIT Press.

_____ and May, R. (1981) 'Questions, quantifiers and crossing', *The Linguistic Review* 1: 41–79.

Hintikka, K. (1974) 'Questions about questions', in M. K. Munitz and P. Unger (eds.), *Semantics and Philosophy*, New York: NYU Press, 103–58.

Jackendoff, R. (1972) *Semantic Interpretation in Generative Grammar*, Cambridge: MIT Press.

Kaplan, D. (1989) 'Demonstratives: an essay on the semantics, logic, metaphysics, and epistemology of demonstratives and other indexicals', 1977, in J. Almog, J. Perry, and H. Wettstein (eds.), *Themes from Kaplan*, New York, NY: Oxford University Press, 481–563.

Karttunen, L. (1977) 'Syntax and semantics of questions', *Linguistics & Philosophy* 1: 3–44.

Katz, J. J. (1972) *Semantic Theory*, New York: Harper & Row.

—— (1981) *Language and Other Abstract Objects*, Totowa, NJ: Rowman & Littlefield, and Oxford: Blackwell.

—— and Postal, P. (1964) *An Integrated Theory of Linguistic Descriptions*, Cambridge, MA: MIT Press.

Kayne, R. (1984) *Connectedness and Binary Branching*, Dordrecht, Holland: Foris.

—— (1994) *The Antisymmetry of Syntax*, Cambridge, MA: MIT Press.

Kripke, S. (1979) 'Speaker's reference and semantic reference', in P. French, T. E. Uehling, Jr., and H. K. Wettstein (eds.), *Contemporary Perspectives in the Philosophy of Language*, Minneapolis: University of Minnesota Press.

Kuno, S. (1982) 'The focus of the question and the focus of the answer', in *Papers from the Parasession on Nondeclarative Sentences*, Chicago Linguistics Society, 134–57.

Ladusaw, W. (1979) *Polarity Sensitivity as Inherent Scope Relations*, Doctoral dissertation, UT Austin.

Lasnik, H. (1976) 'Remarks on Coreference', *Linguistic Analysis* 2.1: 1–22.

Lemmon, E. J. (1962) 'On sentences verifiable by their use', *Analysis* 22: 86–9.

Levinson, S. C. (1983) *Pragmatics*, Cambridge: Cambridge University Press.

Lewis, D. (1979) 'Score-keeping in a language game', in R. Bauerle, U. Egli, and A. v. Stechow (eds.), *Semantics from Different Points of View*, Berlin: Springer. Reprinted in D. Lewis (1998) *Philosophical Papers*, Oxford: Oxford University Press, 233–49.

Liberman, M. and Sag, I. (1974) 'Prosodic form and discourse function', in *Proceedings of the Tenth Regional Meeting of the Chicago Linguistic Society*.

Liptak, A. (2001) *On the Syntax of Wh-items in Hungarian*, Utrecht, the Netherlands: LOT.

May, R. (1985) *Logical Form: Its Structure and Derivation*, Linguistic Inquiry Monograph 12, Cambridge, MA: MIT Press.

Milsark, G. (1974) *Existential Sentences in English*, Doctoral dissertation, MIT.

Napoli, D. J. (1993) *Syntax: theory and problems*, New York: Oxford University Press.

Pears, D. (1967) *Bertrand Russell and the British Tradition in Philosophy*, New York: Random House.

Perlmutter, D. (1971) *Deep and Surface Structure Constraints in Syntax*, New York: Holt, Rinehart, and Winston.

Pesetsky, D. (1987) '*Wh*-in-situ: movement and unselective binding', in E. Reuland and A. ter Meulen (eds.), *The Representation of (In)definites*, Cambridge, MA: MIT Press, 98–129.

Petroski, H. (1992) *The Evolution of Useful Things*, New York: Knopf.

Postal, P. (1971) *Cross-Over Phenomena*, New York: Holt, Rinehart, and Winston.

Quine, W. V.-O. (1960) *Word and Object*, Cambridge, Mass.: The Technology Press of MIT; New York & London: Wiley.

Reinhart, T. (1976) *The Syntactic Domain of Anaphora*, Doctoral dissertation, MIT.

_____ (1983) *Anaphora and Semantic Interpretation*, London: Croom Heim.

Rizzi, L. (1990) *Relativized Minimality*, Cambridge, MA: MIT Press.

Ross, J. (1970) 'On declarative sentences', in R. Jacobs and P. Rosenbaum (eds.), *Reading in English Transformational Grammar*, Waltham, MA: Ginn and Co., 222–72.

Russell, B. (1905) 'On denoting', *Mind* 14: 479–93.

_____ (1918) 'The philosophy of logical atomism', *Monist* 28: 495–527.

_____ (1940, 1962) *An Inquiry into Meaning and Truth*, Baltimore, MD: Penguin Books.

Sadock, J. (1974) *Toward a Linguistic Theory of Speech Acts*, New York: Academic Press.

Safir, K. (1982) *Syntactic Chains and the Definiteness Effect*, Doctoral dissertation, MIT.

Searle, J. (1969) *Speech Acts*, Cambridge: Cambridge University Press.

_____ (1975) 'Indirect speech acts', in P. Cole and J. L. Morgan (eds.), *Syntax and Semantics 3: Speech Acts*, New York: Academic Press, 59–82.

Smullyan, R. (1979) *The Chess Mysteries of Sherlock Holmes*, New York: Knopf.

Soames, S. (1986) 'Incomplete definite descriptions', *Notre Dame Journal of Formal Logic* 27, no. 3: 349–75.

Stalnaker, R. (1974) 'Pragmatic presuppositions', in M. K. Munitz and P. Unger (eds.), *Semantics and Philosophy*, New York: NYU Press, 197–213. Reprinted in S. Davis (1991) *Pragmatics: A reader*, New York and Oxford: Oxford University Press.

Strawson, P. F. (1950*a*) 'On referring', *Mind* 59, 320–44. Collected in *Logico-Linguistic Papers* (1971), London and New York: Methuen, 1–27.

_____ (1950*b*) 'Truth', *Proceedings of the Aristotelian Society, Supplementary Volume xxiv*, collected in *Logico-Linguistic Papers* (1971), London and New York: Methuen, 190–213.

Wittgenstein, L. (1958) *Philosophical Investigations*, New York: Macmillan.

Yngve, V. (1960) 'A model and an hypothesis for language structure', *Proceedings of the American Philosophical Society* 104: 444–66.

Index